# Burnside's Bridge

*The Climactic Struggle of the*
*2nd and 20th Georgia at Antietam Creek*

Phillip Thomas Tucker

STACKPOLE
BOOKS

Copyright © 2000 by Stackpole Books

Published by
STACKPOLE BOOKS
5067 Ritter Road
Mechanicsburg, PA 17055
www.stackpolebooks.com

Printed in the United States of America

10 9 8 7 6 5 4 3 2 1

First edition

**Library of Congress Cataloging-in-Publication Data**


Tucker, Phillip Thomas, 1953-
     Burnside's Bridge: the climatic struggle of the 2nd and 20th Georgia at Antietam Creek
 / Phillip Thomas Tucker.— 1st ed.
         p. cm.
     Includes bibliographical references (p. ) and index.
     ISBN 0-8117-0199-9 (hc)
      1. Antietam, Battle of, Md., 1862. 2. Confederate States of America. Army. Georgia
Infantry Regiment, 2nd. 3. Confederate States of America. Georgia Infantry Regiment,
20th. 4. Georgia–Histroy–Civil War, 1861-1865–Regimental histories. 5. United
States–History–Civil War, 1861-1865–Regimental histories. I. Title.


E474.65 .T83 2000
973.7'336–dc21                                                                    99-048512

# CONTENTS

# ACKNOWLEDGMENTS

MANY PEOPLE ACROSS THE COUNTRY DESERVE CREDIT FOR GRACIOUSLY sharing information on Antietam and Burnside's Bridge for this project. Descendants of both the Georgia soldiers who defended Burnside's Bridge, including General Toombs's family, and the descendants of the soldiers of the IX Corps who assaulted the bridge, were helpful in compiling information. Mr. Keith Bohannon helped to identify the elusive men of the 2nd and 20th Georgia Confederate Infantries. Dr. Perry Jamieson, noted Antietam expert, graciously provided advice in regard to the battle of Antietam and the struggle for Burnside's Bridge.

At Antietam National Battlefield, National Park Service historians Mr. Ted Alexander and Mr. Paul Chiles shared their expertise on the battle of Antietam. In addition, dozens of curators, historians, and archivists across the country provided invaluable assistance, especially those at the Library of Congress, Washington, D.C.

Most of all, I would like to thank Mr. William C. Davis for helping to turn a much too lengthy manuscript into a quality book. In addition to graciously bestowing guidance in regard to both writing and history, Mr. Davis devoted a great deal of personal effort to improving this work.

Special thanks also go to Mr. Davis's competent associate editors, including Michelle M. Simmons and Leigh Ann Berry, who both contributed to making *Burnside's Bridge* a success.

# INTRODUCTION

DURING THE LATE SUMMER OF 1862, GENERAL ROBERT E. LEE BOLDLY ordered his Army of Northern Virginia to advance across the Potomac River and leave the state of Virginia behind for the first time. Thousands of seasoned veterans in faded gray and butternut marched with confidence across the rolling countryside of Maryland in the first Confederate invasion of the North. General Lee was gambling that he could win a decisive victory on Northern soil to gain foreign recognition and independence for the Southern nation. With his army scattered across much of western Maryland in mid-September 1862, General Lee was forced to hurriedly concentrate his forces along Antietam Creek to face the unexpected rapid advance of Gen. George B. McClellan's Army of the Potomac.

General Lee again gambled that the relatively few Rebels at hand would hold firm to buy time until the arrival of his dispersed units. The clash between the armies amid the cornfields, meadows, and woodlots of Antietam on 17 September 1862 resulted in the bloodiest single day of the war. At a little stone bridge, later known as Burnside's Bridge, across the Antietam on the Army of Northern Virginia's right flank, less than 300 Georgia soldiers of Gen. Robert Augustus Toombs's Georgia brigade played a key role in saving the day at Antietam. With hard fighting and inspired leadership these Georgians won the precious time that ensured the arrival of Gen. Ambrose Powell Hill's reinforcements from Harpers Ferry, Virginia, during the army's darkest hour.

The Georgians were uniquely poised to play a crucial role on the day of 17 September 1862. Tactically speaking, they occupied the most vital

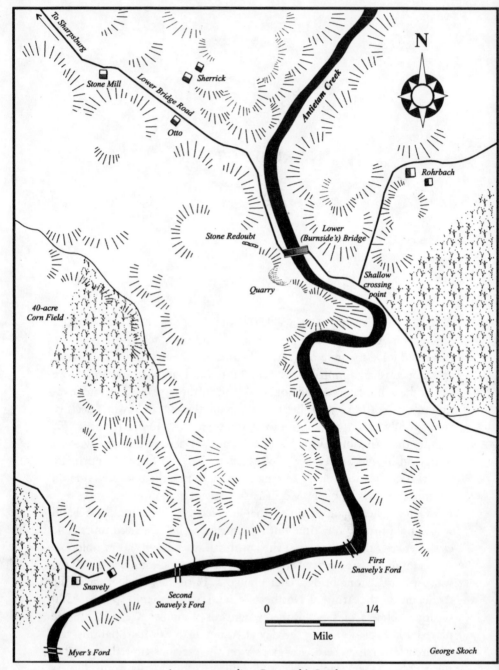

*Area surrounding Burnside's Bridge*

defensive position in General Lee's line. They defended an advanced position on the far right flank of Lee's battle line at the southernmost end of the army's line. Additionally, their position defended  roads leading to Sharpsburg and Harpers Ferry—vital to both protecting Lee's rear and to allowing General Hill's reinforcements to arrive.

It was also by this route that the army escaped back to the safety of Virginia.

The details of the Georgians' performance on 17 September is truly remarkable: Without immediate support or adequate munitions, fewer than 300 soldiers of the 2nd, 20th, and 50th Georgia Infantry held the Federal IX Corps at bay for five hours, repelling five attacks on the bridge. Additionally, later that afternoon these same soldiers spearheaded the counterattack of General Hill's reinforcements that hurled the IX Corps back toward the bridge.

Unfortunately, however, the full story of this tenacious struggle for possession of Burnside's Bridge has never been told in detail until now. The accomplishments of the Georgia defenders have been overlooked by historians who have, in turn, underestimated the significance of their actions on the outcome of the action that day.

The purpose of this work has been to provide a more balanced perspective on the struggle for Burnside's Bridge, to counter the traditional interpretation of events, which has focused almost exclusively on the Union action, by highlighting the role of General Toombs's Georgians. This study also hopes to dispel a number of long-existing misconceptions about the battle. Historians have long failed to recognize the part the Georgia soldiers played in saving the day at Antietam and have misrepresented significant facts such as the number of soldiers defending the bridge (fewer than 300), the amount of time they spent defending it (five hours), the actual number of assaults they faced and repelled (five), and the casualty rate they inflicted upon the IX Corps.

One reason for the distortion of the historical record may be the nature of the heroes themselves. General Toombs, Colonel Benning, and their Georgia rebels were the most improbable of heroes to save the day at Antietam: undervalued troops led by much-ridiculed political commanders.

Non–West Pointers and non-Virginians, they were virtual outcasts because of their individualistic ways. Without doubt, by September 1862, Toombs probably had the lowest reputation of any general in the Army of Northern Virginia.

Historians have traditionally credited a much more likely hero, General A. P. Hill, with "saving the day" at Antietam. Although Hill's timely arrival from Harpers Ferry certainly helped to turn the tide of the action, it was the Georgia soldiers' previous defense of the bridge that bought Hill the time that he needed to save the battle.

An analysis of primary source material indicates that this distortion of the historical record developed primarily after the war. Indeed, General Toombs, Colonel Benning, and their Georgians actually received more recognition than General Hill and his famous "Light Division" for saving the day at Antietam immediately after the battle and during the remaining years of the war than they did in the postwar period. These differences are most apparent when comparing the primary documentation of contemporaries at Antietam who gave the Georgians their due with the pro-Virginian and pro-Hill historians who wrote long after the war. It is the postwar interpretation, however, that has come to be accepted as fact.

Today only a single marker stands on the bluff where a relative handful of Georgia rebels made their last stand, remembering the not more than "600" Georgians who held the bridge for "three hours," In truth, the number of Georgia soldiers was less than half that total and they held firm for five hours, not three. Ironically, the only monument that stands on the slope where Georgia colonel William R. Holmes was killed in an attempt to drive the Federals back across the bridge is a large stone, which informs visitors that the William McKinley monument lies just ahead.

The ultimate irony of history's neglect of the Georgians' role at Antietam is perhaps best illustrated by the name of the bridge itself. General Burnside earned the dubious honor of having the Rohrbach Bridge named after him in a satirical tribute. A more fitting name, perhaps, would have been "Toombs's Bridge" or "Benning's Bridge" in honor of the Georgians who fought and died to defend it.

Phillip Thomas Tucker
Washington, D.C.

# CHAPTER 1

# "For the First Time
# on the Maryland Shore"

## *The Army of Northern Virginia Moves North*

THE BATTLEFIELD VICTORIES OF THE ARMY OF NORTHERN VIRGINIA BY early 1862 revealed a fighting machine with hard-hitting capabilities. Robert E. Lee's Rebels seemed always able to do what other Southern armies, especially those in the Western theater, could not.

General Lee's rise by the bloody summer of 1862 was meteoric. When he took command of the army before the gates of Richmond after Gen. Joseph E. Johnston's wounding at Seven Pines, General Lee seized the strategic initiative and drove the Army of the Potomac from the Peninsula by launching repeated offensive strikes. Union major general John Pope had made the twin mistakes of overestimating himself and underestimating his opponent.

The bloody fighting at Seven Days had served as a launching pad for Lee's more ambitious offensive operations. Amid the summer haze of late August, the Army of Northern Virginia swiftly pushed across central and northern Virginia to descend upon General Pope's Army of the Potomac. Inspired by the Seven Days' success, Lee sent Thomas Jonathan "Stonewall" Jackson's fast-moving troops to advance in a wide-ranging march around the Bull Run mountains and swept into General Pope's rear. Before Pope could turn and strike Jackson, Lee and the rest of his army smashed into Pope, almost annihilating Pope's army at second Manassas during two days of the bloodiest fighting of the war to date. The shattered remnant of the Yankee army limped eastward to the safety of Washington, D.C.

By September 1862, the beaten Federals continued to hover in the safety of the powerful network of defenses around Washington. General

1

Lee's bold decisions and risky gambles seemed to be paying off. Now, convinced that greater audacity could lead to even greater success, he envisioned a bold thrust into Northern territory that would catch the Army of the Potomac unawares. If Lee could then crush that army outside the defenses of Washington, in either Maryland or Pennsylvania, the war might well be won by the Confederacy. And even if decisive Confederate victories on Northern soil were not forthcoming, then at least battles fought north of the Potomac River might strengthen Northern opposition to the conflict. An invasion of the North, combined with ever-lengthening casualty lists, could weaken both political and economic support for the war, and such an advantageous development might give the Confederacy an opportunity to present an attractive peace settlement.[1]

General Lee posed his ambitious plan to Pres. Jefferson Davis on 3 September. "The present seems to be the most propitious time since the commencement of the war for the Confederate Army to enter Maryland," he suggested. The next day Lee was even more optimistic, writing to Davis that he was now "more fully persuaded of the benefits that will result from an expedition into Maryland." So convinced was he of Davis's approval that he wrote, "I shall proceed to make the movement at once, unless you should signify your disapprobation."[2]

By this time, the leaders and the men of the Army of Northern Virginia had proven that they could work together more effectively than the Army of the Potomac. Under Lee's guidance, leadership on every level was performing competently and often brilliantly. After the dramatic successes of the Seven Days and at second Manassas, General Lee and his army of yeomanry and planters were being compared with Napoleon and his grand army. This unbroken string of Confederate victories, however, also fostered a dangerous overconfidence in the army and the young Southern nation. One elated Southern journalist wrote that the opportunity to invade the North "has come at last, and the advance has been made under the most favorable circumstances that it is possible to imagine." Blind to serious manpower losses, Confederate optimism continued to soar to unprecedented levels in the ranks of the Army of Northern Virginia and among its leadership. And such confidence would lead the Army of Northern Virginia to take too many risks north of the Potomac in the days ahead, making Lee and his army more vulnerable than ever before.[3]

General Lee based much of his optimism on the estimation that the beaten Army of the Potomac was in no condition to seriously contest his invasion. One Southerner reasoned at this time that "the veteran forces of the enemy have been either destroyed or demoralized by the battles of July and August. To meet our troops in Maryland, they have little else than raw recruits, many of them averse to the service and all of them cowed and over-awed by the ill-success of the last three months." Gen. William Dorsey Pender believed that the Army of the Potomac was "totally demoralized by the recent whippings we gave them and are now in and around Washington behind their fortifications." Most of the men in General Lee's army shared their commander's sense of invincibility. Georgian brigadier general Robert Augustus Toombs prayed in a 22 August 1862 letter, "I hope the army now will continue onward and reach Maryland before Lincoln raises his large reinforcements [and] I think a quick march into Maryland would cause Washington to be evacuated and close the war."

Even Northerners praised the hard-fighting Rebel soldiers who repeatedly thrashed larger and better-equipped Union armies. A Washington, D.C. newspaper journalist described a common attitude across the North: "No people, with so few numbers, ever put into the field, and kept there so long, troops more numerous, brave, or more efficient, or produced generals of more merit" than the Confederacy. And after the crushing Union defeat at second Manassas, one Northern lady penned with astonishment, "I am lost in wonder, too, at the generalship, the daring and endurance of the Southern army."[4]

Still, many Confederate soldiers pushing north toward Maryland had not enlisted to fight an aggressive war beyond the Confederacy's borders. To many of these conservative soldiers of strong Protestant beliefs, this conflict was about defending their Southern homeland. The idea of invasion did not appeal to them. Certainly this hesitation was felt in General Toombs's Georgia brigade. Many of Toombs's men experienced a sense of foreboding at the prospect of pushing north.[5] Their new role as the invader of someone else's homeland was unsettling. Consequently, even before the Army of Northern Virginia set foot on Maryland soil, numbers of graycoat soldiers dropped out of the ranks and went home. This subtle exodus was only one of the first indications of the army's serious vulnerabilities.[6]

That summer's battlefield losses, combined with shortages in manpower, resources, and matériel in the Army of Northern Virginia, compromised hope for a successful Northern invasion. A Georgia soldier scribbled in July that "you cannot picture in your mind how our troops have suffered under this long protracted fight. Whole divisions have been cut down to brigades, brigades to regiments, and regiments to companies, and companies almost annihilated . . . but the fight must go on!" [7]

After months of rigorous campaigning across Virginia, the army's medical stores and munitions were dangerously low. Even General Lee's "long arm"—the artillery—far from its supply base at Richmond, was exhausted and disorganized.

Ironically, however, the depleted condition of the Southern army played a role in the launching of the Maryland invasion. Lee felt that the move north would replenish his army with badly needed Maryland recruits and provisions, as he wrote to Davis on 4 September: "This army is about entering Maryland, with a view of affording the people of that State an opportunity of liberating themselves." If Lee failed to replenish his jaded army, however, then this ambitious push northward could become a march of folly.[8]

In the balmy days of early September 1862, the lean Rebels embarked upon their first invasion of Northern soil. Around 50,000 eager boys in gray splashed across the shallow, mile-wide Potomac River at White's Ford just above Leesburg, Virginia, as excited citizens yelled to the passing troops, "Hurrah for you! Hurrah! Kill all the Yankees."

A Georgia captain wrote of the crossing: "We stripped our pants and drawers and plunged into [the Potomac's] beautiful waters. This was a grand sight, both novel and exciting; novel because of the peculiar view presented by nature's uniforms; exciting because we were crossing into Maryland . . . " George Washington Hall, of Worth County, Georgia, noted in his diary that "shout after shout rent the air as they put their feet for the first time on the Maryland shore."

For two days, the columns churned across the Potomac. Pvt. Ivy W. Duggan of Toombs's brigade observed, "Our troops were in good spirits [and] confident in the justness of our cause, flushed with victory, and 'Maryland, my Maryland,' was sung by many a tongue."[9]

Reality soon manifested itself to Lee, however. Bolted shutters and downcast looks throughout much of Maryland revealed a marked lack of pro-Southern support. Lee had clearly chosen the wrong stage on which to play the role of liberator. A disillusioned General Pender soon wrote in disgust that "the fact is the people of N.W. Md. are . . . Dutch Yankee . . . and I do not want them."

What little support the troops received was often covert. One of Toombs's disillusioned Georgians, recorded that "we occasionally saw secession flags shown publicly, but frequently the windows would open only a few inches, so that the passer by might see the little flag, concealed from the neighbor of the next door." He continued that "not a soldier wants Maryland, unless Maryland wants to go with us. We want no hand without the heart . . . we want Maryland to be free—to enjoy the privilege of acting for herself. This is all we ask. This is what we intend to have for ourselves, and

Maryland shall have it, if she do not sell her birthright." George Hall added that "some of the citizens of Maryland received [us] in their power [but most were] as strong Yankees as can be found in the New England States." Lee reported the news to President Davis on 7 September: "Notwithstanding individual expressions of kindness that had been given, and the general sympathy in the success of the Confederate States, situated as Maryland is, I do not anticipate any general rising of the people in our behalf."[10]

Resting his army at Frederick, Maryland, near the end of September's first week, Lee planned the next phase of his offensive. The fact that Marylanders had not joined his army failed to deter his ambitions.

Meanwhile, after Gen. George McClellan was satisfied that Lee's invasion was credible, the rejuvenated Army of the Potomac departed the safety of Washington, marching into Maryland. McClellan was confident, writing on 7 September that "I shall have nearly 100,000 men, old & new, & hope with God's blessing to gain a decisive victory [and] I think we shall win for the men are now in good spirits—confident in the General & all united in sentiment."

Lee's army, in contrast, continued to deteriorate. His adjutant, Col. Walter H. Taylor, lamented by September's conclusion that "our present army is not equal to the task" of a Northern invasion. One of Toombs's men explained in a letter of the deplorable condition of Lee's soldiers by the late summer of 1862: "Our knapsacks are beyond the Rapidan [River], and we have but one suit of clothes along with us, and of course, these need washing." Another Confederate noticed: "What a set of ragamuffins they looked! It seemed as if every cornfield in Maryland had been robbed of its scarecrows and propped up against the fence. . . . My costume consisted of a ragged pair of trousers, a stained, dirty jacket; an old slouch hat, the brim pinned up with a thorn; a begrimed blanket over my shoulder, a grease-smeared cotton haversack full of apples and corn, a cartridge box full and a musket. I was barefooted and had a stonebruise on each foot . . . there was no one there who would not have been 'run in' by the police had he appeared on the streets of any populous city, and would have been fined the next day for undue exposure. Yet those grimy, sweaty, lean, ragged men were the flower of Lee's army. Those tattered, starving, unkempt fellows were the pride of their sections."

Lt. Col. James Daniel Waddell, one of Toombs's top lieutenants of the 20th Georgia Infantry, penned a letter telling his wife that "the men are miserably clad and shod. Some have not had a change of clothing since they left Richmond. We have over one hundred men in the regiment barefoot absolutely—with no early prospect of being supplied with shoes." George Hall captured the moment when he said that "our army is in a bad condition at present, the most of it is barefoot and have not but one suit of clothing. I have no shoes nor no clothes but what I have on my back."

The scarcity of supplies among Toombs's Georgia veterans was evident from the words of Pvt. Harvey Judson Hightower, of Muscogee County. Serving in the 20th Georgia, Hightower described being forced by necessity to do what had to be done on the battlefield: "I was in the fight [at second Manassas] with only one shoe and as soon as the battle was over I went up to A dead yankee and pulled off his and put them on. . . . I am in hopes if Ever I get into an other battle I wont have to rob the dead of there shoes. I have Also got A canteen and haversack." So much footwear was taken from dead Yankees that a popular saying among the Army of Northern Virginia was that "all a Yankee is now worth is his shoes."

Despite their tattered uniforms, for the most part Lee's Rebels at Frederick were highly motivated veterans. Ready to accept any challenge, one soldier from Georgia declared: "I am ready to die now if God calls me [but] I am going to sell my life as dear as possible." Sgt. William Robert assured friends at home that he and his 2nd Georgia comrades "bled for a cause they loved better than life."[11] Private Theodore T. Fogle wrote that "we are a dirty, ragged set, mother, but courage & heroism find many a true disciple among us, our Revolutionary forefathers never suffered nor fought as the 'Rebels' of '61 & '62 have fought & suffered."

Righteous indignation permeated the Army of Northern Virginia. One Georgia soldier fought because "our country is threatened [with] destruction by an inveterate enemy that is willing to show no regard for humanity nor the rights of our section and people [and we fight] to defend the rights and interests of our mothers and sisters and homes." Another Georgian affirmed that "the acme of a Southern soldier's ambition consists in the fervent hope that he be afforded the earliest practicable chance of crossing bayonets with the mercenaries of a despotic tyrant who has without a cause forced upon him the alternative of resistance to servilism and drive[n] him in confusion and dismay from the sacred soil of his sunny South!"

Dying in battle was noble sacrifice; one boy swore that "if it [be] my lot to fall in [the] battlefield . . . it will be a just cause . . . for we are fighting for our country and our rights and loved ones left behind." Another Georgia Rebel declared: "We have everything to fight for—our wives, children, land and principles." Another described it as a contest "in defense of innocent girls and women from the fangs of the lecherous Northern hirelings!"

Optimism ran high in Toombs's Georgia brigade. One of his soldiers scribbled in a letter: "Will we go to Baltimore, or towards Pennsylvania?" Another young Georgian crowed: "It is our cry now, Ho: for Washington . . . if we ever get in three miles of Washington City, we will have it or make a heap of death come."[12]

In the Empire State of the South, Georgians, who had no idea of the harsh realities of war, were excited about the invasion north of the Potomac and deep into the heart of Maryland. Already the children of some Rebels had been baptized "Bull Run" and "Virginia" to honor Lee's past victories in the Old Dominion. Soldiers' letters and newspaper accounts informed the home folk of what they might expect after the Confederacy's first major push into the North. A confident Georgia officer wrote to his father in September 1862:

> The fall campaign opens on our part with a brilliancy and success absolutely wonderful. Contrasted with the position the Confederate States occupied three months since, our present is almost incredible . . . and the war is being carried 'beyond the outer confines of our Confederacy' . . . Lee, Jackson, and Longstreet [now] pressing to the rescue of Maryland, Ohio and Pennsylvania will both soon feel the presence of actual, present warfare; while a hasty retreat will be all that is left for the scattered armies of our invaders, who linger in uncertainty and fear in our borders, which they of late overran in such pride, strength, and exultation . . . never in the annals of the world has a nation in such [a] short period achieved such a history. Not two years old, and we have already performed such prodigies of valor, given such assurance of greatness, afforded such examples of moral heroism, individual action, and national prowess, and exhibited such proofs of high-toned patriotism, devotion to principle, and love of truth, that we search in vain among the pages of the past for a record to parallel it. Whatever else the nations of the earth may think or say or do, we have already wrested from them unbounded respect and admiration.[13]

Many wealthy Georgians at home—unlike the community and state leaders serving as Toombs's officers—were sending substitutes to the front to fight for them. By the time of the Maryland campaign, this discrimination based on class and wealth affected the morale of Toombs's Georgians and other Rebels. One Georgia soldier complained that "some men are home, who made the loudest noise to bring on the war, [and] are now speaking and creaking in every hold to keep out of it." Lt. Joseph T. Scott, 20th Georgia, applauded the passing of measures back home to narrow the gap between yeoman and planter: "Now that the wealthy man who owned money and negroes enough to keep his precious carcass out of the reach of the Yankee lead, is reduced to the level of the poor man, with a dozen help-less children, there will spring up a new enthusiasm in the army, and we look forward to a future pregnant with victorious results in our strife against our common foe."

Never before had the soldiers of the 2nd and the 20th Georgia been so far from home. When the war was young, a naive Private Fogle had told his parents that he desired to serve in Virginia. He did not like the idea of "going so far from home, however, I'm in for it now & will go willingly, I have no fear, & want to meet the Northern Scoundrels & help to give them a beating."

During their first major campaign outside Virginia, the Georgians noticed striking contrasts between the eastern border state and the Deep South. It was early September and the nights were now cooler and less humid than in Georgia at this time of year. George Hall noted with surprise that the "vegetation is about one month later here than it is in Georgia."

The bounty of late summer harvests and the extensive crops in the sprawling fields of western Maryland were first evident upon crossing the Potomac. Compared with the backwoods pine forests and red clay hills of the Georgia interior, Maryland was a land of plenty, with seemingly endless fields. Nestled on fertile land, these tidy farms generally produced higher yields than those of the Georgia backcountry.

Stock animals and herds of sleek horses and fat cattle roamed the fields and pastures. Extensive orchards overflowed with fruit. Most important, western Maryland was not dominated by wide stretches of dense wood-lands like most of Georgia, but was well-proportioned with neat woodlots bordering the expansive grain fields. These woodlots looked like parks nes-tled among the sprawling valleys.

The Southerners viewed western Maryland, virtually untouched by war, as an agricultural utopia. Unlike the wealthy Georgia planters, who profited from slave labor on their sprawling cotton and rice plantations along fertile river bottoms and the coastal plain, the vast majority of Toombs's soldiers were mostly lower- and middle-class farmers in Georgia who had struggled to raise small patches of corn, tobacco, oats, or cotton, supplementing their subsistence farming with hunting and trapping game in the forests.

An amazed Pvt. Ivy Duggan described the superior road network of this eastern border state of plenty. "Their turnpikes are great roads among the mountains, graded almost like a railroad, thoroughly imbedded with pounded stones, while even small streams are spanned by arches of solid masonry, capable of sustaining any weight, while they defy the ravages of time and the swellings of tide. To me these splendid bridges are truly wonderful." One of those stone crossings, the Rohrbach Bridge, lay to the west along a creek in western Maryland called the Antietam.

In addition, the Georgians noticed the sturdy stone structures, houses, barns, smokehouses, and outbuildings of western Maryland's farmers. Awed by the prosperity of the countryside, Duggan wrote:

> The barns too are truly an object of wonder. They are generally built of stone, often much larger than our meeting houses, and several stories high. Such forage houses would be unnecessarily large in middle Georgia, but this is indeed a grain country. Such quantities of grain as we see here are really astonishing to the subjects of King Cotton. We often see large fields enclosed with a good stonewall fence. So much labor and money is expended in substantial improvement on a farm that while we admire it, one raised in a Georgia log cabin is reminded of the boy, who went to Augusta [Georgia] and paid his last cent for a fine pocket-book . . . we behold a large valley, stretching far away . . . thickly dotted with large shocks of grain, rich clover fields, fine orchards loaded with fruit and neat white houses . . . I believe I like the little State pretty well. I have never seen apples, pears and quinces so abundant as in Maryland. Good water can be found almost everywhere.[14]

In contrast with the prosperous state, the depleted Army of Northern Virginia badly needed recuperation and replenishment by the end of the first week of September 1862. Now that they had discovered that Maryland's liberation was beyond reach, homespun Georgians concluded: "We may have Maryland, but [we] do not want her . . . there are so many Republicans there that they would always be kicking up a mess, and we would have to whip them."[15]

# CHAPTER 2

# "If We Go Back Bachelors It Won't Be Our Fault"

## *The 2nd and 20th Georgia*

By the time of the Maryland campaign, the 2nd and 20th Georgia Infantry comprised seasoned and reliable troops. These two regiments of General Toombs's brigade hailed mainly from the upper two-thirds of Georgia. The largest contingent originated in the western section of Georgia, especially the fertile lands of the Chattahoochee Valley along the Chattahoochee River, which divided Georgia from Alabama.

Four sections of the state were heavily represented by the 2nd and 20th Georgia Infantry: the counties north of Atlanta including Fulton, Whitfield, Fannin, Banks, Cherokee, and Polk; a scattering of mid-Georgia counties (Meriwether, Bibb, and Telfair Counties); a cluster of eastern counties (Richmond, Jefferson, and Burke Counties); and the western counties bordering the Chattahoochee River (Harris, Muscogee, Marion, and Stewart Counties).

The majority of Toombs's soldiers were young and single. According to one cocky Confederate, his Georgia friends, neighbors, and relatives in gray composed a "company of bachelors." He added that "the ages of the men average from 16 to 25, not a married man among us [but] if we go back bachelors it won't be our fault." These young men went to war during the summer of 1861 "in excellent spirits and expect[ed] to send to Georgia a good account of themselves." When the news of Georgia's secession on 19 January 1861 first swept through the town of Columbus on the Chattahoochee, it "was received with great exultation and welcomed by the ringing of bells—shooting of cannon &c," wrote Pvt. Thomas E. Blanchard.

As naive innocents eager to "see the elephant," wrote one Second Georgia soldier, these volunteers departed with bands playing and citizens cheering. One Rebel described the festive send-off as like a "party going on a pleasure excursion," instead of marching to war. Excited citizens encouraged the Georgians on their romantic adventure by screaming, "Hurrah for Georgia! Bring me a scalp when you come back!"

The 2nd Georgia Infantry was one of the first Georgia infantry units to enlist for service in the Confederacy, thanks largely to its prewar militia nucleus, the Columbus Guards of Muscogee County, which made up one-tenth of the regiment. The company traced a distinguished lineage back to 1836 and the second Creek War. Its members included the social and political elite of Columbus, the largest town on the Chattahoochee and soon to be an important war production center.

Sgt. William Robert Houghton, a teenage schoolteacher from a small Alabama town across the Chattahoochee from Columbus, described the Columbus Guards as one of the "crack military companies of the city, in whose ranks were found the young men of the best talent and blood of this thriving town. It was an old organization with high standards, the pride of West Georgia and Eastern Alabama." The company, which contained at least one French Zouave, equipped its soldiers with red uniform jackets, black pants, and blue caps manufactured at the Eagle Manufacturing Company in Columbus. Most of the Guards' firearms were produced locally, but were supplemented by muskets purchased in New York City by the farsighted Georgians in November 1860.

Capt. Paul Jones Semmes, an aristocratic member of the planter class and a Columbus banker and lawyer, led the company. Semmes was the cousin of both the commander of the famous Rebel raider, *Alabama*, Adm. Raphael Semmes, and Thomas J. Semmes, a Confederate congressman who later advocated one of the most unpopular proposals in the Confederacy's short history, the arming of African Americans to resist invading Yankee armies.

The Columbus Guards included men from across the socio-economic spectrum. One Georgia soldier described the company as consisting of "men of every calling, sailors, soldiers of the Mexican War, a French Zouave who had served in Algiers, men who had been educated in Europe, travelers, circus clowns, poets, authors and musicians." Destined soon to become a sergeant of Company G, 2nd Georgia, Pvt. Lucius Q. Johnson, the son of a future governor of Georgia, also served in the Columbus Guards.

The Guards benefited from the wartime experience of a solid cadre of Mexican and Indian War veterans, as did other brigades in the Army of Northern Virginia. These seasoned officers, both commissioned and noncommissioned, molded the younger volunteers of the 2nd Georgia. During the antebellum period, the reputation of these soldiers from the rich farmlands and plantations along the Chattahoochee was the pride of Georgia. Describing the Columbus Guards, Private Blanchard said "a more clever & sociable set, I never met before. Reserve & Formality was done away with, and we were all 'Boys together.'"

In February 1861 the seventy-man Columbus Guards served as the personal escort for the newly elected president Jefferson Davis at his Montgomery, Alabama, inauguration. They fired the first official salute to honor the new nation from a small cannon known as "Little Red Jacket." Pvt. Blanchard noted in his diary that "having carried our cannon with us, as soon as the [train] cars stopped, we took it out & gave the Pres'd the first official salute he ever recd. [and] I fired the second gun."

The Columbus soldiers then gave "an exhibition of drill, bayonet practice, and firing that the Montgomery Press declared the most proficient ever seen." Impressed citizens exclaimed that the soldiers "move[d] like machinery." During the president's inaugural parade, Captain Semmes led a militia battalion, while the Columbus Guards took the post of honor. Blanchard wrote in his diary of a new democratic experiment at Montgomery: "All seemed to be deeply impressed with the great importance of the occasion—It was indeed an important event well worthy of a serious thought. For it was the formation stone of the new government—a set of people had determined to quit the yoke under which they had been submitting—and make a government to suit themselves. A Government, where liberty as it should be—would reign triumphant."[1]

Before journeying to Virginia, the Columbus Guards united with other Georgia volunteer companies to meet the Union navy's threat to Georgia's Atlantic coast, thus spawning the 2nd Georgia. Among these companies were the Banks County Guards, the Burke County Sharpshooters under the command of an eager young commander, Capt. William R. Holmes, the Joe Brown volunteers of Fannin County, the Cherokee Riflemen of Cherokee County, the Buena Vista Guards of Marion County, the Wright Infantry of Whitfield County, the Semmes Guards of Muscogee County, the Stewart Grays of Stewart County, and the Jackson Blues of Meriwether County.

Rivaling the finely uniformed Columbus Guards' reputation as the best company in the regiment were the Burke Sharpshooters. For years, these marksmen served with distinction as the color company of the 2nd Georgia. In the words of one of Captain Holmes's soldiers, "The Burke Sharpshooters was the first volunteer company from Burke County to the war. Its personnel was representative of the best citizenship of old Burke. In this company there were eight physicians, six lawyers, three printers, and one editor." Improving in quality as the war lengthened, other 2nd Georgia companies began to rise to the level of the Burke County Sharpshooters, wrestling for their reputation as the regiment's finest company.[2]

Anticipating a quick, easy victory, these volunteer infantry companies journeyed southeast by rail to Savannah, where they mustered into service at Tybee Island. "We drilled, [and] fought mosquitoes and fleas for two months," noted Sergent Houghton of the Columbus Guards, who quickly learned that war was not as romantic as he once believed. The newly organized 2nd Georgia then traveled south to Brunswick, Georgia, to help defend the coast. At Brunswick, the organization of the 2nd Georgia was finally completed on 1 June 1861. The 2nd Georgia was destined to fight in more than fifty engagements before the end of the war. Little did these innocent soldiers realize that only eight men would assemble when they formed the final time for surrender four years later at Appomattox.

Eager for action, the 2nd Georgia pushed northward from Brunswick in late July 1861 to reinforce Richmond and join General Toombs's new Georgia brigade. The news of the transfer had "caused a great deal of joy and a stag dance," throughout the 2nd Georgia, observed Houghton. Thereafter, the regiment was stationed in northern Virginia through the dreary winter of 1861–62. While there, Pvt. Thaddeus Oliver of the Buena Vista Guards, 2nd Georgia, composed one of the war's most popular songs. Fated to die in the war, Oliver wrote "All Quiet along the Potomac," while far from the Georgia home that he would never see again.

The level of inexperience among these volunteer rustics of the 2nd Georgia was early evident. Capt. Daniel Gill Candler, commander of the Banks County Guards, was "a gentleman of the old school, and a planter," said another Georgian, who described the Banks County men as Captain Candler's "old neighbors' sons, his personal friends and social equals." On one occasion, when a fence and gate impeded his soldiers' march, Candler—as green as his men—forgot the order "by the right-flank, file left." Instead, he improvised: "Gentlemen of the Banks County Guards! Will you please halt?" After the company stopped, the novice commander continued, "Gentlemen, you will now take a recess of ten minutes. Break ranks! and when you 'fall in,' you will please reform on the other side of the fence."

Rowdiness among the enlisted ranks sometimes made life difficult for the 2nd Georgia's officers. A more refined Virginia infantryman described how "the Georgians were hard but also gay and festive fighters." The city boys of the elite Columbus Guards helped to instill esprit de corps among the regiment's raw volunteers. At the war's beginning, these Georgia rustics knew more about how to plow, shoot wild game, and brag about how many Yankees they could kill, than about the discipline needed to be a good soldier. By the time of the Maryland campaign, however, these rural Georgians had been turned into some of the best soldiers of the 2nd Georgia.

Thanks to his West Point experience and leadership of the Columbus Guards, Paul Semmes was commissioned a colonel and became the 2nd Georgia's commander. Also a University of Virginia graduate, Colonel Semmes was a disciplinarian, soon molding his 2nd Georgia into a dependable fighting machine. Pvt. Theodore Fogle discovered that "Col. Semmes is extremely strict, well I suppose he is right, but (I speak it privately) he is disposed sometimes to exceed his authority, but perhaps he will be all right when things get straight, he has had a rough set to manage, most of the companies in the regiment are composed of the roughest sort of material, even their officers have to be taught everything, I'll venture to say that notwithstanding all the disadvantages we will soon have as good a regiment as is in the service." Semmes enjoyed respect throughout the Army of Northern Virginia by the time of the Maryland campaign. Col. Edward Porter Alexander wrote that Semmes "was well known in Georgia as a man both of military tastes & accomplishments before the war . . . and it is due him to day that there never was a braver or a better."

Semmes became well-known for his "penetrating voice & the short temper." During a September 1861 expedition into northern Virginia during the lull after first Manassas, one Georgia private made the mistake of asking Semmes how long they would remain in the field, far from the comforts of camp. The colonel barked angrily, "We didn't come here to go back to camp sir, we came to fight a battle!" Colonel Alexander never forgot an encounter he observed when riding down a muddy road one night during a campaign. Suddenly he heard Semmes's voice "clear & sharp [bellow] 'Get out of the road, Sir,' & some man in reply said—But I can't. Here's a big ditch on both sides. I can't get off of here.' 'By God! you can and you will,' said Semmes and immediately there was a tremendous splash & floundering in the water & that was all."

To assist him, Semmes relied upon a number of capable subordinates. Lt. Col. Alpheus Harris was born in 1832 in North Carolina. Colonel Harris was a Georgia aristocrat who had married well, taking a judge's daughter as his wife. In addition, Harris owned extensive gold and copper mining interests in Cherokee County, Georgia—a region owned by native Americans before the discovery of precious metal by white settlers. Harris would be killed during the decisive clash of the Vicksburg campaign at Champion Hill, Mississippi.

After the 2nd Georgia's organization, company commanders of the regiment consisted of the following captains: Daniel Gill Candler, Company A, the Banks County Guards of Banks County; William Terrill Harris of Company B, the Jackson Blues of Meriwether County; William Smythe Sheppard, Company C, the Semmes Guards of Muscogee County; William R. Holmes, Company D, the Burke Sharpshooters of Burke County; William A. Campbell, Company E, the Joe Browns of Fannin County; Thomas E. Dickerson, Company F, the Cherokee Riflemen of Cherokee County; Roswell Ellis, Company G, the Columbus Guards of Muscogee County; Jesse A. Glenn, Company H, the Wright Infantry of Whitfield County; Charles R. Wiggins, Company I, the Buena Vista Guards of Marion County; and Jared I. Ball, Company K, the Stewart Grays of Stewart County. Chapl. John B. Dunwoody provided spiritual guidance for the company.

An example of the quality of the company commanders of the 2nd Georgia was Capt. William Smythe Sheppard. He was well liked, if not idolized, by his men. Like many soldiers in Toombs's brigade, Sheppard studied at the Georgia Military Institute at Marietta. Sergeant Houghton described the complex, aristocratic captain as possessing "all the qualities that go to make a fine man, but rather reserved." A onetime private of the Columbus Guards under the then captain Semmes, Sheppard now led Company C, after having been elected captain in July 1862. Heavy losses to come launched Sheppard into the rank of major of the 2nd Georgia, and at Gettysburg, he would lead the regiment into the bloody fighting that swirled through the Devil's Den on the hot afternoon of 2 July 1863.[3]

The regiment's fine brass band from Columbus, under the skillful leadership of Chief Musician Willis Cox, also made its mark. The initial formation of the Georgians' military band came with the first call to arms. In a surge of Southern nationalism and youthful idealism, the pupils of Professor Ryan's music class at Columbus enlisted en masse in the 2nd Georgia. Sergeant Houghton boasted that "the 2nd Georgia had one of the best bands in our army, and it frequently drew immense crowds to our evening parades." Pvt. Ivy Duggan described a rare—and perhaps feigned—demonstration of support from the Marylanders during the late summer of 1862: "There is secession here. I was not a little surprised at the enthusiasm, shown by many of the citizens as our brigade passed along the streets, while the excellent band of the Second Georgia, discoursed sweet music." These musicians played on the front lines and in the midst of battle. High losses were consequently suffered by the Georgia bandsmen during the Seven Days and second Manassas. Soaring casualties eventually resulted in the disbanding of the ensemble in 1862.[4]

The sister regiment of the 2nd Georgia, also destined to play a key role in the defense of Burnside's Bridge, was the 20th Georgia Infantry. The 20th was commanded by Col. William Duncan Smith. Born in Georgia in 1826, he graduated from West Point in 1846, and fought in the Mexican War. [5] Like the 2nd, the 20th was composed primarily of nonslaveholding lower- and middle-class farmers. The regiment began its organization in Richmond during the summer of 1861. One of the first companies to become part of the 20th Georgia was the Southern Guards from Muscogee County. Most of these volunteers were Chattahoochee Valley men from the Columbus area under the command of forty-two-year-old Capt. John Abraham Jones, a Mexican War veteran and Columbus lawyer.

Other Georgia companies arrived at Richmond in time to become part of the 20th Georgia. The Border Rangers of Muscogee County, including volunteers like Pvt. John William Lokey, were led by a reliable Mexican War veteran who had fought with the Texas Rangers, Capt. John A. Strother. Another Muscogee County company, led by Capt. John R. Ivey, became the veterans of Company G, 20th Georgia. [6] Then came the Sparks Guards under the leadership of Capt. Jonathan B. Cumming, who became the lieutenant colonel of the 20th Georgia when Captain Jones left his company to become major of the new Georgia regiment. The organization of the 20th Georgia was completed by the arrival of Roger Lawson Gamble and the Jefferson Guards of Jefferson County, James Daniel Waddell's Polk County Company, Ransom D. Little's Whitesville Guards of Harris County, Eli M. Seago's Confederate Continentals of Fulton County, John A. Coffee and the Telfair Volunteers of Telfair County, Van A. Leonard and the Southern Guards of Muscogee County, and William Craig at the head of the Montgomery Guards of Richmond County. James A. Garrison who served as chaplain, found his work challenging both on and off the battlefield. [7]

Irish, Germans, Frenchmen, American Indians, Jews, Englishmen, and Scotsmen served in both the 2nd and 20th Georgia regiments. But no company of the 2nd Georgia was more ethnically diverse than the Columbus Guards, Company G. Among these immigrants was a well-liked Englishman, Lt. Richard Potter, "a splendid fellow," who was killed during the suicidal assault at Malvern Hill. Also in the ranks was Pvt. William A. Martiniere of French heritage. Ironically, a number of Northerners also fought in the ranks of the 2nd Georgia. One such soldier was good-humored Pvt. William L. Anderson, from Pennsylvania, who was excited about the prospect of perhaps entering his home state after the army pushed into western Maryland, just south of the Pennsylvania border.

Anderson was somewhat of a dandy. A comrade described the fighting Quaker as being "a fop in dress, and had such fine manners, that the boys dubbed him 'Prince of Wales'." Private Anderson's opposite, Sergeant Houghton, joyfully recorded how the dapper Anderson "got to be as dirty and ragged as any of us, although he never complained." The "Prince" received the dubious honor of being the first Columbus Guardsman to fall wounded in action.

Jewish Rebels also served in Company G, including John R. Moses of Columbus, and his young nephews, Pvts. Montefiore J. and William M. Moses. Montefiore performed capably as the commissary officer of General Toombs's brigade and was consequently elevated to a higher position in the Confederate Commissary Department. Later, the multiskilled Montefiore used his medical education as an assistant surgeon of a Mississippi regiment in July 1862.

The 20th Georgia likewise encompassed a diverse collection of nationalities and ethnic groups. Company A, the Sparks Guards, hailed from the town of Macon, southeast of Atlanta. Despite its interior location, immigrants settled in Macon in large numbers. Among the many Celts of Company A, first organized by Captain Cumming, were Patrick Donlevy, Lee R. Hennegan, F. M. S. Filpatrick, Peter McIntyre, and John O. Riley. Company G, Twentieth Georgia, contained even more Celts than Company A, consisting of Celtic Rebels from the busy Chattahoochee port of Columbus. This Muscogee County company included James McCorkle, Absalom D. McDonald, Thomas McEachern, William McElrath, O. McIntyre, Joseph C. McKenzie, Samuel Thomas McKenzie, and Joseph M. McMillan. In addition, some Frenchmen, like musician Bertrand Tissereau, also served in the Sparks Guards.[8]

A solid cadre of General Toombs's officers were graduates of the prestigious Georgia Military Institute, ensuring effective leadership by the time of the Maryland invasion.[9] Despite West Pointers in the ranks, the Georgia Military Institute, modeled after West Point, molded the quality of Toombs's brigade more than any other institution.[10] Many soldiers of this brigade, both officers and enlisted men, were graduates of leading Georgia institutions of higher learning, such as Emory University in Atlanta. One such Emory-educated soldier was Lt. Reuben W. Carswell, a Louisville, Georgia, lawyer, who served as the commander of Company C, 20th Georgia. In addition, some Georgia Military Institute graduates serving as officers in the brigade, such as Sheppard and Hansford Twiggs, were also University of Georgia graduates, as was Col. Henry Lewis Benning. Toombs also attended the University of Georgia. Indeed, the influence of the University of Georgia, then known as Franklin College, in Toombs's Brigade was widespread. Among Toombs's other University of Georgia officers were Maj. William Terrill Harris, a former lawyer and planter who would become the major of the 2nd Georgia, and Capt. James Daniel Waddell, a lawyer from the Class of 1853, who would serve as the 20th Georgia's colonel. Waddell's grandfather, Dr. Moses Waddell, had been the president of the University of Georgia.

Many officers of General Toombs's brigade enjoyed influential political and social connections, which extended to the top levels of the Confederate government. The brother of Vice Pres. Alexander H. Stephens, Linton Stephens, served as the lieutenant colonel of the 15th Georgia Infantry. Many other members of Toombs's Brigade possessed antebellum political or government experience. The 20th Georgia's colonel by the time of the Maryland campaign, Jonathan B. Cumming, had served as the doorkeeper of the Georgia Senate. Maj. William Harris, who would be killed at Gettysburg on 2 July 1863, served in the Georgia state legislature along with the colonel of the 15th Georgia, William MacPherson McIntosh. Many lower-grade officers, as well, were well educated, including some noncommissioned officers of Toombs's brigade. Orderly Sgt. Heman Humphreys Perry, of the Burke Sharpshooters, 2nd Georgia, had received an education at both Georgetown University and the University of Virginia, Charlottesville. Some of the lowest ranking privates boasted of high-quality educations. In the Columbus Guards, Sergeant Houghton never forgot one young 2nd Georgia soldier, "who knew more Shakespeare than any man I ever saw."[11]

Another important influence on General Toombs's brigade was the widespread state militia experience from prewar days. General Toombs and Colonel Benning, in addition, early on emphasized the importance of drill and discipline. The 2nd Georgia, therefore, became famous as one of the best-drilled regiments in the Army of Northern Virginia.[12] Many former Georgia militia members were sprinkled throughout the ranks of the brigade.[13]

Colonel Semmes and his Columbus Guards were known as "one of the best drilled [companies] in the South." Private Theodore Fogle wrote of the hard campaigning in the alternating dust and mud of Virginia that "I cant imagine what it is that the Columbus Guards are made of, they stand all kinds of hardships better than any other company in the regiment, & keep up their spirits under it all, that night they were singing & cracking jokes all the way, some fellow would say a witty thing & we would all break out in a roar, we had our knapsacks & blankets on our backs, our guns on our shoulders, & each man had forty rounds of cartridges in his box, that many cartridges is in itself no mean weight to carry on a march,—well all that weight combined could not keep down our spirits, & we beat the whole regiment on the march." The value of pre-war militia experience was clearly important in training and preparing these young Georgian soldiers for the challenges of war.[14]

The Columbus Guards possessed not only militia skills but also carried the hard-learned lessons of the Indian and Mexican Wars with them to meet the challenges of the Maryland invasion. In 1847, for instance, the Columbus Guards had marched into Mexico City with Gen. Winfield Scott and had been "feted and toasted in the piping times of peace for its superior drilling and the excellent material of which it was composed."

The Mexican War experience of many leading officers helped to make General Toombs's Georgians a dependable fighting force—improving discipline, as well as laying the foundation before the first battle for a veteran cadre of officers. Col. William Duncan Smith fought as a United States officer in General Scott's army of Manifest Destiny during the advance on Mexico City in 1847. As a captain of the 2nd United States Dragoons, he had been wounded in bitter fighting with Gen. Antonio Lopez de Santa Anna's forces. Leading Company F, 20th Georgia, Capt. Eli M. Seago, had also seen service during the Mexican War. Many of the lower-grade officers of General Toombs's brigade also boasted Mexican War experience, such as Lt. Minck Ivey. In the ranks, the Taliaferro County soldiers from the Stephens Home Guards—named in honor of Vice President Stephens—esteemed Lieutenant Ivey because of his distinguished Mexican War record. These Georgia Rebels also drew upon the lessons learned from years of fighting Creek and Seminole Indians on the untamed Georgia frontier and in the wilds of Florida during the 1830s and 1840s.[15]

Having seen Indian combat in Florida during the Seminole Wars and within their own borders, faced the threat of slave revolt especially after John Brown's October 1859 raid on Harpers Ferry, Virginia, and witnessed from afar the black uprisings in St. Domingue, or Haiti, the Georgia Confederates (including Toombs, who strongly denounced Brown's raid) now felt motivated to fight to keep war from touching Georgia. If Union armies eventually invaded Georgia, then the Georgians feared that slave insurrections might consume the state in their absence.[16] Private Fogle, now hundreds of miles from his homeland, confided his worst fears for his people: "I could meet the Yankees now with a great deal of pleasure [because] if Georgia is not well guarded she will suffer."

Fueled by fear, romantic idealism, and Southern nationalism, Toombs's soldiers marched into Maryland, in tattered uniforms and with often

empty haversacks, in pursuit of independence. The 20th Georgia's lieutenant Joseph Scott wrote that this unceasing struggle must be continued
until "our liberties are attained." Scott later expressed the greatest hope for
himself and Toombs's soldiers: "All the heart of the patriot can hope, pray
and fight for, is our independence as a free and untrammeled Confederacy." Worth County's George Hall described the determination of the
Georgia soldiery: "It is far better that they Should lay down their lives at
the Sacrafice [*sic*] of their country and homes than to live and suffer Slavery and degradation below the beast of the forest."[17]

The spiritual faith of the young men and boys of the 2nd and 20th
Georgia was rooted in their strong religious background and frontier spiri-
tualism and revivalism. This faith sprang from the untamed land itself,
with these men growing up close to both gospel and nature among the
hills, creek bottoms, and river valleys of Georgia. Often, it was through
calling on this faith that terrified soldiers were able to summon the courage
to fight. In an 8 August 1862 letter describing the bloody summer battles
around Richmond, Pvt. Harvey Hightower prayed that he might live
through one more battle: "With tearful eyes and A bleeding heart [I] fell
upon my knees and Asked God to spare me that I might hear from you
And meet you Again." Urgently invoking God's mercy, another Georgia
soldier wrote during the slaughter of the Seven Days: "But above all let us
all with one accord as a people give all the praise and honor to God, by
whose help and strong arm alone have we been delivered from our foes."
As the war grew more vicious, faith in God became stronger throughout
the ranks of Toombs's brigade. When a Yankee bullet slammed into one
Georgian's chest and tore through his Bible instead of his flesh, a comrade
observed that "the ball stopped at the 51st chapter and 14th and 15th
verses. He is [now a more] devoted Christian."

By the time of the Maryland campaign, hardships and sacrifices had
transformed General Toombs's men into a much more religious soldiery
than in 1861—a blessing to chaplains such as Dunwoody and Garrison.
George Hall penned in his diary that "I hope and ernestly [*sic*] pray to my
great Redeemer who had carried me safe through so many Battles and hair
breadth escapes, that . . . a glorious peace and independence will [come to]
our unhappy country and all of us poor soldiers who have fought so long
and gallantly for her independence may return home to greet our long
parted friends and relations and to reap the reward that is due us for our
toiling and hardships." Still, one cynical Georgia Confederate understood
that more than God's help was needed to win this brutal war. "Trust in

God is a very good thing in its place, indeed an absolutely essential thing," he said, "but it is also a good thing to keep the powder dry."

Sgt. William Robert Houghton was hardened by the war but refused to forsake either his humanity or Christianity, keeping the faith. He greatly admired the gray-clad brigade chaplains, writing:

> It took a devoted man to be patient in constant hearing of the profanity, ribaldry and general deviltry of camp life, but those who were patient, kind and loving to the men, had their rewards in the affection and respect of the soldiers [but] I think men got to lean towards fatalism after awhile. We could stand on the field looking down into the peaceful, sometimes smiling, faces of dead comrades, so full of life an hour before, and around us, not a tree or a twig the size of a pencil but cut or barked by bullets, and yet we had charged and fought and stood at this very spot for minutes or hours.[18]

As their reputations for combat prowess demonstrated, the young men and boys of Toombs's brigade were tough. They were also sufficiently individualistic to openly question orders, curse an officer, or even knock down a superior on occasion. When a free-thinking young lieutenant was directed by a major to double-quick his company, he "told his men to double-quick, but did not see a damned bit of use in it." Diminutive, red-haired Pvt. John Lindsay of the Columbus Guards was thrown into the guardhouse when he refused to cut firewood for the 2nd Georgia's colonel as ordered. But this was only the beginning. Private Lindsay's arrest immediately incited the 2nd Georgia to revolt against their officers. In the words of Sergeant Houghton, who was one of the insubordinates, "In five minutes a hundred bayonets were fixed and guns loaded to go and get him out. The officers were greatly distressed, but to our relief John came up smiling, and there never was another 2nd Georgian called on to perform such service."[19]

By the time of the Maryland campaign, yet another strong impulse drove the 2nd and 20th Georgia soldiers to stand firm in the fighting ahead. They struggled so that their many comrades who had already fallen should not have died in vain. Battle-hardened Sergeant Houghton never forgot that "the most pitiful of all were the boys, those of fourteen and fifteen years, as they lay dead on the field. We had carried their guns on the march, petted them in rough soldier fashion, and lightened the burdens of the little heroes."[20] Now they were no more.

## CHAPTER 3

# "Not Entirely a Subordinate and Respectful Brigadier"

## *The Impossible Robert A. Toombs*

ALL HIS LIFE, BRIG. GEN. ROBERT AUGUSTUS TOOMBS WAS AN INDIVIDU-
alist as controversial as he was boisterous and opinionated. By the time of
the Maryland campaign, Toombs's brigade comprised the 2nd, 15th, 17th,
and 20th Georgia Infantry, and the 1st Georgia Regulars. At a robust fifty-
one, Toombs was yet in his prime. To both friend and foe, he was a hot-
tempered dynamo. It was said of Toombs that if it would assist the
Confederacy, then he "was for an alliance with Satan himself." The general's sarcasm, vanity, bawdiness, and intellect were already well-known
across the South. An English correspondent of the *Times* of London
described Toombs as "unquestionably one of the most original, quaint,
and earnest of the Southern leaders."

Col. Edward Porter Alexander dryly observed that Toombs "was not
entirely a subordinate & respectful brigadier." Throughout his life, dispute
and controversy attached themselves to Bob Toombs like a magnet, and as
if moved by an irresistible force, Toombs seemed to be drawn to confrontations. He clearly relished personal clashes.

Born near Washington, Wilkes County, Georgia, on 2 July 1810,
Toombs descended from a middle-class family, boasting a line of warriors.
Toombs's Virginia grandfather had served in a French and Indian War, and
his father—Maj. Robert Toombs—fought with distinction during the
American Revolution. As a leader of the Washington Guards of Wilkes
County, Toombs had served in the Creek War in 1836. He and other
Georgians fought to ensure that a Creek-Seminole alliance did not incite
the local slaves to revolt. With typical gusto, Toombs shared the militia
tradition of his family.[1]

Toombs's delinquency began early in life. At the University of Georgia, then Franklin College, in Athens, Georgia, the teenage Toombs was expelled twice for serious infractions. When a pair of brothers badly thrashed him, he attacked them with a bowl, a knife, a pistol, a hatchet, and a club. After being forced to resign rather than face expulsion in 1826 because of gambling, Toombs entered Union College in Schenectady, New York. He graduated from the Northern school in 1828 without incident and later entered law school at the University of Virginia. There, far away again from Georgia, he thrived.

Gaining admission to the bar in Wilkes County in 1830, Toombs soon became one of the leading lawyers in Georgia. He began to amass his own personal fortune in a profession that well suited his antagonistic personality and keen intellect. A smart businessman and investor, Toombs also acquired large plantations not only in Stewart County, Georgia, but also west of the Mississippi River in the rich farmlands of Arkansas and Texas.

Toombs also found time to marry into a wealthy and respected family. Throughout his future political career, the only aspect of Toombs's life that seemed to have any stability was his relationship with his wife and children. Julia Ann DuBose was the quiet opposite of the troublesome Toombs. Despite the mismatch or because of it, the marriage was successful, resulting in three children and a harmony lacking in the rest of Toombs's controversial life.

Fate later upset Toombs's domestic bliss, however. Two of his children died during the antebellum period, one son in infancy, and twenty-one-year-old Mary Louisa, his favorite daughter, in 1855. The loss of this daughter was the most severe personal blow Toombs suffered during his lifetime. Her death apparently increased Toombs's much-publicized drinking both before and during the war. Only one child now remained, Sallie, and she would nearly die giving birth in February 1861.

During the antebellum period, Tombs also developed a lifelong friendship with another young lawyer and a future ally in the rough-and-tumble world of Georgia politics, diminutive Alexander Stephens whom he affectionately called "Aleck." Militia service during the Creek War bolstered Toombs's social standing and his budding political career, which began the same year, 1836.

As a Whig, he was elected to the Georgia state legislature, where he served from 1837 to 1843. Here, notoriety followed his attacks on the governor's policies. Success in local government opened the doors for Toombs to embark upon a career in national government. In 1843, consequently, he won a seat as a Whig in the U.S. House of Representatives, where he served from 1844 to 1852 beside his friend Stephens. In the Southern capital, Varina Davis, the attractive wife of Jefferson Davis, described Congressman Toombs in his prime as "a university man [who] had kept up his classics . . . Mr. Toombs was over six feet tall, with broad shoulders; his fine head set well on his shoulders, and was covered with long, glossy black hair, which, when speaking, he managed to toss about."

In December 1846, Toombs, Stephens, and a young country lawyer from Illinois named Abraham Lincoln ironically became three of the seven original members of the Taylor Club in the House of Representatives. These youthful Whig congressmen, or "Young Indians," effectively campaigned for Gen. Zachary Taylor's successful bid for president. Like Lincoln, Toombs opposed the imperialism of the Mexican War and resisted the temptations of Manifest Destiny. Many years later, Taylor's son, Confederate lieutenant general Richard Taylor, described the unforgettable Toombs as "the most original of men . . . a man of extraordinary energy."[2]

It was not long before Toombs became a leading congressman and influential representative not only of Georgia but also of the entire South. He also joined with Alexander Stephens and Howell Cobb to form the "Georgia triumvirate." In 1850 this influential threesome led a unionist campaign in the state that defeated South Carolina's early secession bid. Despite the rise of sectional tensions and political confrontations, Toombs remained a Southern moderate and Whig. The hot-tempered Toombs would not fan the flames of sectional extremism until 1860. Indeed, he only reluctantly became a Democrat on the eve of the conflict.

During the debates of the Compromise of 1850, Toombs powerfully defended Southern rights in the Western territories. Advocating what he considered to be the South's right to expand slavery, he issued a prophetic warning to the North: "I claim the right of her to enter them all with her property and securely to enjoy it . . . deprive us of this right and appropriate this common property to yourselves, it is then your government, not mine. Then I am its enemy, and I will then, if I can, bring my children and my constituents to the altar of liberty, . . . I would swear them to eternal hostility to your foul domination. Give us our just right, and we are ready, as ever heretofore, to stand by the Union, every part of it, and its every interest. Refuse it, and for one, I will strike for Independence."

After Abraham Lincoln's election to the presidency, a revolutionary Toombs proclaimed in his famous Milledgeville speech of mid-November 1860: "The door of conciliation and compromise is finally closed by our adversaries, and it remains only to us to meet the conflict with the dignity and firmness of men worthy of freedom. We need no declaration of Independence. Above eighty-four years ago, our fathers won that by the sword

from Great Britain . . . make another war of independence . . . fight its battles over again; reconquer liberty and independence."

After South Carolina's departure from the Union in December 1860, a
supportive Toombs saw secession as Georgia's and the South's "best guarantee
for liberty, security, tranquillity, and glory." Toombs denounced Georgia's lingering antisecessionist feeling. "Give me the sword!" he said, "But if you do
not place it in my hands, before God! I will take it!"[3] Thanks in no small
part to persuasive arguments by Toombs, Georgia departed the Union in
January 1861. "I have despaired of the Union," Toombs had written to his
wife from Washington, "and will begin to pack up my own things today."

Toombs demonstrated his support for the South one last time before
leaving the capital. On the night of 10 January 1861, he and Gen. Winfield Scott, the highest ranking officer of the United States Army, clashed
during an elegant dinner party. While seated at a long table of dignitaries,
Toombs declared that whoever had ordered the ship *Star of the West* to
reinforce Fort Sumter deserved being on the ship whenever South Carolina
guns sank her. General Scott, who was responsible for ordering the reinforcement of the isolated Federal garrison in Charleston Harbor, and
Toombs soon had to be physically restrained as they lunged over the dinner
table to get at one another.[4]

As a Georgia delegate, Toombs next attended the convention of
seceded states in Montgomery, Alabama. Some participants favored
Toombs for president of the new nation they expected to found. Toombs
himself coveted the presidency. Stephens thought Toombs the "superior
even of Webster, Clay, and Calhoun in debate, surpassed for raw power
only by Niagara Falls." Despite support among the delegations from Georgia, South Carolina, Florida, and Alabama, however, Toombs's dream of
leading the new nation down the road to independence foundered.

At a party two nights before the delegates were to choose the Confederacy's president, a drunken Toombs behaved foolishly. His support vanished overnight among the skeptical attendees. Instead they made Jefferson
Davis their chief dignitary. A master opportunist, Toombs had missed the
great political chance of his lifetime thanks to an inopportune indiscretion.
Toombs acknowledged this as "the greatest miscarriage of his life."

Smarting from this last minute setback, Toombs proposed his friend
Alexander Stephens for the vice presidency of the new Southern nation. The
humiliating reversal of fortune haunted Toombs, and he never completely
got over it. In the days ahead, Toombs's frustration fueled additional personal clashes within the highest levels of the Confederacy, especially with
President Davis and leading officers of Lee's Army of Northern Virginia.[5]

Toombs was back in Georgia at the bedside of his daughter, Sallie, whose life was in danger during childbirth, when President Davis's telegram arrived to offer Toombs the post of secretary of state. Toombs initially refused, but after much convincing by his friend Stephens, he accepted the position on a temporary basis. Stephens was delighted, declaring that in terms of getting things done, "Toombs would dispatch more in twenty minutes than [Davis] does in three hours."

Toombs found it impossible to be a loyal subordinate to anyone in authority, especially Jefferson Davis, a man he had almost dueled with during the 1850s. Like Toombs, Davis was vain, undiplomatic, and arrogant; trouble between these two strong and uncompromising personalities was inevitable. The president, moreover, set all diplomatic policy and made the appointments, thus reducing Toombs's position to little more than a clerkship. Toombs quipped bitterly that he could carry the State Department "in his hat."

The prophetic Toombs warned President Davis that to unleash the first shot of the war on Fort Sumter would be a psychological, moral, and political disaster for the South. It would stir up "a hornet's nest which extends from mountains to ocean; and legions, now quiet, will swarm out and sting us to death . . . it puts us in the wrong; it is fatal." At the same time Toombs also urged Davis to export cotton abroad to secure as soon as possible the invaluable arms, matériel, and munitions of war, which were essential to support the underequipped armies of the Confederacy.

. The primary difference between the president and his secretary of state was their overall strategic vision. The aggressive Toombs advocated immediate offensive operations that, if successful, could shorten the war and win foreign recognition; the more prudent Davis believed that a lengthy defensive war like the American Revolution would wear down Union resolve. Toombs acvocated carrying the war into the enemy's country. "We must invade or be invaded," he warned. Fearful of the result of a lengthy war on an agrarian nation short on almost everything but bravado, Toombs urged an early strike at the North. In this war of attrition, the Georgian understood that the South had to win this war before the North's superiority in manpower and matériel overwhelmed the Confederacy. What he did not understand was that the South could not appeal for European aid by presenting itself as a nation of isolationists wishing only to defend its way of life, while at the same time invading Union soil.

Bored by paper shuffling and uneventful meetings, Toombs soon realized the uselessness of his best efforts. He increasingly aligned himself with Stephens, who became equally disillusioned with President Davis. A natural team despite opposite personalities, Toombs and Stephens became the most powerful members of the so-called "anarchists," who opposed the Davis administration and their allies, the "monarchists." This personal and political conflict between the two rival factions grew so intense that "the political front in Georgia was almost as dangerous to the Confederacy as was the military front around Richmond," wrote one Southerner. Indeed, it was intimated that Toombs was "capable of leading a palace coup." Certainly in future years he would urge deposing Davis. One observer concluded that the ever rebellious Toombs "is ready for another revolution. He curses freely everything Confederate from a president down to a house boy." Another Confederate who saw the Georgian doing what he did best—raising hell—perhaps best summarized Bob Toombs by concluding: "He was largely a law unto himself."

Toombs resigned on 24 July 1861 after five frustrating months. He had nevertheless retained his seat in the Provisional Confederate Congress after the capital had been shifted from Montgomery to Richmond. Increasingly vocal in his opposition to President Davis and his administration, Toombs was now determined to go where he could make the most direct contribution to the war effort. Like several other Southern congressmen, he decided to take his fight to the battlefield. A week earlier President Davis granted the Georgian's repeated requests for a general officer's rank; Toombs's commission as a brigadier dated from 19 July 1861.

Toombs embarked with characteristic enthusiasm on a new career and his next challenge. And as no surprise, he engaged in a growing list of disputes, controversies, and feuds. Hobbled in the Davis administration, he leaped at the opportunity to command his fellow Georgians on the battlefield. Toombs also felt that it was important to serve as an example to the Southern people because far "too many prominent men . . . were seeking bomb-proof positions, and he was resolved not to be among them."[6]

Toombs welcomed some of his family into his command. His sons-in-law, Dudley M. Dubose, married to his daughter Sallie, and William Felix Alexander, who had been married to his now-deceased daughter, Mary, served as faithful aides on General Toombs's staff. James Madison Dubose, a nephew of General Toombs, also served in the Columbus Guards, 2nd Georgia.[7] Sgt. James Dubose acted more like a common soldier than one with high connections. He occasionally raided the corn reserved for the headquarters horses and earned the envy of the boys, who gave him the nickname "sex" for his nocturnal exploits as the leading ladies' man of the Columbus Guards. Toombs took his black servant, Bob, to war with him, too. At the Montgomery convention where Toombs almost became president, Bob, to Toombs's amusement, was an avid drinker and card-player at the Exchange Hotel.[8]

Even though now in the army, Toombs functioned in a dual role, serving simultaneously as a Confederate general and a congressman, dividing time between the brigade's encampment and the halls of Congress. In both roles, the list of his personal clashes and confrontations continued to grow. Despite being new to the army, he soon criticized its leaders, especially the West Pointers, and even the army's commander.

Toombs believed that many leaders of the Army of Northern Virginia were hampered by antiquated ideas, tactics, and strategic doctrine. From the beginning, Toombs resented these West Pointers' sense of superiority over the non–West Pointers, especially untrained political generals like Toombs.

Toombs also clashed with his fellow Georgians, both at home and in the army. Local committees at home informed him that his considerable Georgia acreage was required for use to raise grain crops instead of cotton and that his slaves were required for work outside his own plantation. In response he blistered: "I refuse a single hand. My property, as long as I live, shall never be subject to those cowardly miscreants, the Committees of Public Safety of Randolph County, Ga., and Eufaula. You may rob me in my absence, but you cannot intimidate me." One knowing Southerner commented: "Bob Toombs disagrees with himself between meals."

More than perhaps any general of the army in Virginia, Toombs repeatedly got into trouble both on the battlefield and off. This gamecock in a Confederate general's uniform, was arrested three times by superiors for doing exactly what he, and not they, wanted to do. Toombs's aggressiveness, ego, and lack of discipline fostered personal difficulties. He chafed under the cautious leadership of his immediate superior, Maj. Gen. David R. Jones, and criticized him to his face. At second Manassas he threw his brigade into the fight without awaiting orders. When Jones reprimanded him, Toombs replied hotly: "The fact is, Sir, I refuse to be tied to a corpse!"[9]

Yet Gen. James Longstreet, despite himself placing the Georgia general under arrest for a minor infraction, admired Toombs for his leadership abilities. Staff officer G. Moxley Sorrell recalled that "Longstreet always had a decided liking for Toombs." In the words of a journalist of the *Daily Constitutionalist* during the winter of 1861–62: "It is the judgement of military men that Gen. Toombs has one of the best, and perhaps the best brigade in the army. The material is no better than we find in other Georgia regiments; it is to the fine administrative talents of the General that the superiority of the brigade is in great measure ascribable. Nothing escapes his attention, from the evolutions of the brigade down to the cartridge box of the soldier."[10]

As early as September 1861, Toombs had proposed to President Davis that the primary eastern army should thrust beyond Virginia and north into Maryland, an idea that was neither new nor original with Toombs. As an early exponent of aggressive strategy, Toombs believed that the Confederacy's foreign recognition and, hence, independence could only result from timely battlefield victories on Northern soil.

In broader strategic terms, Toombs, along with Longstreet and Stephens, opposed President Davis's policy of dispersing the Confederacy's limited manpower and resources in an attempt to defend all reaches of the Confederacy against a vastly superior adversary. Toombs castigated Davis as early as 5 July 1861. "Mr. Davis has fallen into [General] Scott's trap of scattering his forces, and is therefore too weak every where. I should concentrate and fight wherever I had the best chance of success, and let towns and cities go to the flames if necessary." With hindsight, one Southerner overlooked the reputation of the troublesome Toombs to conclude: "I know that he is classed as a braggart and an impractical man. But I believe in my soul that had Toombs governed and Davis taken the field, the Southern cross would be flying yet and Southern Empire a fact."[11]

Toombs wrote a dejected letter to Stephens in late 1861 stating that the "army is dying, and it will not survive the winter. Set this down in your book, and set down opposite to its epitaph, 'died of West Point.' We have patched a new government with old cloth, we have tied the living to the dead." Toombs, thus, early became "an avowed enemy of West Point, and ridiculed the idea, so generally entertained, of the superiority of the officers of the regular army." Unadmitted by Toombs and other amateurs was their jealousy of the higher rank that Davis gave to experienced and trained professionals in preference to politicians-turned-generals. As for criticism of Davis's strategic policy, Toombs never considered the inevitable political explosion should the Confederacy abandon one part of its territory in order to protect another, let alone launch an uncertain—and diplomatically risky—invasion. Despite his intellect, Toombs's ambition and impetuosity made him naive about grand policy.

Growing ever more critical of army leadership, Toombs complained in May 1862, after a visit to the front by Davis and Lee, that "we shall not fight till frost if they can help it. The truth is Davis has no capacity & his [West Point] generals but little more than he has & if it be possible to ruin our cause by imbecility they will do it."[12] As far back as 5 July 1861, he said: "I don't at all like the action of our government as to Missouri. Five thousand men in arms would now save that State, and this government abandons her to her fate . . . five thousand men would enable her to engage fifty thousand Federal troops, and thereby greatly weaken

[Gen. George B.] McClellan in Western Virginia, but Mr. Davis is immovable."[13]

Although General Toombs antagonized the West Pointers and government leaders, he retained the respect of the majority of the common soldiers. One Georgia soldier claimed that "there is no general in the service who has so quickly won the confidence and esteem of his men. At first we were deceived in him, and thought that Davis had missed his mark in leaving the field, to put politicians in command, but if all of his appointments are as good as this, our army will prove invincible [and] there is not a man of his Brigade who does not believe that he is an officer worthy of all confidence, and one that will lead him to victory. So far he has proven a check to tyrants and a private's friend." Private Duggan observed: "Gen. Toombs has always been very kind to his men, and we love him for it. . . . We would not willingly exchange him for any other officer." Another Georgian admired that "Gen. Toombs was a big-hearted man and could not bear for his men, as he put it, to be imposed upon. So when any of the Regulars [of his 1st Georgia] were punished, whether rightly or not, they would report it to the general who would ride over to the regiment [and] curse out the officers." When Toombs eventually left the army in early 1863, a 15th Georgia soldier wrote in a letter: "We only hope to get another Gen. who will treat us as kind and be respected by his command as well as Gen. Toombs was respected & was regarded by his." As Sgt. William Andrews said: "There has never been but one Gen. Robert Toombs. . . . He would have taken sides with poorest private in his command against President Davis if he thought he was trying to impose on him." Toombs, consequently, continued to make enemies at division, corps, and army headquarters. By the time of the Maryland campaign, Toombs suspected a conspiracy within the army to force him out.[14]

Both the 2nd and 20th Georgia reached Virginia too late to fight at first Manassas. These Georgians then spent a relatively quiet winter of 1861–62 along the Potomac in northern Virginia, surprised at how cold and snowy a winter could be in the upper South. Toombs's brigade served in the division of South Carolina–born General Jones, as part of the army's reserve corps, under Maj. Gen. John B. Magruder.

The Georgians first saw action in Richmond's defense before the advance of McClellan's Army of the Potomac up the Virginia Peninsula, by defending the Yorktown line near Dam Number One in April 1862. Then, several miles east of Richmond after withdrawing from the Yorktown line, a nervous General Magruder feared a Federal night attack. On the line defending the approaches to Richmond, he prepared to engage in a holding action south of the Chickahominy, as Lee struck McClellan's right wing at Gaines's Mill north of the river. Unnerved at the sound of the escalating battle to the north, General Magruder desired to ascertain the enemy's intentions and positions. He, therefore, ordered a reconnaissance in force in this sector.

As the roaring guns of Gaines's Mill, northeast of Richmond, cracked to the north, General Toombs was verbally ordered to "feel the enemy" south of the Chickahominy River at dusk on 27 June. Toombs feared the consequences of advancing against a heavily defended position. The veterans of Union general Winfield S. Hancock's VI Corps held defensive positions on advantageous ground around the Golding farm, about three-fourths of a mile to the east. Toombs's Georgia brigade, immediately east of the Garnett house, would have to march across a wide expanse of open wheat and clover fields. Toombs, consequently, refused to obey the ill-advised order to advance unless it came in writing. Toombs's delay was ineffectual. The dreaded written orders soon arrived.

Toombs consequently led his men forward with flags flying, advancing toward defenses overflowing with bluecoats and artillery. The general reluctlantly hurled his brigade forward. Despite mounting losses, the Georgian attempted to force an advantage that only lengthened his casualty list. The one-sided fighting finally sputtered to an end in the humid night amid the Chickahominy lowlands east of Richmond and south of the Chickahominy. The grim result came as no surprise to Toombs. After more than two hours, the Georgia brigade lost more than 200 soldiers for neither gain, victory, nor glory.

Thanks to another uncoordinated offensive effort Toombs's brigade sacrificed more blood on the following day. Magruder, uncertain of the implications of a sudden Union withdrawal, ordered a heavy bombardment of the Federal lines. He then commanded yet another advance to ascertain the enemy's designs. As on the day before, General Toombs's Georgia brigade moved forward on the hot morning of 28 June. As General Jones ordered his brigade forward during the reconnaissance, General Toombs was prepared to advance farther, if the Yankees had vacated their position and retired to their next set of works. When it was determined that the Yankees had fallen back, Toombs consequently continued to lead his troops onward. To support the Georgians and to protect the brigade's flank from enfilade fires, General Toombs directed a fellow Georgian of Jones's division, George T. Anderson, to likewise advance.

The fight soon escalated out of control, with the Georgians encountering a heavy fire and stiff resistance. Toombs's Georgians advanced

piecemeal in support of General Magruder's other units. The uncoordinated offensive effort sapped the momentum of Toombs's advance into the
dense forests along the Chickahominy. When Col. William McIntosh fell,
Toombs complained that "I have been forced, by order of that damned
Magruder, to send McIntosh, one of the best men God ever made, to his
certain death." The Georgia brigade lost almost 300 soldiers during the
second consecutive day of high casualties, with the 2nd Georgia suffering
almost 50 percent casualties during the fighting of 27 and 28 June. No
new names of victories would be painted on the Georgians' battle flags.
Without exaggeration, one of General Toombs's Georgia Rebels recalled
with bitterness how the Seven Days was a "hog-killing time."

General Toombs was furious about the reckless way his brigade was
used in what he deemed an "unnecessary battle". In a letter to Stephens, he
vented:

> I had but 2000 men for duty and was in 400 yards of the
> enemy's entrenchments whom I knew to be in heavy force. I objected
> to the order and required it in writing and preemptory. It was given
> me, and I made the attack. The battle raged with terrific fury for
> about two hours, the [Yankees] trying to drive me from a position I
> was ordered to hold at every hazard by that old ass Magruder. I
> finally repulsed him . . . my men fought like lions this unnecessary
> battle, and the thanks we got for it was a lie sent out from Magruder's
> headquarters before the action was over that I had attacked without
> orders and was repulsed.

The performance of his men, who demonstrated a fighting spirit
despite questionable orders, solaced Toombs. As for Lee, whom he felt had
hurled hundreds of troops to their deaths during his offensive strikes
against the Army of the Potomac before Richmond, he declared to
Stephens that "Lee was far below the occasion. If we had had a general in
command we could easily have taken McClellan's whole command and
baggage."[15]

Continuing to rely on the tactical offensive to drive the Army of the
Potomac off the Peninsula, General Lee's offensive effort at the coming battle of Malvern Hill was to be one of his greatest mistakes of the war. The
Confederates relentlessly charged forward in neat lines across the broad
fields of clover and corn, to be mowed down by the withering Union fire
sweeping down the northern slope of Malvern Hill. Toombs's brigade was
with them. Sergeant Houghton never forgot how "we were very badly led

at Malvern Hill [and] in two ranks touching shoulders with another supporting line just in the rear, [as] we marched through an open field against batteries of many cannons, supported by men armed with rifles. A bullet which struck a front man at close range, was likely to kill the man in the rear." Pvt. Thomas Ware, 15th Georgia, recorded the nightmare of Malvern Hill in his diary: "Our brigade was exposed to a hot fire of bombs & grape. We commenced ascending a hill in front of the enemy, where we suffered awful. . . . Men could be seen falling in every direction, the grape & bombs . . . taking off a great many heads & cutting some half [in two]." Many Georgians either now fought from cover for protection against the leaden storm or continued to push forward in the futile assault. Other 2nd Georgia soldiers, in the words of one Rebel, fell back "for want of leadership in our general, refus[ing] to lie still and be killed for nothing." During the reckless assaults up the high ground, General Toombs's four infantry regiments—the 2nd, 15th, 17th, and 20th Georgia in the line's center—were cut to pieces. They had yet to recover from the fatigue and heavy losses of the fighting at Garnett's farm only days before. But no troops, no matter how rested, experienced, or well led, could successfully storm the high ground of Malvern Hill, lined with 100 Union cannon.

As the slaughter escalated, Toombs tried to get his badly exposed soldiers under cover amid the rain of shell and canister. They had advanced beyond their support, losing alignment with other units during the poorly coordinated assault up the hill. To escape the punishment and reorganize, the general placed his battered troops behind the cover of a rail fence on the northern slope of Malvern Hill.

Then, Toombs rode out into the raging storm in an attempt to rally and then lead forward other portions of his fragmented brigade. Taking severe punishment on the left of General Lee's right flank, a frustrated Maj. Gen. Daniel Harvey Hill soon rode up to the pinned-down portions of Toombs's brigade. Taking command, Hill rushed more of the Georgians to their deaths. Young Pvt. Vincent A. S. Parks of Toombs's brigade described the horror of Malvern Hill: "What confusion and mad rushing into the flood of death, with terrible yells of defiance!" Despite the fragmentation of not only regimental but also brigade and division assault lines, General Hill was surprised to discover that General Toombs was not present with the group of pinned-down Georgians at the fence. By this time, Toombs was in another sector with the remainder of his brigade, rallying his soldiers.

To Toombs Malvern Hill was the epitome of folly. Therefore, when Gen. Joseph B. Kershaw, commanding a South Carolina brigade, asked Toombs to once again assault the fiery rows of artillery on the heights with the promise that the South Carolina troops would support the Georgians, Toombs declined. When General Anderson resumed the attack, Toombs also declined his request for support. Toombs's Brigade lost about 200 soldiers in the inferno of Malvern Hill. The 2nd Georgia suffered the highest casualties, enduring 11 killed and 70 wounded, including its commander. With the colonel of the 2nd Georgia knocked out of action, the capable lieutenant colonel William R. Holmes, the former captain of the Burke Sharpshooters, took command.

After his own troops broke under the ceaseless hammering by shot and shell, General Hill discovered General Toombs in the gathering darkness with a portion of his brigade on the field. Hill denounced the Georgia general before his men for not having been present with that portion of his pinned-down Georgia brigade at the fence. Unable to fathom that the day was already lost, Hill also blamed General Magruder's troops for allowing his own soldiers' mauling by not supporting them on their right.

General Hill might have been equally as ill-tempered, quarrelsome, and difficult as General Toombs. Indeed, Hill's combative temperament would eventually force General Lee to ease him out of the Army of Northern Virginia, despite the fact that he was a hard-nosed fighter. Easy to anger, abrasive, and quick to judge others, especially political generals, a frustrated Hill also sought a convenient scapegoat to explain the mismanagement and poor coordination of his failed attack. Toombs offered an easy target because of his unpopularity and political background. Hill was well aware of Toombs's loudly boasted claims that Lee's respected West Pointers "were generals with so much training they were scared to fight." Hill himself was the epitome of the well-educated, professional West Pointer, serving as the superintendent of the North Carolina Military Institute in the antebellum period.

Not long after Malvern Hill, General Toombs demanded a formal explanation from General Hill of the accusations that he had made on the battlefield. But Hill's curt response angered Toombs. He consequently wrote to General Hill that "it is scarcely necessary for me to say it is not satisfactory [and] I now demand of you personal satisfaction for the insult you cast upon my command and myself on the battlefield." Toombs was determined to maintain his honor in an army that he mistrusted. Hill had misjudged his man; Toombs was not about to let anyone question his courage and that of his Georgians.

Although Toombs had already protested Hill's actions through proper army channels, the paperwork was delayed in headquarters, hence Toombs's challenge to a duel. Eager to clear his name and that of his

Georgia brigade, Toombs requested that Hill immediately see "my friend," Col. Henry L. Benning, the commander of the 17th Georgia Infantry, about arrangements for the duel. Hill refused to accept Toombs's challenge, however. The Georgian was stunned by the West Pointer's reply. Hill responded to Toombs's challenge by writing: "Its acceptance, when we have a country to defend and enemies to fight, would be highly improper." Toombs retorted: "I do not consider a refusal to meet me as satisfaction." So eager was Toombs to defend his own and his brigade's honor that he was prepared to immediately resign from the army for the opportunity to duel Hill. But the duel was not to be. General Hill continued to refuse to accept Toombs's challenge. Not one to forget or forgive, Toombs thereafter continued to rail against Hill, including to his soldiers in camp.

Toombs's penchant for getting into trouble and remaining embroiled in controversy—with the home front, the administration, and the army—continued unabated month after month following Malvern Hill. After the Hill incident, no one in the Army of Northern Virginia again made the mistake of openly questioning the courage of Bob Toombs or that of his Georgia brigade. However, Toombs's image was tarnished by the affair. Indeed, General Hill was a respected fighter, and was the brother-in-law of another idolized Virginian, Stonewall Jackson.

At the end of the Seven Days, General Toombs was not only frustrated but angry. "Our loss has been terrible, and of many of our best men," he lamented. "They were fought without skill or judgement [and McClellan] was not pursued with the least vigor[;] it was Manassas and Shiloh over again, barren victories without results when everything was in our power. McClellan will reorganize his yet powerful army, get reinforcements, and we shall have all this blood and toil to shed over again, and worst of all the poor people cannot see it, and all who will not sing to such blunderers and imbeciles will probably be crushed and dishonored."

By the end of the Seven Days, General Toombs's bloodied brigade was yet reeling after suffering casualties of about one-third its strength in only a few days of fighting around Richmond. With its ranks thinned, his brigade now consisted of the 2nd, 20th, and 15th—composed of men from Wilkes, Elbert, Franklin, Hancock, Taliaferro, Lincoln, and Hart Counties, Georgia—and Colonel Benning's 17th Georgia Infantry, soldiers from Webster, Stewart, Harris, Muscogee, Schley, Decatur, Mitchell, and Dougherty Counties.[16]

The 1st Georgia Regulars Regiment had previously departed Toombs's brigade on the Garnett's farm line for reassignment in General Jones's division. The highly touted Georgia Regulars were transferred to General

Anderson's brigade during the Seven Days campaign partly as a result of friction between Toombs and the Regulars' officers. In the behind-the-scenes political maneuvering that resulted in the ordering of his beloved Regulars from his command, Toombs perceived the schemes of President Davis, his government, and the West Pointers in the Army of Northern Virginia.[17]

Toombs's lack of a military education and his unwillingness to adhere to either military or personal discipline tripped him up at last on 17 August 1862. Then, with Lee's and Pope's forces within striking distance of each other amid the mid-Virginia countryside around the Rapidan River, Toombs ran out of luck during a relatively quiet period not long after the battle of Cedar Mountain and immediately before Lee's advance northward to victory at second Manassas.

Here, when General Lee's army was posted around Verdiersville, Virginia, south of the Rapidan, Longstreet issued orders for Toombs to post two Georgia regiments on the road leading north to Raccoon Ford on the Rapidan River and about a dozen miles above Lee's headquarters. General Toombs's soldiers were ordered to guard this Rapidan ford until Rebel cavalry, which had been ordered to do so, shortly arrived to relieve them. Toombs, however, was absent from his headquarters when General Longstreet's orders arrived. In his absence, the senior colonel of his brigade, Colonel Benning, ordered two Georgia regiments north on the mission as directed. When Toombs later returned to his encampment after visiting a political friend, he heard that another Confederate infantry brigade had moved forward and into a position to protect Raccoon Ford before the arrival of the Confederate cavalry, negating the guardian role of his two infantry regiments.

Toombs, therefore, ordered his two regiments to return to camp, after receiving new orders for all of his regiments to cook three days' rations in preparation for the army's advance northward beyond the Rapidan on the following day. Toombs was still upset that his two regiments—half of his brigade—had been moved forward to Raccoon Ford without his consent, orders, or knowledge. General Toombs had attempted to request permission from Longstreet to return his men to camp before he withdrew his two regiments from Raccoon Ford, but Longstreet had not been located. Toombs, therefore, took the risky move of removing his regiments on his own authority.

Not long after the Georgians had shouldered muskets and marched away from the crossing at the Rapidan River, Yankee cavalry on a scouting expedition thundered across Raccoon Ford. The rumored advance of another Confederate infantry brigade had not occurred. After crossing the river, the

Federal horse soldiers galloped south unimpeded, surging deeper into the domain of Lee's army. The unopposed Union troopers then overran Gen. Jeb Stuart's encampment at Verdiersville, Virginia, almost capturing the Virginian himself. General Stuart's hasty departure damaged his popular image, turning his plumed hat into a Union trophy. Adverse press in both the North and the South turned Jeb Stuart into a laughingstock. Much to the delight of his opponents, Toombs was arrested and confined to his tent.

Toombs characteristically compounded his problems. He again disobeyed orders, either in ignorance or in outright defiance. Seething over his arrest, Toombs buckled on his saber and departed his tent. He then rode behind his brigade on the march. According to Toombs, the cheers of his veterans, as their arrested leader rejoined his command, incensed Gen. Longstreet, known throughout the army as "the old bull of the woods." Longstreet was probably also angered because the former politician delivered anti-Longstreet speeches to his cheering men, as if campaigning for office back in Wilkes County.[18] Slapped with two charges of disobedience for withdrawing his troops from Raccoon Ford without orders and for violating the conditions of his arrest, the contentious Toombs was then ordered to leave the army and report immediately to Gordonsville, Virginia.

Toombs was seemingly near the end of his controversial career as Lee's most maverick general. As the army marched northward amid the hot weather of late August without him, Toombs contemplated resignation from the military. He had already handed over leadership of his brigade to Benning. Toombs now informed Stephens that "I shall leave the army the instant I can do so without dishonor. Davis and his Janissaries (the regular army) conspire for the destruction of all who will not bend to them."[19] Yet now, a strange destiny was to carry the dishonored general toward his finest day far beyond the Potomac in distant Maryland.

General Lee, meanwhile, had skillfully divided his army, converging upon the hapless Union general Pope and his ill-fated Army of Virginia on the field of Manassas during the last days of August. Second Manassas brought more hard fighting for Toombs's brigade (400 soldiers were destined to be killed and wounded). The ravages of summer illnesses and the bloodletting of the Seven Days had greatly reduced the Georgia regiments. Before the attack of the army's right wing under Longstreet at second Manassas, barely 350 soldiers stood in the 20th Georgia's ranks. Indicative of their destitute condition after fighting all summer and marching across much of Virginia, at least 100 of them were now "without a piece of leather on their feet" during the bitter fighting at second Manassas.

During one of the last assaults of a victorious day for the Confederates, Colonel Benning led a desperate attack on a Federal battery. After racing through a hail of fire, the 20th Georgia captured the guns but could not hold their trophies. Hurled back with heavy losses, they relinquished their hard-won gains. Nevertheless, the 2nd, 15th, and 17th Georgia continued forward to storm the Union defensive line. In characteristic fashion, Benning's Georgians hit hard, driving the Union defenders away from their strong positions around the Chinn house. Suffering heavy losses, these bluecoats occupying the Union center were hurled off the high ground of Chinn Ridge by the Georgians. But the Southern charge was too successful, carrying the attackers forward beyond support and into the midst of too many Federal units. Benning possessed the good sense to withdraw. Closing in on another Army of Northern Virginia victory at second Manassas, the Confederates mustered for one final attempt to destroy Gen. John Pope's Army of Virginia on 30 August.[20]

During the day's final advance by Longstreet's Command on the last Union defensive line along Henry Hill, General Toombs suddenly galloped onto the field in the dimming light of 30 August. Eager for action, he had begged Longstreet to release him from his arrest so that he could lead his brigade in battle. General Longstreet, who was perhaps the only senior Army of Northern Virginia general who admired the hot-tempered Georgian, released him.

General Longstreet evidently felt that the humbled Georgian would be less careless in the future. General Toombs dramatically met his troops in the midst of the raging battle. Suddenly appearing out of the drifting smoke at the head of his men, Toombs savored the timing of his last-minute arrival during one of General Lee's greatest victories.

One Rebel long remembered the unforgettable sight when General Toombs rode down the line, and "every Georgian who saw him raised his hat and lustily yelled, 'Hurrah for General Toombs.'" Capt. Henry L. French, 17th Georgia, recalled that "to our great satisfaction, we unexpectedly met our gallant commander, Brig. Gen. Robert Toombs, who, anticipating the fight, had ridden hard all day. He was greeted with hearty cheers, and said, 'Boys, I am proud of the report given of you by General Jones [and now] I [will] lead you.'"[21] With the Georgians "wild beyond description," Toombs encouraged his men during the day's final onslaught: "Go in boys and give the damned invaders hell!" According to another account, he also yelled "Go it, boys! I am with you again. Jeff Davis can make a general but it takes God Almighty to make a soldier."

A Georgian not a member of Toombs's brigade also recalled that moment on the field of second Manassas. "Gen. Toombs passed me going in at full speed and calling on the Georgians at every jump his horse made," he wrote. "A little farther on [he] met his brigade going in to reinforce our line. I certainly felt good all over." Longstreet later complimented Toombs for gallantry in leading his brigade during the last attack at second Manassas.[22]

Despite the losses of the Seven Days and second Manassas, the hardest fighting of 1862 lay ahead for General Toombs and his soldiers, who had yet to learn the price to be paid in winning independence. Indeed, one of General Toombs's men, who earlier wrote that "we are having a jolly good time of it in the Old Dominion," now scribbled in a letter home that "should I die during the war, I hope it will be on some hard-fought battle-field, then bury me where I fall."[23]

# CHAPTER 4

# "Toombs's Skeleton Brigade of Survivors"

## *Toward an Ill-Advised Stand along the Antietam*

AFTER MANY MILES OF MARCHING IN SWELTERING HEAT ACROSS THE rough terrain of western Maryland, and despite rallying at Frederick for several days in hope of gathering Maryland recruits, the Army of Northern Virginia had nothing to show for its efforts by early September. General Lee's army not only had failed to win substantial numbers of Maryland recruits, but also the foreign recognition crucial to the infant nation's future and the subsequent liberation of the state. The nights, meanwhile, were cooler and the dew lay heavier on the fields during the mornings. Days were now shorter, and a paler sun shone upon western Maryland; harbingers of greater woe for the troops who still lacked adequate supplies of shoes, clothing, and food.

During their first northern invasion, the Georgia soldiers in gray and butternut endured weeks of hard marching. One Georgia soldier complained that "in all these weeks we had no change of clothing and we were literally devoured by vermin[,] we had no tents and slept on the ground, and slept soundly even though the rain was pouring in torrents." Another Georgia Rebel exclaimed, "Ma, oh! dear Mother, this place is so lousy I can't hardly keep the lice off of me." These pests spread disease that killed dozens of Georgia soldiers. One Georgia Rebel wrote to his wife that "I am not afraid of the Yanks nor of the rebels, but I am afraid of the innumerable millions of lice that cover the whole face of the earth and everything on the earth. It is perfectly sickening to look at the nasty, filthy things, and the whole army is literally covered with them from the highest officer to the lowest private."

A fatal illness could strike as suddenly as a Yankee bullet. One ill-clad Georgia boy, who survived the ravages of disease in Virginia and Maryland, wrote that "our cloth[e]s has been thin and we have shivered of cold nights and have taken diseases that will carry a great number of us to the grave, where a great many has all ready gone, . . . since I have been in service, I have had the Measles, Mumphs [*sic*], Neuralghia [*sic*], Typhoid fever, Pneumonia, Bronchitus [*sic*], Small Pox [*sic*], Eresipilas [*sic*], and an Abscess in my head which affected my hearing considerable and I think I have got some lung disease that will follow me to my grave." As if these deadly diseases were not enough to kill more vulnerable soldiers, "malaria, scurvy and [the] itch," noted one soldier in a letter, likewise ravaged the army's survivors. "I have seen more suffering men here than ever I saw before in my life," one Georgia soldier lamented. "Their sickness seems to be the hardest to get over that ever I saw. It seems to be the most fatal. Men dies here like sheep with the rot." Another Georgia Rebel observed that "there is a great deal of sickness here and more men dying with it than ever will get killed in the battles of the Confederacy."[1]

The extensive raids on orchards and cornfields by Toombs's Georgia brigade caused their own problems. Pvt. George Henry Abercrombie of the Columbus Guards consumed a total of thirteen roasted ears in one sitting, and then remarked, "Damn a Government that won"t furnish fodder." Also in the ranks was his brother Wiley Abercrombie, likewise a heavy consumer of roasted ears during this campaign. By this time, Rebel soldiers were already beginning to call this raid into Maryland, far away from Virginia and logistical support, the "Green Corn Campaign."

The resulting diarrhea from the diet of green apples and green corn plagued the entire army, effectively cutting down men in record numbers. In a letter, one Georgian in Maryland described the experience of becoming one of the thousands of non-combat casualties during the Maryland campaign. "I was taken quite sick, nausea, living on green apples and corn but little else to eat."

"We live on what we can get—now and then an ear of corn, fried green apples, or a bit of ham fried on a stick, but quite as frequently do without either from morning until night," stated one Georgian. A young officer of the 20th Georgia, now at home and naive to the harsh realities of the Maryland campaign, would ironically soon write: "I thought of the glorious times our boys must be having in Maryland and Pennsylvania, of the good things Stonewall has furnished from the enemy's commissariat at Harper's Ferry for our men." [2] The common soldiers, moreover, suffered in mind, soul, and spirit. The slaughter of the Seven Days and second Manassas swept the thinning ranks with an unprecedented war weariness.

General Toombs would pay an emotional tribute to his fallen Georgians, writing how "nearly one thousand of the brave men who originally composed your four regiments have fallen, killed or wounded, in battle . . . . you have fairly won the right to inscribe upon your tattered war flags, the proud boast of Napoleon's old guard, 'This brigade knows how to die, but not yield to the foe.'"[3] Pvt. Harvey Hightower reflected in September 1862 to his Georgia family: "I have been in two large battles and come out safe but I tell you I am not anxious to be in the third for I have seen as much of war as I went to see. I have seen dead men so thick you could walk on them hundreds of yards and never tutch [sic] the ground." Another disillusioned Georgian said that, "I think we will have to do something before long or we will all perish here soon." Lieutenant Hightower wrote home: "I tell you I am getting sick of this war." This young man in tattered gray admitted after the bitter fighting of 1862, "I have not been to the Regt yet neither do I want to go for nearly all the boys are killed or wounded." In a letter, David P. Taylor of Toombs's brigade, recounted the butchery of second Manassas: "All my company was killed, wounded and missing." Worse, "some shot themselves, but the powder blown into the flesh reveal[ed] the author of the wound," observed Private Houghton.[4]

Lack of adequate provisions further sapped the soldiers' spirits. Maryland's rough roads and turnpikes as well as the deep valleys, steep hillsides, and mountain ranges of western Maryland were simply too rough for thousands of General Lee's ill-shod soldiers. Sergeant Houghton, 2nd Georgia, wrote that "the worst trial besides hunger was want of shoes . . . my shoes gave out at Second Manassas." A Georgia boy accurately described the shape of the Army of Northern Virginia by this time, "Lee's Army is greatly reduced . . . barefooted men are not compelled to keep up or go in battle, thousands being in that condition. I have seen numbers of poor soldiers who could have been tracked by their blood, trying to march over the rough turnpike roads, where a horse could not travel without being shod."

A puzzled sergeant of the 1st Georgia Regulars, formerly of General Toombs's brigade, wrote of the mystery of the Army of Northern Virginia's depletion during the Maryland campaign. "We certainly felt the need of help, with our ranks depleted to almost nothing, . . . not more than 50 in the Regulars. Where are our comrades, . . . numbers were left straggling on the march after we left Manassas. Since we have been in Maryland, it was either keep up or be captured by the enemy. It is reported that there is 30,000 stragglers from Gen. Lee's army, and if the ranks of other commands have been thinned as ours, it certainly must be a fact. There is not a regiment in our brigade 12 months ago that could not muster more men than there is in our whole brigade today."

Much of this straggling across Virginia and Maryland was a case of starving men leaving the column to forage on their own for food and not returning to the ranks until much later. Sergeant Houghton explained that many soldiers departed "the ranks [to] hunt for food . . . generally the straggler wanted something for his 'sick captain,' and for a long time that was a winning dodge [and] whilst . . . famishing for days in Maryland [our] boys would take their ramrods and probe into the gardens and discover cans of preserves, apple butter, and other good things buried against the coming of such visitors."[5]

Private Fogle, Company G, 2nd Georgia, described the gradual reduction of the army when he wrote that "many a hot day & long weary night have I spent in marching during the last two months, sometimes I came near giving up but I managed somehow to keep up with my company, but many a poor fellow had to stop, the work we had to do was almost beyond human endurance, at one time our army had not less than 30,000 stragglers between the Rapidan & Potomac Rivers, the majority were barefoot & convalescent men just returned from home & the hospitals."[6]

One Georgia Rebel described the invasion in a letter home:

> I can't stand the heat in marching . . . our fare, dear, is very rough here . . . our commissaries don't exert themselves to procure provisions as they should . . . the corn crops up here are very good. It is now right for eating and the soldiers play havoc with it [and they] take all the apples they came across, eat them green. When we stop close to a farm, there is always a guard put out to keep them out of it. They get them as soon as they stop before the guard is arranged. There isn't discipline enough in our army. Our troops have their own way too much. I think our army will be compelled to have more discipline. Our regiment is almost ruined.[7]

Pvt. Charles Frederick Terrill, Company C, 2nd Georgia, concurred. "You will hear men complaining of a too strict discipline in the army," he said, "but as far as my observation has extended, it is not strict enough."

As the Army of Northern Virginia grew daily weaker, the Army of the Potomac grew more formidable. General McClellan, once again leading the unified force of General Pope's Army of Virginia and the Army of the Potomac, now marched westward in three long blue columns, after learning on 9 September that the enemy was in large force near Frederick. After successfully revitalizing the Army of the Potomac, McClellan now was slowly but confidently marching forward "Mr. Lincoln"s Army" of 87,000 Federals. The lingering effects of the consecutive defeats around Richmond and Washington, D.C., had faded, shattering much of the foundation upon which Lee based his plan for a successful Maryland campaign. The three long pursuit columns soon converged on Frederick.

With the Army of the Potomac only twenty-five miles southeast of Frederick, General Lee divided his command, assuming that Union garrisons in his rear at Harpers Ferry and Martinsburg would be forced to retire when one of his two wings moved through western Maryland, threatening to isolate them. General Lee dispatched his top lieutenant, Stonewall Jackson, and his troops on a circuitous seventy-five-mile route to capture Harpers Ferry, while the Army of the Potomac was within only a day's march. Lee, meanwhile, accompanied Longstreet's I Corps as it pushed northwest for the mountain gaps, marching toward Hagerstown, Maryland, as Gen. Daniel H. Hill's division served as the army's rear guard.[8]

It was a bad time for Lee to split his army; the march into Maryland threatened to become a folly. Indeed, one officer described that "never has the army been so dirty, ragged, and ill-provided" as on this ill-fated invasion.[9] General Lee lost one gamble after another. Stonewall Jackson was late in arriving before the garrison of Harpers Ferry, which refused to surrender. On 13 September McClellan was handed a copy of General Lee's campaign orders, carelessly lost in the field, that outlined the separation of the army's columns. And the Army of Northern Virginia remained divided. Soon thousands of Federals pushed through the gaps of South Mountain, fighting their way across to the same side of the mountains as General Lee, and in his rear.

The Maryland invasion had proved to be a failure; now it threatened to become a disaster. Lee would be fortunate just to escape to the safety of Virginia. His expectation of the imminent capture of Harpers Ferry by General Jackson impelled Lee, nevertheless, to gamble again. General Lee urgently recalled his units. He now planned to concentrate along a range of rolling hills immediately east of the village of Sharpsburg, Maryland, at the intersection of four roads. On a ridge between the Potomac River, four miles south of town, and Antietam Creek, this small Washington County community of 1,300 was nestled inland of a wide bend of the Potomac about a dozen miles north of Harpers Ferry. Lee now gambled that Jackson would not only subdue Harpers Ferry quickly, but also be able to push north to reach Sharpsburg in time to rejoin him before the Army of the Potomac struck. Until that time, he would stand his ground on the Antietam.

Along a thin defensive line running roughly parallel to the meandering Antietam, General Lee would be outnumbered by almost five to two once all of the contending forces came together. His extended line would stretch roughly in a north-south direction for more than four miles in a long semi-circle along the ridgeline between Sharpsburg and Antietam Creek. This ridge ran roughly parallel to Antietam Creek, averaging about 150 feet above its waters. Here, less than a corps—a mere 12,000 to 15,000 Rebels—were now on hand to make a stand against the Army of the Potomac, about 87,000 troops with more than 300 pieces of artillery. General Lee hoped to buy time for the completion of the capture of Harpers Ferry, which would release the remainder of his six divisions to unite with him along the Antietam. Jackson would then form on the north near a bend of the Potomac to anchor the army's left flank immediately northwest of Sharpsburg; as Gen. D. H. Hill occupied the center, and Gen. James Longstreet the right. Making the best of a bad situation, General Lee's left was anchored on the Potomac as the right was positioned on Antietam Creek.

With General McClellan's forces having to cross the Antietam from east to west to confront General Lee's battle line, this shallow creek was the only natural obstacle standing before the Army of the Potomac.[10] Here, along the Antietam, General Lee was hoping to concentrate his columns, scattered twenty-five miles across western Maryland. Lee was about to risk the life of his army in an unnecessary battle.[11] Lee's nephew ironically recognized as much. Gen. Fitzhugh Lee understood that "the scattered Southern troops could have been more easily concentrated in Virginia" than in Maryland.[12]

Since leaving their encampment in the valley of the Monocacy River around Frederick, General Toombs's Georgia soldiers had marched north-westward for days toward Pennsylvania. George Washington Hall caught the unfounded optimism that continued to pulse through the ranks of the army during the march from Frederick to "liberate" Maryland, especially when they heard of Confederate advances in the West. "Our cause is prosperous everywhere," he wrote. "In Tennessee and Kentucky our army has been victorious and has advanced as far as the State of Ohio and ere this I expect to Surrender Cincinnati." With muskets on shoulders, the Georgians swung onward through the dust rising from the National Road.

Perhaps Toombs felt a sense of history in knowing that his grandfather, a Virginia militia major, had marched this same road in 1755 with Gen. Edward Braddock's ill-fated army that was all but wiped out by the French, Canadians and Indians. Then, the British forces and colonial militia, which included a young and inexperienced Virginia officer named George Washington, had been on their way to disaster in the Monongahela River country against the French, Indians, and Canadians. Toombs could not forsee the fortunes of his brigade in the Maryland hills.

Longstreet's two divisions under Brig. Gens. John Bell Hood and David Jones marched toward Hagerstown, moving deeper into western Maryland to verify the rumor of Pennsylvania militia reported, in the Hagerstown area, to be pushing south from Chambersburg. Undertaking another long trek after departing Frederick, the Georgians pushed across the Catoctin Mountains to enter the broad Midtown Valley, sandwiched between the Catoctin Mountains and South Mountain, or the Blue Ridge. From the top of these mountains the Georgians could gaze upon valleys that reached to the horizon.

Pushing over the mountains, the Georgia boys continued a dozen miles westward through yet another wide valley. Marching past spring-fed creeks that descended from the mountains, Toombs's regiments then passed through the Blue Ridge at South Mountain, before pushing north-westward into the Great Appalachian Valley. The challenge of marching over some of the highest mountains that most of these Georgians had ever seen was unforgettable. Pvt. John William Lokey, 20th Georgia, wrote that "we marched to the top of the mountain [and] the cloud that we were in appeared like a dense heavy fog, and I thought that it was nearly night, but when we marched down the mountain we found the sun shining brightly, and looking back I could see the clouds resting on top of the mountain."

The Georgia solders then pushed onward with the columns of Longstreet's corps. After continuing the march through western Maryland and the small towns of Boonsboro and Funkstown northwest of South Mountain, the dust-covered Georgia troops in the army's advance, reached Hagerstown, exhausted, on 13 September.[13] There Toombs's brigade guarded part of the army's supply trains until Lee dispatched a courier with orders for the Georgians quickly to join the *ad hoc* concentration at Sharpsburg. A dozen miles northwest of Boonsboro, General Toombs received his orders at 10:00 P.M. on the night of 14 September. He immediately ordered his soldiers to prepare to push south to Sharpsburg. This would be an especially demanding march because Toombs's Georgians were now closer to Pennsylvania—less than five miles—than any of General Lee's infantry brigades.

Long before daylight of the next day, the veteran Georgians were on the move. They hurried toward a rendezvous with General Lee at Sharpsburg before McClellan's legions struck an overpowering blow. Lee's other widely scattered units, meanwhile, rapidly converged on Sharpsburg from the north, south, and east.

General Toombs believed, due to his seniority, that he commanded a nominal division consisting of his own Georgia brigade, and the brigades of Brig. Gen. Thomas Drayton, and Gen. George Anderson. By this time,

Col. Henry Benning now commanded Toombs's brigade. On the morning of 15 September the Georgians neared Sharpsburg and the valley of the Antietam. The brigade, however, would soon be without the services of the 15th and 17th Georgia, which Toombs detached to pursue Yankee cavalry near the Potomac crossing at Williamsport. There, the 15th and 17th Georgia were ordered to protect the army's wagon train from Union cavalry, which had slipped out of General Jackson's noose at Harpers Ferry.[14] Fortunately, the Rebels defending the gaps of South Mountain east of Sharpsburg won time in the army's rear.[15]

Worn by more hard marching, little sleep, and scanty rations, the Georgia Rebels finally reached Sharpsburg, a mile east of the winding Potomac and immediately west of Antietam Creek, in the dark before sunrise on Monday, 15 September. Benning immediately led Toombs's brigade to the far right of the gathering army. General Toombs, with only half his brigade, now rejoined Jones's division, which took position along the high ground southeast of Sharpsburg. Behind the Antietam Creek on General Lee's right, the land rose in a series of rolling hills. Three east-west, ridgelike steps, almost equally spaced, led to the plateau upon which perched the town of Sharpsburg.

One Southerner in Toombs's ranks commented that "the country about Sharpsburg is exceedingly beautiful, the farm houses and farms in the best condition." Here, where the Antietam straightened its course above and below the bridge, the broad fields of grain of the German farmers of the Antietam Valley were ready for harvest. In the orchards, the fruit on the trees was now almost ripe. Southeast of Sharpsburg, and unlike the geography north of the community, the gently rolling terrain became more broken and rugged with Antietam Creek cutting deeper into the land.

Here, on the army's right between Sharpsburg and Antietam Creek, the Georgians took an advanced position to guard the vital road leading from Sharpsburg to Rohrersville. They occupied an advanced salient just southeast of Sharpsburg and along Antietam Creek to guard the Rohrbach Bridge at the southern end of the battle line of the Army of Northern Virginia. Toombs ordered Colonel Benning "to place the brigade across the road . . . at the stone bridge across Antietam Creek and to defend the bridge."

Occupying the far end of a Confederate line that stretched more than four miles, the Georgians assumed they had been assigned to a quiet sector. After the hard marching and butchery of the Seven Days and second Manassas, they hoped to avoid another slaughter. If there was fighting to be done, it would probably erupt on General Lee's left or center, and far from the right flank.

Already concerned about the few troops available for the defense of the bridge across the Antietam, Colonel Benning grumbled that the unexpected detachment of the 15th and 17th Georgia now "left me for the defense of the bridge only two small regiments, the 2nd Georgia, under Lieutenant-Colonel [William R.] Holmes, and the 20th Georgia, under Col. John B. Cumming. With these two regiments I proceeded to the bridge and there put them in position as ordered."

Moving into position around the Antietam bridge, some veterans felt convinced that a big battle was imminent. "It was singular that the men would not carry a pack of cards into battle," wrote one. "We pressed forward to form in line of battle, one could walk a long distance on cards strewn by the way." Sergeant Houghton noted the hesitancy that some 2nd Georgia Rebels had about carrying their letters into battle. "When moving into line," he commented, "one could see men tearing up precious missives from loved ones at home, and the way was littered for miles with the fragments." Clearly, Toombs's men would not risk having the Yankees mock these letters from their loved ones should they be killed or captured in the upcoming battle on Northern soil.

With the battle formations of the Army of the Potomac in an extensive semicircle from the Hagerstown turnpike, north of town and near the Potomac's east side, to the Lower Bridge below Sharpsburg, General McClellan was in an opportune position to destroy Lee's army, if he struck with his full might. From right to left, General McClellan's I, XII, II, V, and IX Corps stretched in roughly a fishhook from north to south. His cautious nature, lack of confidence, and a heavy morning ground fog blanketing the Confederate positions west of Antietam Creek early on 16 September, however, conspired to keep General McClellan inactive. Despite the opportunity to destroy what little of the Army of Northern Virginia now stood before him, "Little Mac" failed to strike.

McClellan marked time, unlike Lee's Confederates. Indeed, having finally taken Harpers Ferry, General Jackson's corps was marching rapidly, hoping to reach Lee's army before it was too late. McClellan, therefore, stood idly by while Jackson's three divisions from Harpers Ferry reached the field to bolster General Lee's lines late in the afternoon. Despite being jaded by the rapid march, Jackson's troops added badly needed muscle to Lee's skeleton force. Two additional Southern divisions reached the Army of Northern Virginia on the morning of 17 September, making General Lee so far the undisputed winner of his game of bluff along the Antietam.

General Jones's six-brigade division numbered only around 2,500 men, but General Toombs's Georgians were in the most advanced position on

General Lee's right at the bridge across the Antietam. Besides General Toombs's, there were the brigades of Drayton, Anderson, George Pickett, Micah Jenkins—now under the command of Lt. Col. Joseph Walker with Jenkins yet recovering from a wound at second Manassas—and James L. Kemper. It was Toombs who had to defend the most advanced and vulnerable sector on the army's far right. Meanwhile, to the Georgians' rear, the left flank of Jones's division lay adjacent and south of the east-west-running Boonsboro Pike east of Sharpsburg, as General Jones's battle line extended southward for about a mile and a half before the north-south-running Harpers Ferry Road leading south from Sharpsburg. Only Gen. Jeb Stuart's cavalrymen covered the ground beyond Toombs's right flank, making the Georgians more vulnerable.

Jones allowed General Toombs and Colonel Benning to determine the best defensive alignments on the heights above Antietam Creek. By this time, the brigades of Jones's division were positioned directly behind General Toombs's Georgians and to their northwest on the last stretch of high ground, the third and last ridge between the creek and Sharpsburg. From these heights directly west of the Georgians, General Toombs's lower position around the bridge could not be seen by Jones's troops because of the depth of the Antietam's valley. Here, on General Lee's right below Sharpsburg, a defense in depth was created, with General Toombs's two Georgia regiments holding their exposed salient on the west bank of Antietam Creek, about 650 yards before, or directly east of General Jones's division.

This was a situation that probably suited both Toombs and Benning. Lack of confidence in Jones's abilities was widespread throughout Toombs's brigade, Maj. James D. Waddell saying after Jones's subsequent departure from the army that "I do not think the army will lose much by his absence."

The limitations of the ailing division commander worked to the advantage of Toombs and Benning, however, for now they had the opportunity to fight as they pleased without his interference. Their gear clanging, the soldiers of the 2nd and 20th Georgia began to align in their position on the terrain overlooking the creek. At this point around the bridge, the land dipped sharply down to the creek, making this almost more of a gorge than a valley. With the land behind the bluff continuing to rise toward Sharpsburg, even this eminence above the creek was at a low point on the field. General Toombs and Colonel Benning carefully deployed their meager force along the high ground. Centered upon the Rohrbach Bridge, the Georgians' thin defensive line stretched southward for nearly a thousand yards. Also known as the Lower Bridge, the Rohrbach Bridge was the southernmost of three stone bridges that crossed the Antietam along General McClellan's nearly four-mile front.

On the east side of the Antietam, the Rohrersville road turned southwest to follow the creek's east bank for about a quarter of a mile amid the bottoms of open ground and cornfields before entering the rolling hills leading eastward to Rohrersville, on the western edge of South Mountain between Fox's and Crampton's Gaps. Fortunately for the defenders at the bridge, Antietam Creek was wider here than it was farther upstream, as it began to broaden out before emptying into the Potomac about three miles south of town.

Filing into a defensive line overlooking the Rohrbach Bridge, the 2nd Georgia took position on the right, or south, of the bridge. Along the crest of the bluff, Colonel William Holmes deployed his men in a line for about 300 yards southward and roughly parallel to the creek. Here, the 2nd Georgia's line was shielded by patches of tall timber atop the high ground and along the wooded slope. This naturally strong defensive position was made even stronger by the soldiers' use of fence rails, logs, rocks, and "everything that could give protection."

A hobbled Lt. Thomas M. Beasely moved his soldiers of the Columbus Guards into line, while carrying an old cavalry saber as a walking stick. Along the steep slope of the nearly 110-foot-high bluff rising from the creek's edge, another 2nd Georgia company was positioned above a small rock quarry on the narrow point of land that made a natural defensive salient, looming eastward and about two-thirds of the way up the bluff immediately to the bridge's right.

Colonel Holmes must have been shocked to now see scarcely 120 2nd Georgia soldiers with him at the Antietam. Maj. James Daniel Waddell, 20th Georgia, shortly described his men as "miserably clad and shod [and] we have over one hundred men in the regiment barefoot absolutely."[16] Casualties during the Seven Days and second Manassas, disease, and straggling had reduced the 2nd Georgia to a mere cadre of soldiers.

Meanwhile Toombs and Benning continued to deploy the 20th Georgia, under Col. Jonathan B. Cumming, about two-thirds of the way up the commanding bluff on the left. Colonel Benning estimated there were not more than 250 soldiers in the ranks of the 20th, and Cumming himself would soon write that he placed "about 200 strong" along the banks of the Antietam. The heaviest concentration of 20th Georgia Rebels took defensive positions north of the stone bridge along the bluff's crest overlooking the bridge and parallel to the road running along the west bank. Here, they anchored their right on the 2nd Georgia's left. In addition, along the creek bank leading north from the bridge, Colonel Cumming spread a line of skir-mishers northward to cover the west bank of the Antietam and guard against a Federal crossing that might outflank Toombs's left. Roughly ten to fifteen yards west of the Antietam, a split-rail fence ran northward and parallel to the creek, offering some protection for skirmishers north of the bridge.

A belt of forest lined portions of the Antietam's bank north of the bridge and along sections of the slope, allowing concealment for the men of the 20th Georgia. These defenders took position behind a stone wall, running atop the bluff, and other defensive positions parallel to the creek. North of the bridge, the countryside on both sides of the Lower Bridge Road leading to Sharpsburg was cultivated and devoid of heavy brush and timber. Holding a key defensive position, the 20th Georgia's left was anchored on high ground slightly northwest of the bridge as the Antietam, and the terrain of the bluff, turned slightly northwestward toward Sharps-burg. After the withdrawal of a company of General Hood's Texans who were already in position when Toombs's men reached the Antietam, on the evening of 16 September, the Telfair County soldiers under Lt. Farquhard McCrimmon, Company H, 20th Georgia, replaced them in this sector. These Company H Rebels found good positions along the road, which ran north from the bridge and parallel along Antietam Creek for about 300 yards before turning northwestward at a right angle toward Sharpsburg. Lieutenant McCrimmon's boys also took cover amid a belt of timber immediately above the west end of the bridge. Some soldiers of Company H positioned themselves behind trees along the bank around the mouth of the bridge and along a ten-yard-wide stretch of level ground, where the bridge gained the west bank, an important location in General Toombs's opinion. Others sheltered in a nearby limestone quarry, which was about midway up the slope or about fifty feet above the creek. Like the 2nd Georgia, the 20th Georgia was badly depleted from the battles of the sum-mer of 1862. The veterans of General Toombs's two regiments immedi-ately began digging a network of rifle pits along both the open and the wooded slope as soon as the sun went down. Sergeant Houghton explained that "the men learned to fight according to common sense, and not according to antiquated tactics for smooth bore arms. We took advantage of every defense or obstacle [and] after we were put in position, the officers never interfered with the men to any great extent, and the men knew what to do, and generally did it." The fact that General Lee's army had not brought entrenching tools—picks and shovels—forced the Georgians to improvise once again. They now used bayonets and the halves of tin Yan-kee canteens to excavate the earth.

Under cover of darkness, the Georgians cleared away brush and timber before their defensive positions to open fields of fire. They left most of the natural cover of light woods and underbrush lining the slope in place, however, to provide protection and to mask their dispositions. Heavy foliage along the slope combined with the network of rifle pits almost totally obscured the Georgians from the Federals' view.[17] Initially, Benning was more optimistic than Toombs, sensing the possibilities for a successful defense of the new position:[18]

> For a long distance below the bridge, and for some distance above it, the ground rose very steeply from the creek for fifty or sixty yards. The face of this slope was clothed with rather thinly scattered trees, and in one place on the left it had a sort of pit large enough to hold twenty or thirty men. Behind the trees at the top of the steep slope ran a rail fence. Along the face of this slope among the trees, in a rather irregular line, to suit the ground, I placed the two regiments, the Second on the right and the Twentieth on the left, with the line of the Twentieth extending forty or fifty yards above the bridge. Thus the greater part of the general line was placed below the bridge. This disposition was adopted because the road to the bridge on the other side of the creek ran from below up the bank of the creek near the water for 100 or 200 yards . . . the hill-side occupied by the regiments was on its left commanded by a sharp ridge about 200 yards beyond the creek.[19]

With the regiment's left resting on the right of the 20th Georgia, the 2nd Georgia's line spanned southward from the bridge before the regiment's line turned southwestward at a right angle, following the contours of the bluff and the Antietam at its base. Here, the bluff jutted eastward, forming a salient in a loop of the creek. This was the highest point of the bluff, which was more precipitous and rockier than the terrain above the bridge. Perched on high ground above the Antietam, the right of the 2nd Georgia overlooked the road on the other, or east, side of the creek, where the road turned sharply west at a right angle to flow parallel to the creek. This dirt road on the east side of the creek led a quarter mile northwestward along the east bank to the bridge: a seemingly easy avenue of attack for the Yankees. But this enhanced the Georgians' defense because the road paralleled the elevated position of Colonel Holmes's regiment aligned across the high ground. An advancing bluecoat column could thus not only be raked by a frontal fire but also could be hit by a flank fire for a length of 300 yards at relatively close range. Such a plunging fire sweeping off the high ground from a long line of 2nd Georgia soldiers could be devastating. The high ground 300 yards south of the bridge was even more advantageous for its defenders than for those men holding the bluff around the bridge. The more commanding ground below the bridge was more of a rocky perch or overlook than a bluff, offering the defenders an ideal shooting gallery across the creek.

General Toombs, in his somewhat less accurate battle report a month later, said that "upon examining the position, . . . I then ordered the Twentieth to take position, with its right near the foot of the bridge extending down the river near its margin, and the Second Georgia on its right, prolonging the line down to the point where the road on the other side from the mountain approached the river." Despite holding the high ground, Toombs was still concerned about his line's vulnerabilities. He had far too few men to hold an overly extended front of nearly a thousand yards. Describing this handicap with some understatement, Toombs wrote that "this required a more open order than was desirable, on account of the smallness of the regiments," which were also vulnerable because they held an exposed salient, jutting before the main line and dangling beyond the army without immediate support on the south end of General Lee's battle line. The Georgia Rebels, moreover, did not like the looks of the high ground of the parallel ridge on the opposite side of the creek directly over the bridge. Union artillery there could dominate the Antietam's narrow valley, and the Georgia defenders could be blasted off their bluff by a concentrated fire of massed artillery.[20]

Clearly, Colonel Holmes's 2nd Georgia now held the most vital defensive sector with its left flank protecting the bridge and its right overlooking the most fordable section of the creek immediately below the bridge. Here, about 300 yards below the bridge, the banks of the creek decreased in height and the Antietam's width narrowed immediately above the wide bend in its course. In addition, the bottoms on the east side of the Antietam narrowed at this point. This topography would work to the Federals' advantage, allowing any attackers to leave the protection of the slight elevation, covered in brush and trees bordering the creek, and advance only a short distance to gain the Antietam's east bank without crossing the wider stretch of open ground to the north.On the east side, the creek bottoms became ever wider upon approaching the bridge from the south. That made this a good fording point below the bridge and before Snavely's two fords about three-fourths of a mile below the bridge. This crossing point just beyond sight of the defenders around the bridge was well known to the Federals, and General McClellan's engineers identified this shallow point as a potential crossing site immediately below the bridge. Unfortunately for them, however, this first ford below the bridge fronted the highest section of bluff, which rose up almost like a wall on the creek's west bank.

In the fight ahead Colonel Holmes could rely on Maj. William Terrell Harris, who had repeatedly proven himself in combat from the Seven Days to second Manassas. He also could depend on natural leaders such as Sergeant Chaffin, described by Private Houghton as having "never had a furlough, never swore an oath, never was in the hospital, and never received a wound, though he had the seams of both sides just below his pockets cut out at Chickamauga, and his sword belt was shot off, and his canteen punctured on other occasions. In a fight he always got a gun, and if coolness accounted for anything he did execution." The struggle for possession of the Rohrbach Bridge would be the sergeant's most harrowing day.[21]

Taking charge of the 2nd and 20th Georgia in defense of the bridge was General Toombs's dependable top lieutenant, Col. Henry Lewis Benning. In his late forties, Benning was only a few years younger than General Toombs. The third of eleven children, Benning was born on a plantation in Columbia County on 2 April 1814, when Indians and British still waged war on the eastern Georgia frontier. Like other soldiers of General Toombs's Brigade, he possessed a fair percentage of Cherokee blood. A number of full-blooded Indians also joined the 2nd Georgia in 1861. Their influence was often felt during attacks through wooded terrain in which the Georgia Rebels charged from tree to tree while "yelling like an Indian," wrote one soldier.

Like Bob Toombs, Colonel Benning also attended the University of Georgia at Athens, graduating at the top of his class. After graduation, Benning moved to Columbus on the Chattahoochee, where he returned after the Civil War and lived for the remainder of his life. During the antebellum years, Benning became a wealthy planter and successful attorney, serving as solicitor general for the Chattahoochee Circuit. He soon entered the Georgia legislature, married the only daughter of a prominent Columbus attorney, and became a law partner with his respected father-in-law, serving as a key member of a formidable legal team in Columbus. As an esteemed antebellum leader of the Columbus community, the tough-minded Benning early became a defender of Southern rights and nationalism, long before Toombs abandoned the Union. In 1850 Benning was elected to the Southern Convention at Nashville, Tennessee, where he advocated an immediate withdrawal from the Union, becoming a leading fire-eater not only in Columbus, but also in the South at large. After a narrow defeat in an election to Congress in 1851, Benning set his sights two years later on a seat on the Georgia Supreme Court.

During a span of six years on the court bench, Benning's legalistic mind thrived on the challenges presented by the defense of states' rights. In one memorable decision, supported by an original eighty-page treatise, Benning argued that the Georgia Supreme Court could not be overruled by the United States Supreme Court, because they were "co-equal." This was the famous 1854 case of *Padleford v. Savannah,* which cemented Benning's reputation across the South as a leading states' rights advocate.

Like a Roman patriarch, he lived on an estate of more than 3,000 acres, which were worked by eighty-nine slaves. One of these blacks, "Old Billie," served beside Colonel Benning throughout the war, helping to nurse him whenever he was sick or wounded. Benning's family life proved as fulfilling as his legal and political career. He fathered ten children, nine daughters and one son. But, tragedy suddenly struck as four infant daughters died of disease in rapid succession. Ironically, this tragedy was not unlike Toombs's loss of two daughters before the war. For both men, it was almost as if family setbacks counterbalanced the levels of success in their professional, social, and political lives.[22]

Serving as a delegate to the Democratic national convention during the last week of April 1860, Benning led the Georgia delegation's walkout at Charleston, South Carolina, after Northern Democrats rejected a platform proposed by Southerners. In June Benning then acted as a vice president of the reconvened convention in Baltimore that nominated Stephen Douglas for president. With Lincoln's election in November 1860, Benning argued that "the meaning of Mr. Lincoln's election . . . is the abolition of slavery as soon as the Republican party Shall have acquired the strength to abolish it." When South Carolina departed the Union in December, Benning was elected to Georgia's secession meeting after both he and Toombs signed a 15 November 1860 resolution calling for a state convention. There, in a rousing speech a few days later, the pragmatic Benning emphasized that "another remedy is to fight in the Union, [but cautioned] if we do, we fight to great disadvantage." Benning then ended with a war cry that brought an enthusiastic response: "Ho! for independence!"

During the summer of 1861, Benning formed the 17th Georgia Infantry, a regiment that consisted of many of his closest friends and neighbors. The soldiers of the 17th Georgia hailed from the counties of Webster, Schley, Muscogee, Decatur, Mitchell, Dougherty, Harris, and Stewart. With his rowdy, young volunteers, Colonel Benning headed northeast for Virginia to join the principal Confederate army in the East. In barely seven months from the time of the Maryland campaign and because of his performance at the Antietam, Colonel Benning would earn the rank of brigadier general in April 1863.

Benning was nicknamed "Old Rock" and "Old Bull," evidence of his stubborn nature and hard-fighting qualities. By the time of the Maryland campaign, he was considered throughout the Army of Northern Virginia as a model colonel. "Not only the brigade, but the whole division are enthusiastic in his praise," said one Southerner.

The nickname of "Old Rock" was first applied to Colonel Benning at Thoroughfare Gap, where he commanded Toombs's brigade on 28 August. Benning led his Georgians forward with flags flying, to drive the Federals out of the gap in the Blue Ridge, allowing Lee and Jackson to converge on the hapless Pope at second Manassas. One of the wounded Georgians under the command of General Anderson (known as "Old Tige") was inspired by Colonel Benning's advance and shouted, "Drive up, Old Rock, old Tige's treed over yonder." In response, Benning shouted back, "Attend to your wound; I"ll attend to Tige." Shortly thereafter, the men in the ranks tagged Benning with what was to be a lifelong nickname. By the time of the Maryland campaign, the name "Old Rock" and its meaning were known throughout the Army of Northern Virginia. One amused Rebel wrote, "I don't think Gen. Benning ever fully appreciated this intended compliment from the boys, but it stuck to him all the same."

"Old Rock, as the boys loved to call, had a good many oddities," said Sergeant Houghton. "Among them, he was very plain of speech, and would talk back in kind with compound interest to any of his men." During one long march Benning eagerly drank from the waters of a creek without noticing the body of a dead horse immediately upstream, or that the waters rushed through the putrid carcass. When the colonel was informed of the tainted water, "Old Rock" snapped, "I don't care a damn, it was as good a drink of water as I ever had in my life!" Benning also openly criticized the Confederate government, cursing the new conscription act with such vehemence "as to court arrest." [23] In his Milledgeville speech in November 1860, he had emphasized that in defending Southern soil, the Rebels would fight against the odds with the spirit of Leonidas when he and his band of 300 Spartans defended the pass of Thermopylae against the invading Persian hordes. Now, along Antietam Creek, "Old Rock" was about to redeem his prophecy.[24]

When not fighting Yankees, Colonel Benning was especially fond of the 2nd Georgia's brass band. Whenever the bandsmen serenaded him at headquarters, Benning sat silently, smoking his pipe and savoring both the tobacco and the good music. Before the close of a concert, he often jumped up to yell, "Now, give us, 'The Gal I Left behind Me.'" As the band played the tune, the Georgia colonel kept time "with a vigorous patting of his foot whilst his favorite was being played, a distinction given no other air."

By September 1862, Benning could claim a rare distinction in the Army of Northern Virginia: He was one of the army's only officers who had neither clashed nor bickered with Bob Toombs. As could be expected, the rest of the team was as combative off the battlefield as on. One confrontation began when Capt. Daniel B. Thompson resigned and 2nd Lt. P. W. Gittinger was elected by the soldiers of Company F, 17th Georgia, to fill the void. But an angry 1st Lt. Henry McCauley, a hard-headed Irishman, had already applied for a captain's commission based on seniority to take Captain Thompson's place. Secretary of War George W. Randolph upheld McCauley's promotion. Experienced as a Georgia judge, a defiant Benning declared that the secretary of war's decision "was unconstitutional, that it was infringing on the rights of the States, that he would fight it and would make short work, with the Secy. of War." Before his 17th Georgia soldiers, Colonel Benning proclaimed that he would "fight it with the Bayonet" on this states' rights issue if necessary.[25]

In the summer of 1862, Benning arrested Lieutenant McCauley to circumvent the secretary of war's directive. To settle the issue, General Lee ordered Toombs to give Lieutenant McCauley his captain's rank. General Toombs balked, however. He and Benning continued to hold firm against even Lee's orders, and the Georgia soldiers stood behind them. Benning and Toombs, meanwhile, stalled for time, with each telling Lieutenant McCauley that the other possessed his captain's commission, which of course was nonexistent. Finally a frustrated Lieutenant McCauley resigned in disgust in July 1862.[26]

Commanding the 20th Georgia, Colonel Cumming could count on a top lieutenant in Maj. James Daniel Waddell, the scholarly University of Georgia graduate. A lawyer, writer, and planter from Cedartown, in Polk County, he had been married less than four years when he left his practice to march off to war. Now, Major Waddell's leadership abilities would be tested along the Antietam Creek.[27] Standing atop the commanding high ground above the Antietam, he confidently watched his 20th Georgia soldiers take good defensive positions. In a letter to his wife he said he was anxious to give General McClellan and the Army of the Potomac "a good wholesome drubbing." What he wanted most of all to see was the day when his children were "smiling in peace, prosperity & plenty—the Yankees defeated everywhere & our independence established."[28]

Quite unexpectedly, the small cadre of the 2nd and 20th Georgia received a much-needed reinforcement on 16 September with the arrival of Lt. Col. Frank Kearse and 100 men of his 50th Georgia. This timely addition bolstered General Toombs's thin lines, allowing an extension southward across a wider front in guarding the creek's west bank.

Colonel Kearse was an experienced commander, known as much for his leadership qualities as for his patriotic speeches in the Toombs tradition. The 50th Georgia first took shape near Savannah, formed primarily of volunteers from the piney woods of south Georgia. Many of Kearse's officers were veterans of the Creek and Seminole Wars, and others gained early militia experience in such units as the Macon Volunteers during the antebellum period. Along with the 2nd Georgia, the 50th Georgia served in the defense of the Georgia coast until the summer of 1862. Then, these Georgians hurried north to Virginia to assist in Richmond's defense during the Seven Days.

During the early phase of the Maryland campaign, the 50th Georgia was led by thirty-two-year-old Col. Peter Alexander Selkirk McGlashan. A native of Edinburgh, Scotland, McGlashan was the son of a Waterloo veteran and the grandson of the last chief of the McGlashan highland clan of Scotland.

The transplanted Scotsman moved into the interior of frontier Georgia to start a new life. But the allure of gold suddenly attracted him to California in 1849. Returned to Georgia no richer but considerably wiser, McGlashan left again in 1856 to serve in William Walker's filibuster expedition to Nicaragua. After its failure and Walker's execution, the adventuresome highlander returned to Thomasville, Georgia, where he established a mercantile business.

Like the 2nd and 20th Georgia, the 50th contained a cadre of officers educated at the Georgia Military Institute, including Capts. William Frederic Pendleton and Frank Fontaine. Pendleton was the son of Maj. Philip Coleman Pendleton, a Seminole War veteran who was one of the regiment's most experienced officers. The major's son William had led a militia company in Savannah before the war. Major Pendleton was a Macon lawyer who had served as a newspaper editor in both Macon and Savannah. The veterans of the 50th Georgia had fought well from Virginia to Maryland, struggling on the battlefield to the motto of "In God Is Our Trust." On 17 September in defense of the arched bridge across the Antietam, yet another battle cry of the 50th Georgia would inspire Colonel McGlashan's soldiers: "Men, remember that you are Georgians!"[29]

Knowing that he must judiciously place the few 50th Georgia soldiers at hand, Toombs ordered some of these grayclads to take concealed positions at the southern edge of a forty-acre cornfield, about halfway between the Rohrbach Bridge and Snavely's Fords. After learning of the exact location of Snavely's Fords on his right flank far to the south, however, Toombs then ordered them to about-face, and march south into a clover field, where they were ordered to take a defensive position and lie down. Capt. Thomas H. Jackson, commanding part of the 50th Georgia, now occupied a good high ground position overlooking Snavely's Ford. With these veteran troops in their new position closer to the Antietam, General Toombs could now count on a hidden strategic reserve on commanding ground to defend the two vital fords on the Snavely farm, about three-fourths of a mile below the bridge.

The 50th Georgia's defensive line extended south to a wide bend in the Antietam, before turning west to follow the creek as it sharply shifted course. A skirmish line of Georgia veterans was aligned along the top of the bluff in an inverted fishhook that stretched southward from the bluff overlook above the first, or northernmost, ford immediately below the bridge, and continued until the bluff culminated on a hilltop that overlooked and commanded both of Snavely's Fords. Kearse's regiment was spread so thin that it amounted to little more than a skirmish line by this time.

From this position, Kearse extended his skirmish line downstream another 600 yards to protect the westernmost Snavely's Ford, or Snavely's Ford proper, to guard his regiment's rear, as well as the right flank and rear of the 2nd and 20th Georgia. In addition, the far right flank of the 50th Georgia protected the road leading up the high ground toward Sharpsburg from the second, or westernmost, of Snavely's Fords, which was the main ford. Colonel Kearse also dispatched a company of skirmishers to guard the creek around the ford. Then, he ordered another skirmish company of 50th Georgia boys to take defensive positions even farther west, or downstream, to watch the creek for any crossing and cover the right flank of his over-extended position. In total, General Toombs's defensive line now stretched nearly a full mile. Clearly, this was far too much for scarcely 300 soldiers to hold.

The final diminutive band of infantrymen to stand beside General Toombs's defenders along Antietam Creek were "the Palmetto boys," who had reached the army during the late morning hours of 15 September. These soldiers from Brig. Gen. Micah Jenkins's South Carolina brigade consisted of a company of about twenty to twenty-five Palmetto sharpshooters armed with Enfield rifles who ensured that the defense of the brigade was not solely a Georgian affair. Formed in early 1862 by the then colonel Jenkins, the regiment now was known simply as the Palmetto Sharpshooters. The South Carolina outfit was one of the first specialized units of Lee's Army, consisting of men who had qualified by meeting high standards of marksmanship. Ordered to relieve Lieutenant McCrimmon's Company H of the 20th Georgia around the bridge and along the road in this sector, the South Carolina marksmen were directed by General Toombs to hold the commanding high ground above the creek. Here, between the 2nd and 20th Georgia, the "Palmetto boys" were to take a position from which their fire could sweep the bridge and its approaches on the east bank.

General Toombs's orders to the Palmetto Sharpshooters, however, were not delivered, not fully understood, or simply not obeyed. McCrimmon's men consequently remained in their line immediately above the bridge. Angry that his order had not been obeyed, General Toombs made one final defensive adjustment on the morning of Wednesday, 17 September. In his own words, General Toombs then positioned "the captain and one-half of this [South Carolina] company between the Second Georgia and Fiftieth Georgia, and the other half, under a lieutenant, near the lower ford, to prevent or retard the passage of the enemy at this point . . . this position was important, and had been guarded by a cavalry regiment with an infantry brigade in its rear, up to Tuesday evening when both were removed to another position on the field of battle, and left the crossing unprotected, except by the small force I was thus enable[d] to place there."[30]

Toombs ordered the sections to take two separate defensive positions: Capt. Franklin Kilpatrick and one-half of the Palmetto company were placed between the 2nd Georgia and the 50th Georgia, while the other half-company of the South Carolina marksmen, under a trusted lieutenant, guarded the shallow crossing of the creek at Snavely's Fords along with the 50th Georgia skirmishers. With Enfield rifles on shoulders, the South Carolina sharpshooters positioned themselves along the west bank, as the 50th Georgia soldiers stood above them on the bluff to guard the road, which led from the main Snavely Ford to the Rohrbach Bridge and General Toombs's right and rear.

As with Toombs's Georgia regiments, prewar militia experience and early training were factors that explained the high quality of this South Carolina sharpshooter regiment. Many of them had served in a militia unit known as the Palmetto Riflemen of Charleston. The young, handsome Jenkins had served with distinction as the Tidewater captain of the Jasper Rifle Guards—named after an Irish hero who was killed in the American

Revolution—and then as the colonel of the 5th South Carolina before forming the Palmetto Sharpshooters. A hero of the battle of Seven Pines, where he led a fierce attack that smashed through four Union lines and repulsed a fifth, General Jenkins was a graduate of the South Carolina military academy—The Citadel—in 1854. He then established his own military school, the King's Mountain Military Academy, a year later in the up-country of South Carolina at Yorkville.

The Palmetto Sharpshooters were formed from the transfers of volunteers from the 2nd, 5th, and 9th South Carolina Infantry , who were able to meet Jenkins's tough standards. Consisting of a blend of college boys, graduates of military schools like The Citadel, and Mexican War veterans, the Palmetto Sharpshooters were among "the very best Carolina could give her cause," wrote one Southerner. The Seven Days' battles proved their combat reliability, where during a fierce flank attack, one Palmetto Sharpshooter captured nearly 140 Pennsylvania soldiers.

At Gaines's Mill on 27 June 1862, the sharpshooters drove the Yankees into the swamps of the Chickahominy and captured the colors of the 16th Michigan. During the fighting at Frayser's Farm, in the Seven Days, the Palmetto Sharpshooters lost 69 percent of their strength in capturing a Pennsylvania battery and driving back units of a Union division, one of the highest regimental losses of the war.

Along Antietam Creek, consequently, the 2nd and 20th Georgia veterans possessed confidence in these South Carolina soldiers. In the words of one Rebel of General Toombs's Brigade, "the Palmetto boys are made of the right material." As with the Georgians, a sense of idealism and personal motivation were yet high among these Palmetto Rebels. As one South Carolina soldier wrote: "We are now in the land of danger, far, far from home, fighting for our homes and those near our hearts."[31]

General Toombs now had in hand all of the troops that he would have on 17 September to defend the bridge and its surrounding sectors, and to cover the fords. For good reason, one Virginia soldier felt pessimistic about the chances for success in the upcoming struggle for the possession of the Rohrbach Bridge, referring to the over-extended band of Georgians as General "Toombs's skeleton brigade."

After one of the hottest and driest summers in memory, the Antietam was now fordable at several points along Toombs's front. One of Stonewall Jackson's staff officers would later say that the Federals "might have waded that day without getting their waist belts wet in any place." Colonel Benning reported that "the creek was fordable everywhere above and below the bridge; in most places was not more than knee-deep."

The Georgians quickly discovered that the creek was too low to offer a formidable barrier for a fording of the Antietam. That forced Toombs and Benning to spread their line extremely thin to cover more than a thousand yards, the 50th Georgia and the South Carolina company protecting the west bank southward to not only cover the creek before them, on the east, but also Snavely's Fords to the south. Below the Rohrbach Bridge, the Georgians extended in a widely dispersed line. Only a single soldier now stood at every forty to fifty yards or so in this southernmost sector. Spreading their lines thinly below the bridge allowed Toombs and Benning to concentrate as many defenders as possible around the bridge itself.

The exact number of Georgia soldiers defending the Rohrbach Bridge is difficult to determine, with accounts varying. Colonel Benning estimated that the 2nd and 20th Georgia consisted of only 350 soldiers at Antietam, but even Colonel Benning overestimated his strength. Pvt. Theodore T. Fogle, 2nd Georgia, wrote ten days later that "at a bridge on the Antietam Creek our Regiment & the 20th Ga., in all amounting to not over 300 muskets," held the line. Private Fogle thought the 2nd Georgia "went into the fight with only 89 muskets." By contrast, the average Confederate regimental strength at Antietam was 166 men.

Like Colonel Benning, Toombs also overestimated the number of his Georgia troops defending the bridge, hardly realizing how few soldiers had reached the Antietam because of straggling, disease, and battle losses. He thought that the 2nd and 20th Georgia totaled "about 400 muskets strong" at Antietam. Yet, while General Toombs wrote that 250 men of the 20th Georgia stood in line along the Antietam, Colonel Cumming reported within a week of the battle that his regiment consisted of only 200 soldiers. And lower-ranking 20th Georgia soldiers thought even fewer were actually present.

Clearly, the exact number of General Toombs's defenders was less than generally believed. The exact number of Georgia defenders was probably 280 to 290 soldiers. The safety of General Lee's right flank and the all-important bridge would depend almost solely upon these thinly spread men in a defensive line of around 1,500 yards in length. Even though the 50th Georgia and the handful of Palmetto Sharpshooters extended the length of General Toombs's defensive line southward along the creek, these units would play relatively minor support roles in the bridge's defense.[32] Fortunately for the defenders on the far right, although the top of the bluff was open and cleared of timber for cultivation, the slopes were heavily timbered all the way down to Snavely's Fords, offering good concealment.

Lieutenant McCrimmon's soldiers of the 20th Georgia intermingled with the Burke County Sharpshooters of the 2nd Georgia in the sector around the west end of the bridge, while Company H, 20th Georgia, held an advanced position above the bridgehead. Some Rebels took defensive positions in the roadbed, which turned sharply north from the west end of the bridge and led to Sharpsburg. The slightly sunken dirt road provided yet another strong defensive line that paralleled the creek. The Georgians thus created a four-tier defensive line at the bridgehead: the lower position along the bank; the midtier position along the road north of the bridge; another along the long slope; and the upper level position along the stone wall at the bluff's crest. Rifle pits between each level enhanced the stronghold.

Colonel Holmes placed the Burke County Sharpshooters, the best riflemen in the 2nd Georgia, at the most vulnerable sector at the west end of the bridge. They were armed with the .577 caliber Enfield rifled musket, a deadly weapon with greater velocity and accuracy than the .69 caliber smoothbore muskets carried by most of Toombs's soldiers. Other Burke County soldiers, meanwhile, took position farther up the slope in the quarry and its environs. Some men selected firing positions along the bank, behind fallen logs and towering sycamores, or amid the cover of the thick stands of willows and saplings. This dense growth along the bank south of the bridge was ideal for cover, especially after the defenders dug slit trenches.

The 20th Georgia also boasted a dependable company of sharpshooters, Lieutenant McCrimmon's Company H, who now held the high ground around the bridgehead. Like the Burke County Sharpshooters of Company D, 2nd Georgia, the soldiers of McCrimmon's company were also armed with the deadly Enfield, and so two companies of veteran marksmen anchored the Georgians' defensive line around the bridge.

Marksmen of both of these companies held positions at intervals in and around the quarry. With the quarry large enough to hold twenty or thirty defenders, in Colonel Benning's estimation, both Captain Dickerson's and Lieutenant McCrimmon's soldiers exploited the natural bunker, which effectively commanded the length of the bridge and its approaches from above.

This strong point anchored the line immediately south of the bridge. Situated at the apex of a shelf about two-thirds the way up the bluff, the Georgians' rock salient extended slightly from the bluff and loomed above the bridge. The steep slope of the bluff above the Antietam rose almost vertically like a wall behind these quarry defenders, while immediately before the quarry the slope dropped off sharply, descending to the creek.[33]

Toombs and Benning would receive limited support from two guns of Capt. John B. Richardson's 2nd Company of the famous Washington

Artillery of New Orleans. These Louisiana gunners prided themselves on hailing from the best families of Louisiana.[34] Instead of wearing their standard red kepis at Antietam, some of Captain Eshelman's artillerymen wore tall, bell-crowned beaver hats. These hats were once fashionable but now out-of-date for men so young. Dressed in gray uniforms with red piping, the Washington artillery cannoneers were prepared for the challenge of Antietam.[35] Richardson was a veteran of first Bull Run, serving as a lieutenant in command of a two-gun section that fired the battery's first shots of the first battle of the war. This Louisiana battery was attached to the Georgia brigade and positioned to Toombs's left-rear in support of the 20th Georgia. Unfortunately, the usually reliable guns of the Washington Artillery were placed too far to the rear to offer much support.[36] Toombs would ask Longstreet for more guns, but Richardson is all he would get. The only additional artillery support that he would receive on 17 September was long-range, from Capt. John Lewis Eubank's Virginia battery, which galloped into position along the high ground in the 50th Georgia's rear and unlimbered to face both east and south to guard the creek on the morning of 15 September. Thus, defending the Rohrbach Bridge would depend most of all upon the marksmanship of the Georgia soldiers.[37]

By the beginning of the battle, the batteries of Richardson and Benjamin Franklin Eshleman would hold positions on commanding terrain around 500 yards west and northwest of the bridge. Positioned among the trees of an orchard atop a ridge west of farmer John Otto's lane, would be Captain Richardson's two 12-pounder Napoleons, which stood to the left, or north, of Captain Eshleman's cannon. Eshleman's four guns, two 12-pounder howitzers and two bronze 6-pounder smoothbores, stood beside Captain Richardson's Louisiana cannon. Eubanks would be positioned several hundred yards southeast of Richardson and Eshleman by the morning of 17 September.[38]

The dominant landmark of General Lee's right flank was the 125-foot stone span over the Antietam. The Rohrbach Bridge was distinguished by handsome proportion and symmetry. It was named for Henry Rohrbach, whose modest two-story stone house stood on the east side of the creek, northeast of the bridge. The German Rohrbach family, among the first to settle in the valley of the Antietam, sought peace and prosperity far from the religious persecution, political authoritarianism, and perceived moral corruption of Europe. Along with their German neighbors, the Rohrbach family worshipped at the Dunkard Church north of Sharpsburg. For generations, Dunkards baptized their flock in the waters of the Antietam. The twenty-six-year-old Rohrbach Bridge was the creation of John Weaver, almost as much of an artist as an engineer. Weaver's distinctive stone bridges were highlighted by three arches that became progressively larger from the base to the bridge's midpoint. Two sets of rounded piers supported each side of the central arch of the bridge. He incorporated this design into the Rohrbach Bridge in 1836 and at the cost of barely two thousand dollars.[39]

Constructed by Irish laborers, this bridge was built here because the National Road cut through Washington County, linking the eastern seaboard to the Ohio and Mississippi River Valleys. Thanks to the early republic's emphasis on internal improvements to hasten development, the nation maintained a good wagon road that led west to the Ohio country. Fueled by the progressive spirit of the Jacksonian Period, these stone bridges facilitated the nation's growth for decades during the antebellum period. Most of the bridges of Washington County were built during the 1820s and 1830s as public works. More than a dozen such limestone bridges spanned Antietam Creek, as it descended south toward the Potomac. Of the three stone bridges that stood between the two opposing armies at Antietam, only the Rohrbach bridge would play a prominent role 17 September.

At the stone bridge, the quick-flowing Antietam was about sixty feet wide. To the north, Antietam Creek was formed from the confluence of the Black Andes, Gum, Chestnut, and Cold Springs of Franklin and Adams Counties, Pennsylvania. Along its western bank timber and smaller willows and oak saplings shaded the bank. A belt of forest and thick underbrush covered much of the slope of the high ground above the creek below the bridge. A split-rail fence along the crest was soon adapted for defense. Benning reported that "the rails were taken from the fence and built up against such trees as were in suitable situations, and where there was no such trees the rails were laid in simple piles. These rude barricades, few and far between, afforded to men lying behind them tolerable shelter against small-arms." Commanding Company C, Capt. Abner McCoy Lewis wrote how the 2nd Georgia deployed themselves "behind trees and barricades made of fence rails."

Fortunately McClellan's indecision granted the Confederates plenty of time to strengthen their defensive positions and utilize the natural cover. Certainly the most effective structure they erected along the Antietam was a V-shaped stone redoubt, solidifying and anchoring the 20th Georgia's line on the right flank. After being erected at about the same elevation of the bluff as the rock quarry-bunker, it dominated the length of the bridge. Both the quarry-bunker and the stone redoubt stood close to, and at about the same distance from, the west end of the bridge.

Complementing the stone redoubt, and only a few yards south of the bridgehead and two thirds up the slope, the stone quarry likewise loomed above the bridge. It stood at the point where most needed by the defenders. The 2nd and 20th Georgia soldiers used the limestone rock in and around the quarry to strengthen the stone redoubt. The Georgians also gathered rock to erect individual, fortified firing positions along the slope. In addition, they collected logs and fence rails to strengthen their defensive positions, creating lunettes, three sided redoubts with a narrow opening in the rear. In essence, these were miniforts, scattered at various elevations along the slope to cover the bridge and its approaches from multiple angles.

The late summer season also aided Toombs's soldiers in the bridge's defense. The fair weather of mid-September in western Maryland, provided a veil of late summer foliage. The first cold of fall had not yet dropped the mostly green leaves from the trees or the underbrush. The steep hillside above the bridge, consequently, was densely green despite a slight tint of yellow in the hickories and sycamores along the creek bottom.

Harvest from the fields of early fall also enhanced the Georgians' defense, as haystacks atop the bluffs, where the split-rail fence ran the length of the crest, offered concealed positions. As it became increasingly obvious to both Toombs and Benning that the Rohrbach Bridge provided the quickest and easiest avenue for the Yankee IX Corps to turn the Army of Northern Virginia's vulnerable right flank and gain General Lee's vulnerable rear, the Georgia soldiers worked with renewed urgency.

But the Georgians were less optimistic. The open avenue of the Rohrbach Bridge held the promise that the Federal columns attacking across the span would be funneled by the narrow bridge to make compact targets for the concentrated fire of the concealed Georgia Rebels. Twenty months before, Bob Toombs had mistakenly celebrated his election as the president of the Confederacy. He missed destiny once. If and when it called again, he was determined to be ready.[40]

## CHAPTER 5

# "Our Only Hope Is Providence"

## *Standing Tall at the Rohrbach Bridge*

BY THE WARM AFTERNOON OF SEPTEMBER 16, THE GEORGIANS COULD SEE more IX Corps units converging toward the Antietam. Bluecoat infantry pushed forward to secure the advanced ground opposite the bridge necessary for the emplacement of artillery to command the bridge. As ordered by McClellan, Maj. Gen. Ambrose E. Burnside was attempting to unlimber his guns. Union artillery fire earlier in the morning had already warned Toombs's veterans of the appearance of these Federal units.[1]

Now additional IX Corps troops poured forward, taking positions amid the pastures, hills, and fields of the Rohrbach farm, on the east side of the Antietam. The 2nd and 20th Georgia Rebels were understandably anxious. One 2nd Georgia private misread the role his regiment was destined to play on 17 September, for he had written to his parents in frustration that "I dont think the Columbus Guards will have much fighting to do." The soldiers of the 2nd and 20th Georgia were about to experience more than their fill of warfare in the next five hours.[2]

The long lines of advancing IX Corps skirmishers shortly swarmed forward on the east side of the Antietam. Under mid-September sunshine, the blue-clad skirmishers peppered General Toombs's position on the west bank with musketry. To ascertain the strength, dispositions, and intentions of the approaching Yankees, as well as to slow their advance, Toombs and Benning decided to take the offensive. The Rebels' retention of the high ground on the east side of the creek would deny General Burnside the advantage of Union artillery emplaced on the heights that dominated the bridge.

As the September 16 skirmishing increased, Col. Jonathan B. Cumming sent some 20th Georgia boys forward to reinforce Toombs's advanced skirmishers, who were yet holding their own and fighting on the east side, supported by Eubanks's battery. With gunfire escalating in early afternoon, gray-clad skirmishers of the 20th Georgia and the Texas company fell into line. With full cartridge boxes, the graycoat skirmishers were ordered across the creek several hundred yards to the front. At the double, the Rebels raced across the bridge, spilling over the open bottoms on the east side of the Antietam to meet the boys in blue.

The surging Georgia and Texas skirmishers engaged the Yankee skirmishers east of the Antietam, exchanging a brisk fire. Loading and firing on the run, the Confederates gained ground. After the minor success on the east side of the creek, the Rebels now occupied the valley of the Antietam before the bridge for a distance of several hundred yards. But soon the skirmishers encountered large numbers of arriving IX Corps troops. The first Confederates to fall in defense of the bridge thus fell on the east side of the creek. As the Georgia and Texas skirmishers were pushed rearward, the Federal gunners exploited the advantage, moving forward to sight their cannon on the Georgians' positions. Union cannon continued to shell General Toombs's position throughout the early evening of 16 September, alerting the Georgians to the possibility of an impending attack for 17 September.

Meanwhile, about 500 soldiers of Anderson's Georgia brigade and Brig. Gen. John G. Walker's division arrived from Harpers Ferry on the afternoon of 16 September to bolster General Lee's right. Walker's division took position to Toombs's right-rear, to guard the area around Snavely's Ford, proper. Just west, and beyond the extreme end of Toombs's line, Col. Thomas Munford's Virginia cavalrymen held the line on the high ground overlooking the Antietam above Myer's Ford, farther downstream and west of Snavely's Fords. Strung out in a thin gray line that extended south to the mouth of the Antietam, where it entered the Potomac, these cavalrymen could primarily only scout any unexpected threat.

Despite the arrival of Walker's division and the high ground positions occupied by Jones's division near Sharpsburg to the Georgians' rear, Toombs continued to hold a vulnerable salient, with Jones, especially, well beyond supporting distance. Leadership also presented problems. Walker should have taken command of the Antietam Creek defensive line but did not, leaving Toombs in charge. Evidently Confederate leadership continued to believe that the Georgians would be unable to long hold their advanced position and that Toombs's role was primarily that of a trip wire to slow the IX Corps's advance on Sharpsburg.

As the sun dropped behind Sharpsburg, Toombs felt satisfied in having gained time with his skirmishers. In the dimming light, the worn Confederates took defensive positions around the bridge's east end. Most important for the Rebels in this sector, an ill-prepared IX Corps did not strike on 16 September because McClellan was not yet ready.

During the firefight of the sixteenth, the Southern skirmishers learned definitely that the Federals had arrived in force in their front. This was no feint. In fact, in preparation for the next day's attack, the IX Corps's Union artillery east of the Antietam continue to shell Toombs's position. In the fading light, General Burnside's soldiers overlooking the valley of the Antietam now got their first good look at the stone bridge as Confederate skirmishers retired.[3] They could not know that McClellan had missed an opportunity to strike with his overpowering forces on 16 September. General Toombs, however, realized that the following day might be his chance, with only a few hundred soldiers, to somehow stop the IX Corps.[4] Throughout the Army of Northern Virginia, Toombs was "notorious" for having "a thousand times expressed disgust that the commanding general did not permit [him] to fight," wrote Gen. Daniel H. Hill.[5]

Six months earlier an angry Toombs wrote to his wife, Julia: "So far as I am concerned, Mr. Davis will never give me a chance for personal distinction. He thinks I pant for it, poor fool. I want nothing but the defeat of the public enemy and to retire with you for the balance of my life in peace and quiet in any decent corner of a free county . . . I shall not quit it [the army] until after a great victory, in which I shall have the opportunity of doing something for the country. The day after such an event, I will retire if I live through it."

Because of the mass straggling and the campaign's shortcomings, Toombs was not optimistic about the upcoming fight, or even of the war's outcome; he now believed that "our only hope is providence."[6] A light, drizzling rain had fallen during the night. The Georgians huddled in wet blankets under arms amid their rifle pits and in the rock quarry. "We [had] slept in our clothes, taking off our shoes with a cartridge box for a pillow," wrote Sergeant Houghton of the Columbus Guards. Captain Ross, 20th Georgia, scribbled in his diary every day now that he, along with many other defenders, was "Sick all day."

The pale sunrise of 17 September augered the war's bloodiest day. Light skirmishing almost immediately shattered the quiet morning.[7] A misty fog, meanwhile, rolled off the creek below the defenders perched across the bluff. In the foggy half-light the mist bathed the land along the creek with a surreal glow. With a bright sun rising, brisk enemy skirmishing forewarned the Georgians of a big fight. The dark clumps of cedars on the high ground of the knolls opposite the bridge were now full of Yankee troops of the IX Corps.

The 2nd and 20th Georgia battle flags fluttered in the light early morning breeze. The first battle flag presented to the 20th Georgia had been light colored. The colonel feared that the Yankees might interpret it as a surrender banner. Gen. Pierre G. T. Beauregard, therefore, immediately ordered the colonel to "Dye it with blood, sir!"

As the Georgians waited for the IX Corps to strike, they heard the first heavy fighting begin to roar about three miles north of them around six o'clock. After having just returned from the capture of Harpers Ferry, Stonewall Jackson's troops on the army's left were steamrolled by assault waves of a Union corps in the early morning hours. To secure possession of the commanding ground north of Sharpsburg on the west side of the Antietam, both sides hurled brigade after brigade into the escalating struggle. Thousands of casualties on both sides piled up in record time. Some of the most savage fighting of the war raged on General Lee's left this morning, swirling through the fields of the East Wood, the Miller Cornfield, the West Wood, and around the Dunkard Church.

Despite the mauling of General Lee's left, Stonewall Jackson somehow held firm under the pounding. Skillfully maneuvering his troops to bolster weaker sectors, Lee held McClellan's overpowering legions at bay by eventually concentrating more than half of his twenty-four brigades on the north to resist the relentless hammering. Fortunately for the Army of Northern Virginia, McClellan failed simultaneously to strike Lee's weak right with a crushing blow during the morning's early hours.

To General Toombs's soldiers, the escalating volume of musketry on Lee's left sounded "as though you had set fire to a cane brake of a thousand acres," penned one rural Georgian in a letter. In the respite, the Georgians continued to strengthen their defenses. General Burnside's IX Corps, meanwhile, mustered its considerable muscle, getting into position and preparing to smash across the Antietam. The fierce fighting to the north, unfortunately, acted like a magnet, pulling three Rebel brigades from the Confederate right to reinforce the left as General Lee committed more troops to the battle. With each passing hour on 17 September, therefore, Toombs's position became more vulnerable.

Utilizing frontierlike tactics, Colonel Benning now ordered snipers to climb the tallest trees along the slope and to take up good firing positions. From their treetop positions these Georgia sharpshooters commanded a view of the valley of the Antietam.[8] And based on their reports, Toombs did not like what he saw in the limited support for his small command. He found Capt. John B. Richardson's two 12-pounders were positioned too far from the bridge to be effective. In addition, the angry responses from the graycoat gunners were too brief. The Rebel cannoneers, far from their supply bases, knew that ammunition had to be conserved for the inevitable Union attack upon the Rohrbach Bridge. Union firepower, superior in range, caliber, and ammunition, soon excelled that morning to dominate the Confederate artillery.

Not all of the inviting IX Corps's targets in the valley below, nevertheless, could be resisted.

Shortly before 8:00 A.M. Capt. John Lewis Eubanks discovered a large body of the enemy opposite him in a wood within range of his guns. He opened fire and drove them away in confusion, with some loss. But then Eubanks was ordered away, and with his infantrymen now more vulnerable, a frustrated Benning found his Georgians left at the bridge without any artillery supports whatsoever.[9]

General Toombs watched sullenly while "on Wednesday morning, [17 September, the Federals] threw forward his skirmishers and light infantry in greatly increased numbers, and before 8:00 A.M. o'clock drove in my pickets and advanced in heavy columns to the attack of my position on the bridge."[10]

Around 7:00 A.M. Burnside had ordered the corps forward to the heights above the Antietam "in readiness to cross the stream, carrying the bridge and the heights above it by assault."

Throughout 16 September the IX Corps, except one division, had moved forward, converging on General Toombs's position in overwhelming numbers. This experienced corps contained veterans of the early fighting in the rugged mountains of what would soon become West Virginia, the North Carolina coast, second Manassas, Chantilly, and most recently at Fox's Gap on South Mountain. Now, they methodically carried out General McClellan's orders for the IX Corps to advance to the high ground opposite the bridge and within striking distance of the Georgians.

General Burnside, the heavily whiskered Rhode Islander who inspired the name "sideburns," only awaited General McClellan's specific directives to carry the bridge and the heights above it by assault and perhaps bring decisive victory to the Army of the Potomac's left.[11]

The personable General Burnside was respected for his successful amphibious operations—the first large Federal landing by water of the war—and victories first at Roanoke and then at New Bern and Beaufort on the North Carolina mainland during early 1862. For his successful North Carolina expedition, Burnside won a major general's rank and McClellan's

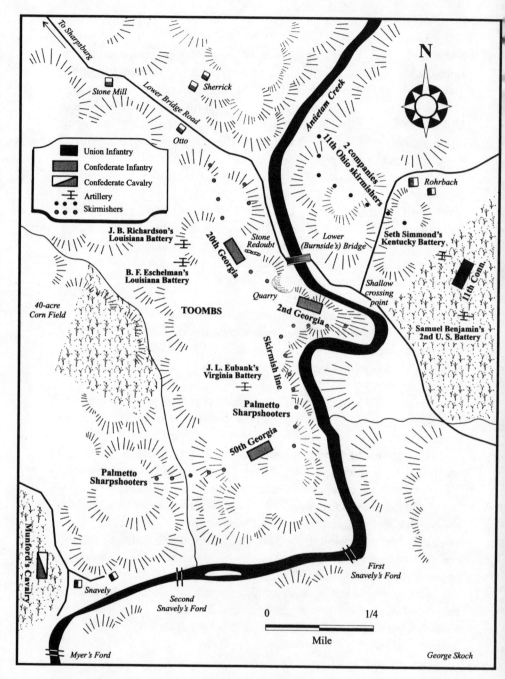

*Situation at 8:30 A.M.*

accolade that "everything goes well with us but your success seems to be the most brilliant yet." Burnside was not only one of Little Mac's top lieutenants but also one of his best friends.

A handsome Mexican War veteran with prewar experience as a general of the Rhode Island militia and the son of a slave owner, Burnside had organized the 1st Rhode Island Infantry at the war's beginning. He then commanded a New England brigade at first Manassas, and led the Army of the Potomac's right wing during the recent pursuit of General Lee's army into western Maryland.

Both Toombs and Burnside, strangely, felt uncertain about exactly what and how many troops they commanded that day. The Georgian believed he continued to command a provisional division, consisting of his own, Drayton's, and Anderson's brigades. Hence, Colonel Benning now exercised direct command of the regiments of Toombs's own brigade, the 2nd and 20th Georgia, at the bridge. Burnside, meanwhile, continued to believe that Gen. Jacob Dobson Cox retained direct command of the IX Corps, and would act as the tactical commander in the forthcoming contest, and that Burnside continued to command the army's left wing of two corps, the I and IX, as he had during the pursuit of Lee across Maryland. McClellan, however, had made abrupt organizational changes, including the elimination of the wing commands after South Mountain, without officially notifying Burnside. With the I Corps now anchoring the army's right flank to the north and the IX Corps anchoring the army's left flank at the opposite end of the battlefield, the two components of the now divided wing could not function together, hindering communication in the IX Corps leadership during the upcoming battle. Both Burnside and Toombs, thus, ironically believed that they had more responsibility and commanded more troops than were actually available. Toombs would not command a division, as he believed, but a mere brigade—his own. Burnside commanded only the IX Corps, and not a wing, as he now believed.

Still, Burnside could hardly complain about the disparity in numbers between his forces and Toombs's. Against a few hundred Georgia defenders, Burnside could hurl 13,000 soldiers from almost thirty battle-tested IX Corps regiments, supported by the firepower of the corps's nine batteries.

Unlike the Toombs-Benning team, the IX Corps's command arrangement was untested, partly because General Cox was a relative newcomer to the Army of the Potomac and although McClellan considered "Burn" to be the IX Corps's commander, Burnside yet considered himself a wing commander. Command decisions would thus have to flow from McClellan to Burnside, and then from Burnside to Cox. General Cox was a philosopher-soldier, author, and the former commander of the "Brigade of the Kanawha," which secured the Kanawha Valley in western Virginia in 1861. In addition, the Ohio politician and former lawyer recently performed well at South Mountain.

General Cox found the task of carrying the bridge in front of Burnside a difficult one. The IX Corps was spread out along an extended front, and ill-prepared for a heavy offensive effort. The depth of the valley and the shape of its curve made it impossible for Confederate gunners on the high ground below Sharpsburg to reach the enemy's position near the bridge by artillery fire. Not so from the enemy's position, for the curve of the valley was such that the Georgians' position was especially vulnerable to Union artillery fire.

Additionally, the rough topography—the two twin knolls on the other, or east, side of the narrow valley—and the bridge's approaches would funnel the attackers as they advanced closer to the bridge. Worse for the IX Corps, the line of defenders along the west bank as it spanned southward could lay down a converging and overlapping cross fire from the front, right, and left.

Even if the Union troops successfully ran the gauntlet to reach the bridge, the Georgians' fire would then concentrate at the spout of the funnel at the bridge's east end. Promising high losses among the attackers, the open bottoms before the bridge widened to create an ideal field of fire for the Georgians who overlooked the level terrain from the dominating heights.

General Cox had never commanded a corps in a major battle, and none of his IX Corps commanders—Isaac Peace Rodman, Eliakim Parker Scammon, Samuel Davis Sturgis, and Orlando Bolivar Wilcox—possessed sufficient experience in leading divisions on the battlefield. "I fear Coxe [sic] is slow," McClellan wrote two months before. In another letter shortly afterward, a disgusted McClellan complained that "unless I command every picket & lead every column I cannot be sure of success." On 17 September, however, the greatest mistake was committed by McClellan and Burnside in overestimating the capabilities of the IX Corps and underestimating the Georgians before them. As early as late 1861, McClellan complained that "the policy of the rebels has been as a general rule to remain on the defensive & receive our attacks in their positions chosen & fortified beforehand."[12] Much like Lee, McClellan viewed this war in moral terms, a struggle of right against wrong, and he condemned this "traitorous conspiracy dignified by the name of the Southern Confederacy."[13]

With McClellan making his main effort on his right, Burnside and Cox on the left feared that an impatient Little Mac would soon order the

IX Corps to attempt to storm the Rohrbach Bridge.[14] Both Burnside and Cox realized that the IX Corps was not yet thoroughly prepared nor in position for an attempt to storm the Rohrbach Bridge. North of the bridge, meanwhile, the vicious fighting began to die down around mid-morning. The first of the three phases of the battle of Antietam sputtered to an end with both sides exhausted from the bloodletting. Frustrated on the north, McClellan gradually began to focus his attention toward Lee's center, the second phase of the battle, and farther south, toward the Rohrbach Bridge sector.

Such an offensive effort was calculated to pressure Lee's right to complement the pressure already applied to his left throughout the morning, thus weakening his center. The cautious McClellan, however, would not issue orders for an attack on the little stone bridge across the Antietam until after 9:00 A.M.

Just before that hour a bugle blared over the Antietam, echoing through the narrow valley, and a long wave of New England soldiers stood at attention across the two knolls, their mission to drive the advanced Georgia skirmishers from around the mouth of the bridge on the east bank prior to launching an attack on the bridge. Here, around the mouth of the bridge, Colonel Holmes had placed his Burke County Sharpshooters in positions behind the stone wall on the east bank above the bridge and along the chestnut fence bordering the stream to the south. If the Federals quickly swarmed across the 300 yards of open fields west of the twin knolls, then the Georgians in this advanced position would only have time to unleash a single volley before being forced to make the long 125-foot run across the bridge to the safety of the west bank.

A long line of Companies A and B, 11th Connecticut Infantry, surged forward on the double. After advancing through the small stands of cedars and scrub oaks along the two knolls, the attackers rolled down the slope opposite the bridge. The onrushing Yankees on the left surged across a plowed field south of the bridge, and soon they and Colonel Holmes's advanced skirmishers began exchanging a fire. As the Connecticut soldiers continued down the slope, the Georgia skirmishers of Company D, 2nd Georgia, raced across the bridge and back to their defensive positions around the bridgehead and along the high ground on the west side of the Antietam. Most of these Burke County soldiers crossed at the bridge instead of fording the creek, probably to hide the Antietam's shallowness from the attackers. Some retiring graycoat skirmishers forded the creek, however, amid the heaviest cover along the bank, concealing the movement from the Yankees' view. With the Federals surging forward on the double,

Georgia drummer boys buglers signaled that the attack was underway. Seconds later Georgia soldiers atop the bluffs grabbed their muskets and rushed forward to rejoin their comrades in their defensive positions inside the network of rifle pits, the quarry-turned-bunker, and the stone redoubt. In the most advanced line of his 2nd Georgia, as usual, Colonel Holmes was near the east end of the bridge and beside his newly deployed Company D soldiers from Burke County.[15]

Toombs watched the surging bluecoats advance with heavy columns to attack his position. Despite holding the high ground, he and Colonel Benning understood that there were vulnerabilities in their isolated and advanced location. "This position was not strong," wrote Toombs. "The ground descended gently to the margin of the river, covered with a narrow strip of woods, affording slight protection to the troops. Its chief strength lay in the fact that, from the nature of the ground on the other side, the enemy were compelled to approach mainly by the road which led up the river for near 300 paces, parallel with my line of battle, and distant therefrom from 50 to 150 feet, thus exposing his [left] flank to a destructive fire the most of that distance."[16]

The first Union attack of the day was wisely not ordered forward up this road following the east bank below the bridge. Instead, Cox ordered the two companies of Connecticut soldiers to pour across the fields east and southeast of the bridge. After sweeping off the southernmost knoll, the attackers on the left turned north toward the bridge and neared the road. It was early morning and the wooded hillside lined with defenders remained cool in the first light of day, the sun yet low on the eastern horizon. The trees along the bluff consequently cast long shadows that helped to conceal the Georgians' rifle pits and lunettes.

Upon signal and with the Yankees near the creek, Holmes's 2nd Georgia unleashed a volley, dropping the first of many New Englanders. Soon, more blue-clad bodies began to litter the bottoms along the Antietam. Rather than a battle, this was a turkey shoot for General Toombs's veterans, and in record time, their fire chewed the attack into fragments. Punished by the fire pouring off the high ground, the Connecticut soldiers fell back.

The Georgians resoundingly cheered when the New Englanders began to retire, leaving their dead and wounded behind. Hurriedly, the Rebels reloaded muskets in case the Federals wanted to try their luck again, then rested in the shade of the trees and in rifle pits.[17] No aid from Jones's division was forthcoming during the first attack, but the firing had alerted a group of Georgians who had been dispatched to the rear to secure beef (the 2nd and 20th Georgia soldiers had not been issued rations in two days).

When "the battle opened up in all of its fury," wrote Pvt. John William Lokey, 20th Georgia, "we threw away our half-cooked beef and hurried on to the front." This would be the only reinforcement for General Toombs's defenders at the bridge during 17 September.[18] Realizing the damage that they could inflict from the high ground, the Georgia boys celebrated prematurely. The fighting on his right had been so severe that McClellan decided to order his left to strike a blow in the hope that Lee had weakened his right to reinforce his left. His 9:10 A.M. order reached General Burnside probably around 9:30, directing him to hurl his IX Corps forward to storm the stone bridge during the third and final phase of the battle.

Designated to lead the second advance upon the Rohrbach Bridge was the 11th Connecticut of Gen. George Crook's brigade, Kanawha division, IX Corps. Instead of sending two companies as during the first attack, the entire regiment would now swarm forward as skirmishers to feel out the enemy's strength and to cover the advance of the balance of General Crook's brigade, the right wing of the IX Corps assault. General Crook's three regiments of the 2nd Brigade were to descend off the high ground and charge westward toward the bridge, overwhelming the bridge defenders with one rush. The division of Gen. Samuel Davis Sturgis was to support the attack and exploit any success by advancing across the plowed field south of the bridge to take forward positions from which to deliver a covering fire.

The orders to General Crook instructed him "to march under cover of the Eleventh Connecticut and attempt to carry the bridge by assault, deploying to right and left as soon as the bridge should be carried, and taking the heights above it." General Burnside complimented the Kanawha division for its gallantry at South Mountain by now allowing these tough Westerners to lead the attack on the Rohrbach Bridge.

Meanwhile Burnside ordered the left wing of the IX Corps, the division commanded by Gen. Isaac Peace Rodman, to try to outflank the bridge defenders from the south. Instead of directly assaulting the bridge, Rodman was to move down the Antietam and ford the creek at the head of the bend about a third of a mile below the bridge because of the natural strength of Toombs's position. According to plan, the two wings of the IX Corps would hit the Georgians in a combined punch, with General Crook's Ohio brigade attacking in front as General Rodman's division of two brigades would flank the Georgians from the south. General Rodman's Quaker middle name, Peace, belied his mission. Today, General Rodman would have to kill as many Georgians as possible to flank Toombs and

Benning out of their positions. Col. Hugh Ewing's Ohio brigade, Kanawha division, now under Col. Eliakim Parker Scammon, a tough West Pointer and Seminole and Mexican War veteran, would follow in support of General Rodman's 3rd Division.

For the IX Corps to achieve success today, it would have to orchestrate a well-timed movement based upon the premise that General Rodman's troops could quickly cross the Antietam immediately below the bridge. Here, General McClellan's engineers had already discovered the first ford south of the bridge, a natural crossing during one of the driest summers on record.

Indeed, at this fording point, the creek narrowed and became so shallow as to form a slight rapids on the otherwise placid Antietam. This shallow point below the bridge acted almost like a dam that created a wider stretch of open water up to and beyond the bridge to the north.

Here, the east bank of the Antietam suddenly decreased to a level of around five feet, about half as high as the east bank extending north to the bridge. In addition, the level expanse of bottomland on the east side of the Antietam all but ended opposite this first crossing point below the bridge and upon meeting the creek's edge. Such gently sloping ground on the east side of the creek would make it relatively easy for General Rodman's troops to reach the water. They would also be protected by the wooded strip of the slight ridge, which was the southern extension of the southernmost knoll that almost touched the creek at this crossing point. Unlike the terrain directly across the bridge to the east, the nature of the ground below the bridge would enable Rodman's bluecoats to reach the creek without receiving a heavy fire. Then, if all went right, the Federals could cross the creek at this shallow point, at the southern edge of the bottoms, unseen from the bridge to the north. Rodman's division could then scale the high ground of the Antietam's west side and push General Toombs's defenders off the heights, after delivering a flank attack.

Usually competent Union engineers from McClellan's headquarters, under Capt. James C. Duane, senior IX Corps engineer, had discovered this ford during the previous day. During the hasty reconnaissance, however, these engineers had scouted only a short distance down the Antietam. Discovering one ford about a third of a mile below the bridge, they made no effort to locate a better crossing point farther south, and apparently failed to reconnoiter the Antietam north of the bridge. The IX Corps consequently now knew nothing of the two Snavely's Fords below the bridge. Indeed, the first ford on the Snavely farm was a little less than 1,200 yards south of the bridge. Farther down the creek, the main Snavely's Ford was located about three-fourths of a mile in a direct line downstream below the bridge, or about two miles along the Antietam's meandering length south of the bridge.

If the frontal attack on the bridge was repulsed, then crossing the Antietam below the bridge as soon as possible would be even more important for Union success. Indeed, once across the creek and atop the bluff, General Rodman's left wing of Burnside's corps would then link with its advancing right wing after it outflanked Toombs's position, uniting for a combined push northward to Sharpsburg. According to the battle plan, the combined might of these Federals would capture the town and gain General Lee's rear in one stroke, cutting off the Army of Northern Virginia's withdrawal across the Potomac and into Virginia. Much of the IX Corps battle plan, therefore, now depended upon the accuracy of the information gathered during the brief reconnaissance by McClellan's engineers, who were themselves unfamiliar with the terrain, the battle plan, or the importance of a successful fording of the Antietam below the bridge.

Worse, no one ordered a follow-up reconnaissance to make sure that the battle plan rested upon an objective that could be easily obtained: the fording of the Antietam below the bridge.[19] Opposite the Middle Bridge north of the Rohrbach Bridge, General McClellan massed a full division of his cavalry reserve in his center to exploit any advantage. His Napoleonic vision of a cavalry attack also ensured that these mounted troops would not reconnoiter the Antietam south of the Rohrbach Bridge.[20]

Finally, the IX Corps right wing stood prepared to unleash its offensive effort at the stone bridge. Generals Crook and Sturgis were now relying upon Col. Henry Walter Kingsbury and his New Englanders to lead the way to victory in this sector. Kingsbury and his 11th Connecticut were a good choice. In May 1861 General McClellan had been so impressed with him that he wrote to Gen. Winfield Scott, requesting him for his personal staff. The young colonel was blessed with ability, looks, and winning ways. High expectations accompanied Kingsbury wherever he went. When his father, a United States army major, died in 1857, future Confederate general Simon Bolivar Buckner and the family's close friend Ambrose E. Burnside became the legal guardians of the teenage soldier. At first Manassas, Kingsbury acted as aide to the Union commander, Gen. Irvin McDowell, serving with distinction on his first battlefield.

By the time of the Maryland campaign, Colonel Kingsbury, a young West Pointer, possessed not only a promising career but also a fulfilling personal life. He had married a Kentucky girl in December 1861 but the war now kept them separated by hundreds of miles. His wife's sister, ironically, was married to Gen. David R. Jones, now commanding the division that included Toombs's Brigade. When Kingsbury drew up his will barely six months before the Maryland campaign, he named General Burnside his executor.

Here, along the Antietam, Kingsbury possessed an opportunity to distinguish himself. With his veteran 11th Connecticut soldiers, he planned to focus his primary offensive effort on crossing the stone bridge. The Federals did not fully realize what they were about to attack, for in many ways the Georgians' defensive network was an ambush. To the Yankees, this alluring bridge seemed to be an open avenue leading not only across the creek but also to Sharpsburg, General Lee's rear, and most of all, decisive victory.

To the IX Corps soldiers, especially from a distance, the sixty-foot wide creek at the bridge appeared much deeper than it actually was, especially with a swift current distinctly visible to the naked eye. Working in the defenders' favor, a slightly murky color—from the muddy banks and plowed fields farther upstream and the light stain of the first leaves felled early by an exceptionally dry summer—also helped to obscure the creek's shallowness to the Union engineers who had discovered the first ford. The Georgians now high in the treetops and along the bluff could see exactly how shallow the creek actually was on 17 September, however. All along the length of this stretch of the Antietam, the creek bottom could be clearly seen from bank to bank, with rocks, logs, and currents clearly distinguishable, after the dry summer. Colonel Benning described that "the creek was fordable everywhere above and below the bridge [and] in most places was not more than knee-deep." The fact that the Antietam could be easily forded was perhaps one reason why Toombs and Benning decided to leave the bridge open, inviting an attack there and dissuading fording attempts.

Around the bridge by the early morning of 17 September, however, the Yankees could not get close enough to test either the depth of the stream or to determine a crossing point. General Burnside was sulky over his sudden demotion as wing commander, and uncooperative throughout the morning. Most of all, he did not like the prospect of unleashing assault formations against defensive positions on high ground. He was therefore hesitant to attack, which evidently explains the lack of thorough IX Corps preparations to launch an assault until so ordered by McClellan. General Cox was likewise hesitant about hurling his troops against the Georgians along the Antietam. As for the past several days, Generals McClellan and Burnside were not communicating closely. General McClellan had not offered a detailed plan about when or how to achieve victory on General Lee's right. Burnside and Cox, therefore, initially believed that the IX Corps would be employed in only a diversionary role this morning.

McClellan, later seeking scapegoats, would claim in his rewritten battle report that the IX Corps had been designated an early and leading part in attacking the bridge at 8:00 A.M. In fact, McClellan only issued his orders to attack at 9:10 A.M., and these probably reached General Burnside no earlier than 9:30 and perhaps even later. The delay in launching the attack on the Rohrbach Bridge on the morning of 17 September was the fault, therefore, not of Burnside, but of McClellan.

The uninformed Burnside was disgruntled. Neither Burnside nor McClellan—nor the team of Burnside and Cox—would work effectively together on the army's left flank. This leadership malaise filtered down through the ranks. Within the dysfunctional IX Corps, the mismanagement, lack of direction and coordination, and miscommunication was so pervasive this morning that both Generals Burnside and McClellan deserve blame for failing to rise to the challenge at the Rohrbach Bridge.[21]

The first Yankee regiment to pay for the IX Corps command failures was Colonel Kingsbury's 11th Connecticut. Having recently forced a passage through the gaps of South Mountain, the 11th Connecticut had been forged into a dependable regiment. But it had not been an easy transformation. Nearly driving his men to mutiny by imposing West Point standards, Kingsbury had turned raw recruits into soldiers. Behind his back, the colonel had been derided by his disgruntled New Englanders as "the damned West Pointer." The 11th Connecticut soldiers, consisting primarily of young men from the small, agricultural communities around Long Island Sound in western Connecticut, were now ready to push the Georgia defenders off the high ground as at South Mountain. With his staff trailing behind him, General Burnside had galloped over to the regiment to issue orders to launch the attack around 9:45 A.M. "Gen. Burnside came to our Col. and said the stone bridge over the Antietam Creek must be taken and held until troops could be thrown over and assigned the duty to the 11th Conn," wrote one private. Their admiration for General Burnside raised the resolve of the Connecticut soldiers. The trusting Yankees were misled because they could see neither the number of General Toombs's concealed defenders, nor the 2nd and 20th Georgia men lying low and unseen along the stone wall atop the bluff.

The 11th Connecticut soldiers deployed in a long line across the high ground of the two knolls between the creek and the Rohrbach house, northeast of the bridge. Before the bridge and the creek bottoms, the right of the Connecticut regiment began aligning on the north end of the northernmost knoll. The regiment's left, meanwhile, where Colonel Kingsbury prepared to lead his men forward, was forming on the southern end of the southernmost knoll. Georgia snipers in the treetops along the high ground carefully aimed at officers and color-bearers. One 11th Connecticut soldier who now realized that hard fighting lay ahead reflected in his diary: "Now comes the tug of war on our left."

Elements of the IX Corps right wing meanwhile prepared to strike Toombs's advance position, after Lee's sudden redeployment of General Walker's division had pulled away thousands of Confederates from the key assignment of guarding the Snavely's Fords below the bridge. The sight of thousands of Rebels hastily departing General Lee's right made the Union commanders believe that they could more easily smash through the bridge defenders. This crucial reduction of his already diminutive force below Sharpsburg left General Lee with only Jones's Division of around 2,000 soldiers on his right, behind the Georgians, to defend more than one mile of front before Sharpsburg. As General Walker's Rebels entered the fighting amid the West Woods to stabilize Lee's battered left, the Georgians remained on their own, awaiting reinforcements that would never come. Colonel Alexander realized that now only a miracle could save the day on the army's right because "there was very little left there but Toombs's small brigade guarding the bridge."[22]

Colonel Benning was worried about the increasing vulnerability of his increasingly vulnerable position, which he described as "so far in front of that line—a place so untenable as was the bridge." Feeling abandoned, the Georgia colonel said that at this time, "The general line of battle of our army was nearly, if not quite, three-quarters of a mile in rear, and not a soldier was between them and that line. The intervening ground for a great part of the way was a long slope facing the enemy's batteries, and thus commanded by those batteries, so that re-inforcements, if they had been sent, would have been cut up by shells before they could have reached their destination . . . thus the two regiments were also without infantry supports, and without the expectation of receiving any re-enforcements."[23]

Indeed, here was the central paradox of Toombs's position: Although his was the strongest natural position at Antietam, it was also the weakest in numbers. In the absence of Walker's division south of the bridge, only a relative handful of 50th Georgia soldiers, half of the Palmetto Sharpshooter company, and some of Colonel Munford's Virginia cavalrymen guarded Snavely's Fords. Clearly, this was not enough to stop the Yankees from crossing the Antietam. The Confederates at the bridge were now on their own. For General Toombs, Colonel Benning, and their relative handful of Georgia soldiers, disaster at the stone bridge on 17 September now seemed as inevitable as it appeared imminent.[24]

CHAPTER 6

# "Over the Bridge
# at a Double Quick!"

## *Federal Assault on the Georgia Defenders*

THE SITUATION REMAINED CRITICAL: CAPTURE OF THE ROHRBACH BRIDGE
by the IX Corps would lead to the imminent destruction of Lee's army.[1]
The assault column of the 11th Connecticut prepared to lunge forward,
targeting the stone bridge. With a bugle's call cutting the air, and with a
shout of unfounded confidence, at about ten o'clock Col. Henry Kingsbury led 440 Connecticut soldiers down the gradual slopes of the knolls
toward the bridge. The Federals' frontal attack complied with McClellan's
instructions. As the New Englanders surged onward across the open
ground, however, the Georgians prepared to concentrate their field of fire
on the most direct approach to the bridge.[2]

In Colonel Benning's words, "the fight opened in earnest." With
artillery supporting the assault, Kingsbury advanced. Remaining motionless, the Georgians prepared to open fire on the hundreds of bluecoats
spread out in a long line as they began pouring off the high ground and
entering the open fields of the level creek bottoms. Rolling onward on the
double, the 11th Connecticut's right swarmed toward the Antietam, as the
regiment's left surged across the plowed field to the south and the creek's
level flood plain. Benning himself thought the Yankee attack was "bold
and persevering."

From the Georgians' heights, the blue-clad targets could not have
been more exposed after the Federals emerged from the brush and timber
of the twin knolls. With the approaching Yankees spread out in a long line
across the open fields, Colonels Benning, Holmes, and Cumming gave the
order to fire. A sheet of flame erupted from the greenery of the bluff and

slope. The concentrated fire savaged the onrushing ranks of the 11th Connecticut. In the words of one Federal, "the Rebel guns were pouring in a destructive fire . . . while continuous volleys from an unseen enemy in the woods were also showered upon . . . this 'valley of death.'" Still the Connecticut soldiers continued to surge through the blistering fire, ignoring the increasing numbers of their dead and wounded comrades littering the ground. Almost side by side on the high ground on either side of the bridge, the quarry-bunker and the stone redoubt belched lead across the open fields. With each passing minute, more Yankees dropped to the ground when hit by the .577 and .69 caliber bullets. A chorus of groans and screams meanwhile filled the air along the east side of the Antietam, now dotted with blue-clad bodies. One Connecticut soldier mourned that during the assault they could not answer cries for help. Instead, the New England attackers kept moving onward into the face of the Georgians' blistering fire.[3]

The foremost Connecticut soldiers advancing north of the bridge survived to near the east bank of the Antietam.[4] They took cover along the bank behind a stone wall that stretched northward along the creek from the bridge's mouth. The wall was low, providing insufficient protection for the Connecticut soldiers on the regiment's right, leaving heads, shoulders, and upper chests exposed whenever they stood up to fire. Still, having no time to rest or even catch their breath, those Yankees north of the bridge steadily returned fire from farmer Rohrbach's stone wall. In this sector, meanwhile, the remainder of the 11th Connecticut stayed under cover while awaiting the arrival of the bulk of General Crook's Ohio brigade, which the New Englanders expected to be following close behind. They would be disappointed. In fact, not even the 11th Connecticut was mounting a closely coordinated offensive effort by this time, sapping the attack's strength and momentum. Because of the rougher terrain below, or south of, the bridge and a longer stretch of ground to traverse, the regiments left under Kingsbury had yet to reach the creek.

Kingsbury's attack received accurate fire support from the artillery of his West Point classmate, Lt. Samuel N. Benjamin. On the crest of a larger knoll commanding the Antietam's valley, behind the twin knolls and directly east of the bridge, Lieutenant Benjamin's guns boomed with authority, raking the Georgians' position with blasts of shell. "Benjamin's battery, posted on yon hill, which overlooks the whole space between our advance bodies and the wooded hills where the enemy lay, is belching forth a severe fire," a Pennsylvanian attested. More than the Yankee cannoneers realized, Benjamin's artillery caused considerable damage among the Georgians, cutting down more Rebels that day than the Union musketry.

Benning reported that "the fire not only from their infantry, but from the artillery, was incessant, the artillery being so placed that it could fire over the heads of the infantry."[5] At long range, the guns of the Washington Artillery dropped a few shells among the exposed Federals along the east bank, but to little effect. More deadly to the Federals was the vicious plunging fire exploding from the Georgians' Enfield rifles and smoothbores. Worse, the Georgia snipers in the treetops fired down from their perches, hitting an increasing number of Connecticut boys behind the rock wall. In less than fifteen minutes after the New Englanders' attack began, a full third of the 11th Connecticut was cut down. With his soldiers continuing to drop around him, Capt. John Griswold realized that something must be done before it was too late.[6]

The daring Connecticut captain, therefore, stood up to encourage his men, then urged them across the creek immediately north of the bridge, planning to take advantage of the creek's fordability to cross there and to bypass the narrow bridge, clearly a death trap. Leading Company A himself, Griswold leaped over the wall with a shout, waving his saber. A group of soldiers followed him down the slippery bank into the shallow waters of the Antietam. The graycoat defenders turned their attention on this renewed effort. Exposed in the open, the first New Englanders in the water found the footing was treacherous with submerged tree limbs and large rocks along the creek bottom proving to be greater obstacles to a crossing by infantry than the current's strength. As the bullets splashed around them, the Federals struggled onward to gain the west bank. As they drew closer, the stream became deeper, the mud more clinging, and the defenders' fire more accurate.

Around the bridgehead, meanwhile, the Burke County Sharpshooters easily shot down the foremost Yankees, while from the high ground, the fire of the Georgia veterans continued to create more Connecticut orphans and widows. Knowing that the bridge was suicide to cross, Captain Griswold and his bluecoats gambled by taking the shortest, and seemingly less risky, route across the stream by wading the creek in this sector, thinking the defenders' fire had been trained primarily on the bridge. In reality, however, Captain Griswold's band pushed directly toward the stone redoubt, the most formidable stronghold on the Georgians' line north of the bridge. In the confusion, Griswold also mistakenly assumed that the entire regiment was following behind him. In fact, the Georgians' fire kept most of the 11th Connecticut's survivors pinned down along the east bank. As a result, the Georgians cut Captain Griswold's attack to pieces in record time. Those Yankees who tried to wade the creek were slaughtered. About midstream, Captain Griswold, encouraging his men, was mortally struck by more than one bullet. The Connecticut officer nevertheless continued toward the west bank, where General Toombs's defenders, inspired by the New England captain's efforts and perhaps because of Colonel Holmes's orders, held their fire. Upon gaining the west bank just north of the bridge, exhausted and bleeding, Griswold expired on the Georgia shore. The sight of every single Federal soldier who had boldly entered the stream being either killed or wounded ended all efforts by the remaining New Englanders to ford the Antietam near the bridge.[7]

Despite the systematic elimination of Captain Griswold's men, the most severe loss for the 11th Connecticut occurred farther south. As the regiment's right wing reached the creek above the bridge, Kingsbury led his left wing south of the bridge across open ground and over a longer distance. The West Pointer wore a finely tailored blue uniform with brass buttons and buckle, a conspicuous target. The best Georgia marksmen consequently concentrated their fire on Colonel Kingsbury as he urged his soldiers onward.

The advancing left wing poured through Rohrbach's cornfield and then across the open, level ground of the plowed field to reach the east bank of the Antietam. With more open ground to traverse than those attackers north of the bridge, Colonel Kingsbury's soldiers took a worse beating, suffering higher losses in crossing the level bottoms. One soldier wrote of going forward on the double quick under fire that "many of our brave boys [were] killed. [O]ur Col. was very calm and told us not to get excited."

The Connecticut soldiers below the bridge found cover behind the five-rail fence along the road bordering the east bank. Capt. Abner McCoy Lewis, 2nd Georgia, recalled that the enemy attacked the center of the regiment.

Along the east bank beside the fence, meanwhile, Kingsbury hurriedly spread his men out. He then implored his soldiers to return fire. After seeing the decimation of the boys north of the bridge, these Connecticut soldiers maintained their advanced positions and blasted away at the high ground above the Antietam, now covered with smoke and the flashes from the Georgians' Enfield rifles and smoothbores. Passing up and down his line, Colonel Kingsbury exhorted his soldiers to stand fast and return fire more rapidly, while awaiting General Crook's follow-up attack.

Determined to provide an example to encourage his soldiers across the stream, Kingsbury himself attempted to wade the creek, despite the destruction of Captain Griswold and his followers to the north. Unlike Griswold, the young colonel did not get far in his attempt. Almost immediately, a bullet smashed into his foot, inflicting a painful wound. Nevertheless, the hobbled Connecticut colonel continued encouraging his soldiers forward. But then another minié ball soon tore into Colonel Kingsbury's body, dropping the New Englanders' commander.

With their colonel down, a handful of blue-clad soldiers rushed to his side. They then attempted to get Kingsbury to the rear for medical attention. As bullets whistled around them, a handful of volunteers lifted their commander, but yet another bullet smashed into Colonel Kingsbury's shoulder, and then one more bullet tore into Kingsbury's stomach, the mortal wound. Kingsbury would die the next day at the Rohrbach house, never to see his son, Henry Walter Kingsbury, born in December 1862. Upon learning of the mortal wounding of Colonel Kingsbury from Union prisoners, Gen. David R. Jones, the enemy commander as well as his brother-in-law, broke down in tears.

Besides Kingsbury, another thirty-seven officers and enlisted men of the 11th Connecticut were killed or mortally wounded during the attack.[8] Some Connecticut survivors continued to maintain a fire from the slight cover of the road and the chestnut fence below the bridge. Other Yankees fired from the cover of a wooded ravine north of the northernmost knoll. Increasing numbers of Federals began to retire to the protection of the wooded knolls, however, which they had only recently left with such confidence.

All told 139 11th Connecticut soldiers went down, about one-third of the regiment destroyed in less than one half hour. When the 11th Connecticut's attack was repulsed and most of the New Englanders fell back, Georgia shouts of victory echoed across the hillside above the Antietam, mocking the IX Corps attempt to storm the bridge. Rejoicing in their bloody victory, the 20th Georgia veterans unleashed their distinctive regimental war cry to celebrate their success. Colonel Cumming's soldiers clapped their hands in rhythm to the shouts of "one, two, three, four, hip! hip! hurrah!"

Despite repulsing two assaults, the Georgians' losses were relatively light. Some Georgia Rebels were hit by the rain of shell bursts above their rifle pits and the stone wall, quarry, and rock redoubt, but they were few. The Georgians' medical personnel consequently served at the front instead of the rear, tending to the injured to enable the less seriously wounded to remain at their posts. In fact, during what would end as an intense five-hour battle, and despite suffering high casualties, only one injured Georgia soldier would walk out of the valley on his own this day. As the fighting intensified, and casualties increased, the most severely wounded Georgians would be taken rearward a short distance to the shelter of a long row of haystacks. There, a handful of injured Georgians would be made as comfortable as possible by their comrades, who then quickly returned to the firing line.

So far, the 2nd and 20th Georgia suffered the majority of casualties. Playing only a minor support role in defending the bridge, Colonel Kearse's 50th Georgia was yet to suffer from Union artillery. Musicians in gray, meanwhile, played a more active role during the emergency. Some, having left their instruments in the rear, helped their comrades to shoot down attacking Yankees. So many of General Toombs's musicians were already killed and wounded in the battles around Richmond that the brigade band was officially disbanded in the late summer of 1862 before the Antietam campaign. The only music that they heard along the Antietam this morning was the whistle of minié balls and shells. Some Georgia bandsmen died beside the infantrymen in defense of the Rohrbach Bridge.[9]

After the second attack, the Georgia soldiers used a brief respite on a warm morning to prepare for the next onslaught. They rested, cooled their rifles, and refilled cartridge boxes from those of their dead and wounded comrades because of a growing shortage of ammunition. Neither Lee, Longstreet, nor Jones sent even a handful of troops or extra ammunition throughout the day. Thousands of Rebels in Jones's division behind the Georgians, and within easy support distance, meanwhile, remained idle with full cartridge boxes and without firing a shot or losing a man to assist Toombs and Benning. The smoke and roar of musketry and cannon on both sides should have awakened Toombs's superiors to the need to resupply the Georgians with ammunition and reinforcements. General Lee's ammunition wagons, moreover, stood in the army's rear in and around Sharpsburg not far from General Toombs's advanced position. But the proximity of the army's munitions train would not prove beneficial to the Georgia Rebels this day.

During the respite between assaults, Benning, Holmes, Cumming, and other Georgia officers hurriedly checked their defensive lines before facing the next attack, encouraging their boys to stand firm. Colonel Holmes "was as brave a man as I ever saw," wrote Private Fogle. "He was perfectly cool & calm & did not seem to know what the word danger meant, he had won the confidence of the regiment."

The worst was yet to come for the Georgians, and all the while, they continued to fall from the steady fire of small arms and artillery that pounded the bluff and slope after the attack. From the high ground above the Antietam, the men of the 2nd and 20th Georgia now saw yet more right wing units of the IX Corps moving forward in preparation for the next assault.

As could be expected, the escalation of the fighting before the bridge drew most of the defenders' attention away from the danger of being out-flanked on the south by General Rodman's division. And even if the Georgians were concerned about their vulnerable right flank, there were simply too few defenders to do anything to alter the tactical situation. General Toombs could not worry about his vulnerable flanks.[10]

It was after 10:00 A.M. now, the day was growing hotter, and the main column of Crook's brigade was yet attempting to get into position for the assault. Marylander George Crook, West Point Class of 1852 and the former colonel of the 36th Ohio, was now leading his Ohio troops on his own ancestral soil. General Crook was hampered by having neither a guide nor detailed knowledge of the terrain before the bridge. That Burnside, Cox, and Crook failed to thoroughly reconnoiter the approaches to the Antietam now proved costly. Even worse, General Crook, although not entirely clear on the exact requirements of his assignment, did not seek a clarification of his orders from his superiors.

General Crook's column consisted of the 11th, 28th, and the 36th Ohio, Kanawha division. The commanders of these tried units, respectively, were Lt. Cols. Augustus H. Coleman, Gottfried Becker, and Melvin Clarke, all destined to become casualties during today's bitter fighting. Having gone without dinner the previous day and breakfast on 17 September, these Buck-eye bluecoats were angry.

To cover the assault of General Crook's Ohioans, elements of General Sturgis's 2nd Division, IX Corps, had advanced to draw the defenders' attention and then unleashed a diversionary fire. Crook's troops, mean-while, continued to trudge northward through the dark, tangled wood-lands adjacent to the bridge. Without a guide the Ohioans soon became lost amid the terrain behind the twin knolls, and moved too far north beyond the bridge. After losing time, Crook's men finally headed in the proper direction, westward toward the creek.

The Ohio regiments still approached the creek about 350 to 400 yards north of the bridge, however. The plan of assault was quickly improvised to meet the new situation. Now Crook's main attack would descend off the high ground primarily from the northeast, hoping that the tactical advan-tage of striking the bridge from this angle might work in their favor, for advancing in this direction rather than straight westward would cause the Ohio brigade to avoid the worst frontal fires, unlike Colonel Kingsbury's head-on assault.

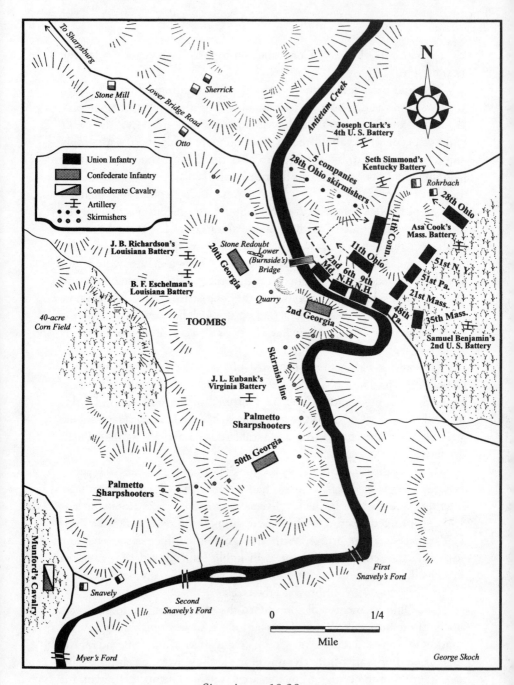

*Situation at 10:30 A.M.*

Crook was, however, actually preparing for yet another suicidal frontal assault. If Crook's troops had continued marching north to more level ground beyond the northernmost knoll to ford the Antietam closer to Sharpsburg, they would have faced Toombs's left, the weakest point in his line. This spot would have offered the quickest and easiest route to decisive Union victory, if only Crook had known where to go. One of the great opportunities of Antietam was thus overlooked. A crossing there would have allowed the IX Corps to take a shortcut to Sharpsburg, gaining the town and General Lee's rear more quickly and easily than Rodman's much longer approach over the rough terrain to the south. Crook had been ordered to assault the bridge, however, and so he would launch another attack.

Among General Crook's soldiers were many Germans, including veterans of the 1848 liberal European revolutions. Teutonic blood ran so thick in the 28th Ohio that it had once been known as the 2nd German Ohio Regiment. These patriotic freedom fighters of the 28th Ohio Volunteer Infantry had been molded into soldiers by a Mexican War veteran, Col. August Moor.

Another combat unit with Crook was the 36th Ohio, trained and once commanded by Crook himself. Lt. Col. Melvin Clarke succeeded Crook as a capable leader. Most of the 36th Ohio, which hailed from Marietta in the eastern part of the state on the Ohio River, was formed by Crook not long after the first clash of amateurs at first Manassas. These Westerners, now under the command of Lieutenant Colonel Clarke, were armed with .58 caliber Springfield rifled muskets, the worthy counterpart of the Georgians' .577 caliber British Enfields. In addition, the IX Corps Ohioans knew how to bayonet, as they had recently demonstrated at South Mountain. General Crook was finally ready to assault the bridge. With flags waving and the sound of drums echoing across the Antietam, hundreds of Ohio soldiers surged off the twin knolls and approached the stone bridge primarily from the northeast. The sight of the level ground near the creek did not encourage them. The bottom ground of the Antietam was strewn with the bodies of Kingsbury's 11th Connecticut. Some soldiers lay motionless in clumps, as others cried out in pain. The Ohio soldiers kept their advancing formations neat and tight, charging onward with momentum.

As during the first two attacks, the Georgians grimly braced for the next one. To General Toombs's rear, the booming guns of the Washington Artillery encouraged the diminutive band of defenders with a fire that was loud but largely ineffective.[11] As Crook's Ohio regiments surged toward the Antietam with colors waving in the September sunshine, Rodman's

division supported by Colonel Ewing's brigade of more than 3,000 men
marched to the east side of the creek in the area around the first crossing
point below the bridge. This ford was located at the head of the first bend
in the Antietam as identified by McClellan's engineers, who may have mis-
taken this shallow crossing point for Snavely's Ford, which was farther
downstream. General Burnside believed that the two strong assault
columns would be enough to crack Toombs's undermanned positions.
Even if the attack of the IX Corps right wing was thwarted, Rodman's
3,000 troops of the left wing fording the creek to the south should easily
carry the high ground on the Georgians' vulnerable right flank, especially
after the hasty departure of Walker's division. Seemingly all that Rodman
had to do was to wade a few feet of water to gain the high ground on the
Antietam's west side. Then, the advancing bluecoats could enfilade and roll
up General Toombs's line from the right flank, surging northwestward to
hit the defenders from the rear and capture the bridge, as General Crook's
attackers struck the Georgians in front in a combined effort.

Fortunately for Toombs, a combination of the rugged geography and
the accurate fire of both the Georgians and the half-company of South
Carolina marksmen along the west bank thwarted General Rodman's crossing. After pushing south along the high ground running parallel to the east
bank of the Antietam, and then a short distance west in an attempt to gain
the Antietam's east bank, Rodman's soldiers approached the ford about
one-third of a mile below the bridge. At this first ford below the bridge, the
water was low, but McClellan's engineers had not considered the steep and
rugged terrain on the west bank. It was now obvious that this rock wall was
simply too steep to be scaled under fire, making a creek crossing at this
point an impossibility. From the bluff's highest elevation opposite the first
crossing point, and where the creek made its first loop below the bridge,
hidden Rebel marksmen delivered a plunging fire over the treetops below
to shower the road and the bottom ground to the east with a hail of bullets. In the face of the rugged terrain and the Georgians' fire, Rodman
decided to move his troops farther downstream in search of Snavely's Ford.
A local farmer acted as a guide in his search for the next ford, but marching southward only wasted more time.

With General Rodman unable to strike from the south, General
Crook's assault was now on its own. Even after determining the bridge's
location, a confused Crook later swore that he "received orders from the
general commanding corps to cross the bridge over Antietam Creek after
General Sturgis had taken the bridge; but upon my arrival in the vicinity of
the bridge I found that General Sturgis's command had not arrived."

As the Union batteries continued to target the Georgians' position and Crook's lines surged forward, Sturgis's division of two brigades—Gen. James Nagle's 1st Brigade in front and Brig. Gen. Edward Ferrero's 2nd Brigade—pushed northeastward through the cornfields while moving roughly parallel to the creek and toward the bridge. These support troops advanced only tentatively, however, going forward under the protection of the wooded ridges south of the Rohrbach house, encountering rough terrain that slowed the march. Immediately northeast of General Sturgis's advancing division, meanwhile, stood Gen. Orlando Bolivar Willcox's division in reserve.[12]

After surging forward only a short distance, Crook's Ohioans met fire, as the Georgians allowed the Yankees to get close before unleashing their first volley. The isolated half of the 28th Ohio—the regiment's right wing of five companies—was moving on the double toward the creek about 350 yards north of the bridge, suffering heavy losses from the fire of the 20th Georgia defenders as the Yankees charged over the creek bottoms northeast of the bridge. Leading the 11th Ohio on the left wing farther south and east of the bridge, meanwhile, Lieutenant Colonel Coleman was mortally wounded by a minié ball. Capt. John B. Weller was also hit about the same time, falling beside his colonel. After the fall of Colonel Coleman, the riddled Ohioans' ranks were thrown into confusion by the fire pouring off the high ground. Maj. Lyman Jackson now took command of the Ohio regiment. Meanwhile, Lieutenant Colonel Clarke, leading the 36th Ohio forward, was also felled by a fatal bullet.

Like Crook himself upon first receiving his orders to attack, his regimental commanders had been confused about their offensive roles. Major Jackson reported that when his regiment had been first ordered "to move toward a bridge across Antietam Creek . . . I [did] not know the duty assigned, but as two of our companies had been sent forward as skirmishers to the woods and hill-side on our side of the creek, I suppose it was to support them."

To escape the roaring Rebel muskets, Jackson hurriedly shifted his section of the 11th Ohio eastward, retiring under fire across more open ground to find cover along the brushy knoll. The surviving members of the 11th Connecticut covered the Buckeyes, helping to save lives. All the while, these New Englanders below the bridge assisted the westerners by firing from the slim shelter of the twin chestnut fences bordering the road near the stream. To the north, meanwhile, the five companies of the 28th Ohio on the right wing also continued to fight from the cover of a rail fence located near the east bank and a low, sandy ridge above the bridge. Here, the Ohioans exchanged hot fire with the 20th Georgia.

General Cox was especially frustrated as the rapidly firing Georgians took full advantage of Federal mistakes. Now three uncoordinated Union attacks had ended with the same result, blue-clad soldiers dying largely because of their leaders' errors. A thin line of 20th Georgia skirmishers had been hurriedly extended farther northward from the bridge sector by Colonel Cumming and beyond the 20th Georgia's left to cover the creek. Positioned there just in time to meet General Crook's unexpected thrust so far north of the bridge, these Confederates helped to break up the Ohioans' assault. For the Georgians around the bridge, however, the fighting several hundred yards upstream drew manpower from the defensive sector around the bridge, making it more vulnerable for the inevitable next attack.[13]

Despite meeting with heavy losses, General Crook was not yet ready to concede defeat. He ordered the 28th Ohio, above the bridge, to reconnoiter farther north for a crossing of the Antietam at the most shallow point, while holding Lt. Col. Clarke's 36th Ohio in reserve. Toombs's soldiers meanwhile continued to shoot down more bluecoats who maintained their advanced positions on the east bank, resulting in further dwindling of the Georgians' limited ammunition as the morning lengthened.[14]

Despite much effort and losing hundreds of men, the IX Corps had not succeeded in altering the tactical situation to its advantage. Burnside and Cox continued to expect to hear the sound of Rodman's attack rolling up General Toombs's right flank, but it did not come. The front remained silent below the bridge, mocking the failed flanking strategy. With an impatient McClellan fearing that General Lee might launch a counterattack on his battered right, another IX Corps attack would now have to go forward.

It would be General Sturgis's turn. Unlike Crook, Sturgis was clear about his objective this morning. Burnside personally ordered Sturgis forward to capture the Rohrbach Bridge. General Burnside correctly realized that the Rebels had concentrated the most defenders—the left of the 2nd Georgia and the right of the 20th Georgia—to hold the bridgehead and the high ground above the bridge. To avoid the same devastating frontal and oblique fires suffered by the New Englanders and Ohioans, respectively, Burnside ordered Sturgis to charge from the south and straight up the Rohrersville road leading to the bridge. Also the bayonet would be used in the next attack to unnerve the Georgians and expedite the assault without attackers halting to return fire. No Federal attack had yet surged up the road along the east bank of the creek, partly because it was originally assumed that most Rebel firepower was massed for several hundred yards along the west bank below the bridge to cover the easiest approach and the first fording point. But now that General Rodman's troops had moved even farther south along the creek below the first ford, General Burnside hoped that some defenders in this sector might have redeployed to bolster the heavily pressured 20th Georgia north of the bridge, creating a vulnerability below the bridge that now could be exploited.

By employing this tactic, the Federal attack hoped not to go astray like General Crook's attempt. The plan for the right wing of the IX Corps was as simple as it was direct, with General Sturgis's division leading the way. As the 2nd Maryland and 6th New Hampshire of Gen. James Nagle's brigade attacked the bridge from the south, with the 48th Pennsylvania and 9th New Hampshire Volunteer Infantry in support, other Union regiments would shift to the right to align along the knolls and rake the defenders from the high ground opposite the bridge. If this fourth assault was successful, then eight Michigan, New York, Pennsylvania, and Massachusetts regiments of the 1st Division under General Willcox were to follow Sturgis over the bridge and then onward to Sharpsburg and victory.

Unable to ford the creek below the bridge, meanwhile, General Rodman's division of New York, Connecticut, and Rhode Island troops—one-fourth of the IX Corps—continued south along the high ground parallel to the creek in search of Snavely's Ford. Rodman's guide proved to know little more about the terrain than did the Yankee engineers. Out of desperation to cross the Antietam, Rodman continued to move south in pursuit of the rumored Snavely's Ford. In fact, the main Snavely's Ford, proper, lay about two miles distant by way of the creek below the bridge. After General Rodman sent a party of scouts to ascertain a possible crossing of the creek, rifle fire cracked down the long line of the 50th Georgia skirmishers, reminding him that additional resistance lingered even farther south of the bridge.[15]

As Rodman's forces eased southward, the ground on the Confederate side of the creek gradually became more level after the IX Corps left wing passed the dominating heights of what is today called the "Georgia overlook." This terrain seemed more advantageous for a crossing, making it increasingly possible for General Rodman's Federals to wade across the Antietam and then ascend the more gradual opposite slope to gain the top of the bluff on the Antietam's west side. The gunfire exploding from the high ground, however, made such a crossing impossible during the march southward. Unable either to halt or cross the Antietam to turn General Toombs's right, General Rodman continued southward in the time-consuming hunt for Snavely's Ford. Rodman's Federals, however, would continue to be fooled by the snarled terrain along the east side of the Antietam, finding neither a fording point nor a more favorable ground for a crossing by thousands of infantry. Instead, the ground on both sides of the creek became higher and more rugged, especially after the Antietam turned west in the second great loop below the bridge and toward Snavely's two Fords. And at the one point where some relatively level land lay inside this bend, the ground suddenly rose higher on the east bank,hindering both a crossing and the advance uphill as it became more heavily wooded and brush covered. Still, two companies of the 8th Connecticut struggled onward.[16]

General Sturgis, meanwhile, was mindful that General McClellan had personally issued the order for him and his two-brigade division to "Carry the bridge at once." Sturgis, however, was also guilty of minimizing the task before him. He ordered his troops to charge "over the bridge at a double quick and with bayonets fixed!" By launching his attack up the Rohrersville road, he was determined that the assault of his division would not go awry or be delayed in attacking the bridge. Sturgis personally directed his troops forward, refusing to take chances by delegating authority. When he found the 48th Pennsylvania experiencing difficulty in getting to its assigned position in one of Rohrbach's cornfields, he exploded at the regimental commander, "God damn you to hell, sir, don't you understand the English language? I ordered you to advance in line and support the 2nd Maryland, and what in hell are you doing flanking around this corn?"

More Union artillery was brought up to pound the Georgians. One of the artillery units that hurried forward to unlimber on high ground was Lieutenant Benjamin's Battery A, 5th United States Artillery, under Lt. Charles P. Muhlenberg. Lt. Col. George Washington Getty, chief of artillery for the IX Corps, ordered Muhlenberg to put his battery in position on the crest of a hill on the east side of Antietam Creek, and some 400 to 500 hundred yards from its bank, and then immediately open fire on the woods to the right and left of the bridge, along with a heavy concentration of other IX Corps batteries massed on the high ground southeast of the bridge, and below Lieutenant Benjamin's guns, which were the northernmost IX Corps cannon.

General Nagle, a Mexican War veteran who commanded an experienced brigade of veterans, was not optimistic about another assault on the bridge. "The position was a strong one for the enemy, as he was posted in strong force on the banks of Antietam Creek, on the wooded banks of the stream, with precipitous banks that afforded them shelter from our artillery and infantry," he found. "A deadly volley could be easily poured from the enemy in ambuscade on the other side of the bridge. The topography being of such a nature that the whole brigade could not be posted to advantage."

Nagle's brigade consisted of the 2nd Maryland, 6th New Hampshire, 9th New Hampshire under Col. Enoch Q. Fellows, and the 48th Pennsylvania under Lt. Col. Joshua K. Sigfried. Born in 1822, the idealistic Nagle, a former painter and former militiaman, had organized the 48th Pennsylvania. Now facing his greatest challenge, he rode a cream-colored charger down the lines to a loud chorus of cheers from his men.

Seemingly with a will of their own, General Nagle's formations surged onward toward the bridge. Hundreds of fresh Yankees advanced roughly parallel to the Rohrersville Road. Once again, Union leadership continued its fatal mistake of hurling infantry headlong against the bridge. Despite the Georgians' dwindling ammunition and increasing losses, this was exactly what Toombs and Benning desired. By this time, less than 300 ragged Georgia soldiers, spread out in a thin skirmish line, were denying General McClellan his victory. After three-fourths of General Lee's army had been spread along the battered lines north of Sharpsburg to counter the fierce Union onslaughts on the left, Burnside's powerful IX Corps of 13,000 men now only had to charge across the bridge to win it all.

General Rodman's troops meanwhile continued to push steadily south and toward the two virtually unguarded Snavely's Fords. Fortunately for Rodman, Walker's soldiers had evacuated the key high ground position guarding Snavely's Ford, proper, except for a young South Carolina lieutenant and a handful of Palmetto Sharpshooters. Not a single company was sent from Generals Lee, Longstreet, or Jones, to replace Walker's division. In addition, General Lee had also dispatched Anderson's brigade to Stonewall Jackson on the army's left. Meanwhile, the steady fire from the high ground along the west bank continued to place Rodman's men in jeopardy, as Cox and Burnside looked south in vain for any indication of Rodman's successful crossing of the Antietam. But, time was running out for the defenders of the bridge. The farther Rodman's troops pushed south toward the lightly defended twin fords on the Snavely farm, the greater the likelihood that the Georgians' position would be flanked and compromised.[17]

General Sturgis's division, meanwhile, continued to advance, surging toward the bridge. One New England soldier in this division recorded the appearance of the Georgians' position. "The other bank presented a steep hill-side, rising precipitously from the water," he wrote. "The rebel bank to the left of the road was also covered with thick woods near the water. On the hill-side, a few yards above the bridge, there was a heavy stone wall running parallel with the stream, and in the woods and at the turns of the road as it wound up the hill were rifle-pits, and the light breastworks of rails and stones, all making an excellent cover for the rebel riflemen defending the passage. Take it altogether, it was an exceedingly difficult place to carry by assault, and the . . . poor fellows, dead or cruelly wounded, who lay in front of it served as powerful remonstrants against the practicability of the attempt."[18]

Among the attackers were the soldiers of the 48th Pennsylvania, who felt as cocky as "roosters." These men were "perfect in drilling" and tough, including among their ranks mulattoes and free blacks.[19] Many of Colonel Sigfried's men of the 48th Pennsylvania had come from the coal mining regions or the "Dutch" country of south-central Pennsylvania, including Gettysburg.[20] The 2nd Maryland Volunteer Infantry led Nagle's brigade, with the 6th and 9th New Hampshire and the 48th Pennsylvania following and moving into firing positions to support the attack. Most of these 2nd Maryland soldiers hailed from Baltimore, which certainly would be captured if Lee defeated the Army of the Potomac at Antietam. They now advanced toward the bridge and through the southernmost Rohrbach cornfield, southeast of the bridge. With a clatter of accoutrements, the 2nd Maryland soldiers quickly unslung their gear amid the tall corn. In neat piles, soldiers stacked their knapsacks, with regimental designations and names stenciled on them, as if each man knew that he would be among the lucky ones to return to retrieve his own.

On a day in which nothing was going right for the IX Corps, Sturgis galloped over to the 2nd Maryland, pulling up hard. As was his custom, Sturgis encouraged his boys in blue, hoping for the best in the final outcome of this next assault. In fact, the regiment's ambitious and aggressive young lieutenant colonel, Jacob Eugene Duryea, was especially ready for the challenge. When Sturgis asked him earlier this morning if he wanted an opportunity to earn the star of a brigadier general, he instantly jumped at the chance. At that, Sturgis had presented a Faustian bargain: "Well, there is a bridge around the other side of this hill, and the Lieutenant Colonel of the 6th New Hampshire thinks his regiment too small to head the assault on it, so I offer it to you." Hardly realizing what he was getting into Duryea responded, "All right, General, I'll make a try for that star anyhow."

A good choice for the assignment, Duryea would win a brevet and a brigadier general's rank for skill and coolness demonstrated in battle. But the slaughter at the Rohrbach Bridge would be too much for this promising Maryland leader. After surviving Antietam, he would resign in barely two weeks, leaving the carnage of this war behind him but not its memories.[21]

Toombs and Benning prepared their men to meet the attack as General Nagle's brigade pushed forward. Behind Nagle's brigade came General

Ferrero's brigade, and Willcox's division was waiting in reserve to exploit any weakness or breakthrough. The repulsed Ohioans meanwhile continued to exchange fire with the Georgians, spraying the hillside with bullets. For the first time, it seemed that perhaps the IX Corps had finally marshaled sufficient might to overwhelm the defenders.[22]

The 2nd Maryland now marched upon the stone bridge, through the hot cornfield adjacent to the wide bend in the Antietam southeast of the bridge. Determined to capture the bridge at all costs, Duryea's Marylanders moved by the left flank and toward the creek. As the first of Sturgis's division to attack, hundreds of these Maryland veterans advanced with fixed bayonets in a column of fours.

Behind the 2nd Maryland marched the 6th New Hampshire, under Col. Simon Goodell Griffin, a lawyer and legislator who first won distinction at first Bull Run. Ironically, the first Rebels that these New Englanders had fought were Georgia Rebels at Camden, North Carolina, during Burnside's coastal expedition. After battling at second Manassas, Chantilly, and South Mountain, these soldiers of the "Bully 6th" were well honed by 17 September.[23]

After midmorning, the late summer day had become more like a July day than one near autumn. Patiently awaiting the fourth attack of the day, meanwhile, the Georgians sat quietly in their rifle pits and lunettes and in their treetop perches. The soldiers chewed tobacco, thought of home and family, and prayed that they would survive. The Georgians' loaded Enfield rifles and smoothbore muskets were steadied on rocks, fallen logs, and trees, from the quarry, stone redoubt, and stone wall, and all trained on the creek bottoms and the Rohrersville road.

In the valley below the Georgians, the Maryland assault column made last minute preparations. Then, with a shout and the blast of a bugle that echoed across the valley of the Antietam, around 10:30 A.M., 300 veterans of the 2nd Maryland suddenly charged forward across the plowed field below the bridge and toward the Rohrersville road. This narrow dirt track meandered through woodlands and pastures until reaching the cornfield opposite the wide bend in the creek. Then the road made a sharp, ninety-degree turn northwestward, running north along the east bank and straight to the bridge, through the open plowed fields north of the cornfield. The 6th New Hampshire followed behind the Marylanders, as the remainder of Nagle's brigade opened fire on the heights above the Antietam to pin down the defenders. Other remaining bluecoats from the earlier attacks added a steady fire on Toombs's position that caused casualties and impeded the volume of the Georgians' fire.

Maryland surgeon, Dr. Theodore Dimon, recalled that "as we got to level ground on the border of the stream, the bridge was in sight to the right some two or three hundred yards off. The Regiment flanked off some ploughed ground towards the bridge, the Colonel at the head."[24]

Like the doomed attackers before them, the onrushing Marylanders and New Hampshire soldiers poured across the open fields of the creek bottoms, the fast-moving Marylanders in their column of fours. Then they encountered the split-rail chestnut fence that ran along the creek to the bridge. Led by Duryea, the foremost Yankees broke ranks to tear down the fence, stacked five rails high, to create a gap for the attackers to surge through to gain the Rohrersville road. They made ideal targets for the Georgia marksmen. The gap they opened in the fence became a bottleneck for the 2nd Maryland. The Georgia Rebels blasted away as fast as they could from behind their lairs of rocks, fallen trees, and standing timber. Many bluecoats were cut down there by Confederate fire so dense that one soldier remembered that "the hills blazed with musketry." The congested blue ranks at the gap presented a compact target for the Georgia marksmen. Yankee bodies began piling up like cordwood. Maryland officers struggled to steady their men while trying to squeeze them through the narrow opening in the fence. There was no time for the Marylanders to tear down additional rails to widen the gap in the fence because the Georgians' severe fire was dropping them so rapidly. The enfilade fire especially riddled the left of the blue column. Worse, the Marylanders were unable to return an effective fire because the Rebels were so well concealed in the timber covering the bluff.[25]

Yankees, therefore, fell as rapidly as paper cartridges could be ripped by teeth, rammed down Enfield rifles, capped, and fired. Indeed, the feeling that fueled this ruthless destruction of the attackers on this day was captured by one of General Toombs's soldiers, who soon wrote home that "In my own heart . . . I felt very bitter against these men who had invaded our soil, as I believe against every principle of right, and yet in the hour of victory we soldiers were touched with pity for those wounded and dying enemies." Of the first hundred Marylanders spearheading the assault, ninety were destined to be cut down.[26]

The Georgia Rebels were far from escaping unscathed for killing so many Yankees. Supporting General Sturgis's assault with an effective fire, Lieutenant Benjamin's guns continued to pound the Rebels, delivering a raging fire storm. With guns lined up almost hub-to-hub along the long ridge southeast of the bridge, a trio of IX Corps batteries roared below Lieutenant Benjamin's cannon, as Capt. Seth J. Simmond's section of

Kentucky guns blasted away from the northernmost knoll northwest of Lieutenant Benjamin's guns.

In all, the massed firepower of seven full batteries unleashed their wrath upon the Georgians. Shell fragments ricocheted off the stone wall and smacked into trees, cutting off tree limbs and clumps of leaves from branches. Shells exploding above the rifle pits rained iron fragments on the Rebels below. The barrage caused havoc with the snipers in the treetops, as midair explosions hurled iron fragments in every direction.

In a letter, Pvt. Theodore T. Fogle, described this "artillery hell," as the Union gunners of seven batteries "had every advantage of position, their artillery was placed where we could not charge it & it was used on us with terrific effect, but we just used up their infantry wherever it met us. We suffered badly, eight cannon just five hundred yards off were pouring grape shot, shell & cannister into us & our artillery could not silence them."[27]

Meanwhile, the Marylanders refused to break under their punishment, despite wavering in the leaden storm. The turning point for the 2nd Maryland at the gap in the fence came when Duryea had just thrown down the last rail and, looking back, saw the regiment ready to break. The lieutenant colonel turned to his hard-hit soldiers and screamed, "What the hell you doing there? Straighten that line there, forward!" A Federal recorded in his diary that amazingly, "the line straightened, like straightening your arm, and on it went for the bridge." The Marylanders rebounded to resume the attack with vigor, after finally passing through the narrow opening in the fence. With a cheer, they pushed forward into the fire sweeping down from the heights, and on toward the bridge. Gaining momentum, the soldiers finally reached the dirt road bordering the east side of the creek. On the double and without halting to rearrange ranks or return fire, they turned up the Rohrersville road around two hundred yards below the bridge.[28] However, as more soldiers were cut down, it became obvious that the 2nd Maryland could not get to the bridge and have any men left.

With his regiment being destroyed Duryea had no choice but to order his boys to take cover between the road and the chestnut rail fence and behind logs and trees along the creek's east bank only thirty to forty yards below the bridge. At this point, and finally under some cover, the hard-hit Marylanders returned fire.

Two captains of Companies A, H, E, and F, 2nd Maryland, were killed by the musketry pouring down from the high ground. One Union officer never forgot the sight of the slaughter before the bridge. "There were dead men all along the row," he said, "and up at the head lay the Adjutant and numbers of others." From the beginning, the Georgia veterans had concentrated their fire on the color guard, cutting down some of the regiment's best soldiers. The surviving color guard members, nevertheless, maintained their advanced positions at the Maryland column's head, leading by example. The 2nd Maryland would lose 44 percent of its strength along the bloody banks of the Antietam and the Rohrersville Road.[29] Dug-in across the fortified high ground, the Georgia Rebels continued to load and fire as rapidly as possible, shattering the van of the 6th New Hampshire's column as well. The 6th New Hampshire took severe punishment on the open ground before the bridge, and as could be expected, losses were especially high at the fence opening. It only got worse for the foremost New Hampshire bluecoats who charged past the fence and continued toward the bridge. One New Hampshire infantryman recorded of the 6th New Hampshire soldiers:

> With fixed bayonets [at] the double quick, [they] passed through a narrow opening in a strong chestnut fence—which there was no time to remove—and charged in the most gallant manner directly up the road to the bridge. As the attacking party, led by Colonel Griffen, debouched from the field into the road, the rebels, from their entrenched position, redoubled the fury of their fire, sweeping the head of the column with murderous effect. Of the first hundred men who passed through the opening in the fence, at least nine tenths were either killed or wounded. Such sweeping destruction checked the advancing column, but the men sheltered themselves behind logs, fences, and whatever other cover they could find, and bravely held the ground already gained.[30]

In fighting back as best they could, the mauled units of Nagle's brigade were now aligned in a long north-south diagonal line with the 2nd Maryland at the head, followed by the 6th New Hampshire, the 9th New Hampshire, and the 48th Pennsylvania, at the southernmost tip of the bottoms opposite the loop in the Antietam. The following regiments in the advance learned the folly of charging headlong up the road. Consequently, the 9th New Hampshire sensibly took cover instead of pressing onward into the open fields.

Col. Enoch Q. Fellows, a thirty-six-year-old West Point dropout from Sandwich, New Hampshire, led the 9th New Hampshire. It was a large and well-equipped regiment, about 900-strong, its total manpower nearly five times the number of Georgians who were left alive in defense of the Rohrbach Bridge. The 48th Pennsylvania also blasted away from the shelter of the cornfield and the road below the bridge, pouring a flank fire on the defenders around the bridge. All along the road and fence line, the Federals continued to fight back and fall to Rebel fire. So desperate was the fighting that some frustrated officers, including Lt. Col. Herbert Bradwell Titus, grabbed muskets from their dead and wounded men and blasted away. As could be expected under such punishment, the surviving bluecoats near the bridge fell back to escape, running the gauntlet in retreating.

The IX Corps courage rose to the fore, however, and a renewed effort was soon launched to carry the bridge by storm. This attack was also beaten back. A Federal officer wrote that the shattered Maryland and New Hampshire regiments "were driven back like sheep," with some survivors retiring to the shelter of the brushy knolls. Nearly 45 percent of the 2nd Maryland were cut down on this bloody morning, with 67 Marylanders falling on home state soil. Of the 150 attackers of the 6th New Hampshire, nearly 20 went down. By this time, "New Hampshire blood flowed freely," one soldier later wrote. Here, along the knolls, the regiment seemed to suffer losses "every minute."[31] The extent of the killing led one unnerved 9th New Hampshire soldier to shoot off two of his fingers so that he would not have to attack the fatal bridge. Other men earlier threw down their rifles, and headed rearward to escape the destruction in the valley. One Union general, disgusted by the waste of life, complained that McClellan "threw away our power by impulsive and hasty attacks on wrong points."[32]

Storming the Rohrbach Bridge was proving to be more difficult than either General McClellan or the IX Corps leadership had imagined. One young officer of the 48th Pennsylvania, Henry Pleasants Jr., pinned the failure on the lack of support from General McClellan. Pleasants asserted that Burnside's men "began to understand the bitter hatred on the part of certain other leaders against our corps commander . . . we learned that reinforcements had been refused at a time when not only were some fifteen thousands troops instantly available, but also at the very time when the rushing of those troops to Burnside's assistance might have meant the capture of Lee's whole army."[33]

After the double repulse of the 2nd Maryland and the "Old Bully" 6th New Hampshire, some survivors continued to blast away at the hillside, but the Yankees' fire only occasionally hit the nearly invisible graycoat targets. A slight breeze easing down the valley caused some of the dense clouds of battle smoke to drift away, slowly rising to conceal Confederate firing positions. Not even the Confederate battle flags waving from the heights could be clearly seen by the attackers who were attempting to storm the strongest natural position they had ever encountered.[34]

With each repulse, and in a continuation of IX Corps folly along the Antietam, numbers of Federals moved forward to replace those who fell to the deadly Georgia rifles. Lee's army, meanwhile, remained in trouble. One Confederate officer described the Rebels as "outnumbered at every point [and] we had no troops in reserve."[35] To the decreasing band of defenders, meanwhile, it seemed as if the IX Corps numbers were endless. An amazed Capt. Abner McCoy Lewis, 2nd Georgia, wrote that the Federals assaulted the stone bridge with "how many regiments we are unable to ascertain. They were repulsed . . . but their reinforcements continually came pouring in." Toombs desperately dispatched messengers to his division commander, General Jones, begging in vain for reinforcements from his idle brigades. Still, the wall of fire sweeping down the hillside acted like an impenetrable barrier to the IX Corps. One Federal described the tragic fate of the 2nd Maryland: "The brave fellows reeled and fell back as if smitten at the bridge with the blast of Hell. . . . At this bridge the murderous balls and bursting shells were appalling destruction hovered in the air, death environed it; the approaches were strewn with dead men. It spanned the Antietam, but all who attempted to cross it had found eternity." Across the lines Private Fogle of the 2nd Georgia later wrote home in disbelief that this was, without doubt, "the greatest battle which ever occurred on this continent."[36]

## CHAPTER 7

# "With a Coolness and Tenacity Unsurpassed in History"

## *Holding the Federals at Bay*

AGAINST THE ODDS THE GEORGIANS HAD ALREADY HELD THE IX CORPS AT bay for three hours, repulsing four distinct attacks, buying more time for General Lee and his battered Army of Northern Virginia. As the hot mid-September sun rose high, an impatient McClellan continued to shift his main effort from General Lee's center to his right flank, and toward Toombs and Benning, waiting for the bridge defenders to be pushed aside before he unleashed his massed reserves to attack west up the Boonsboro Pike and across the Antietam, capture Sharpsburg, and gain Lee's rear. So far, the Georgians were thwarting General McClellan's vision of success.

The next attack launched by the IX Corps leaders would be more determined. Colonel Benning could hardly believe the sight, when "toward 12 o'clock, the enemy made preparations for a still more formidable attack." And, with ammunition running low and with fewer defenders left to resist the assault, the Georgians would be forced to hold their fire until the Federals pushed closer to the bridge than before to maximize the effect of their first volley. No longer would the first Yankee who appeared within killing range on the east side of the Antietam become a target for Colonel Benning's sharpshooters.

With cartridge boxes almost empty by this time, long-distance shots could not be wasted. The last remaining rounds were quickly gathered from the cartridge boxes of the dead and wounded, but this was hardly enough to meet the strongest assault yet launched. Still the Georgians retained at least two distinct advantages. One was the buck and ball loads the defenders used. "The boys had a lot of buckshot cartridges," wrote one. "Thirteen buckshot in each cartridge [was] a terrible shot in close quarters." The Georgians also had canteens full of Antietam Creek water, and they could get more if they ran out, unlike most soldiers of the IX Corps. As the hot day wore on, this water was a godsend for the Georgians, washing away the choking black powder residue.

With low supplies of shot evident from early in the campaign, Confederate artillery officers had taken the precaution to collect scrap iron along the way into Maryland. One fifteen-inch-long chunk of railroad rail whistled over the heads of the 9th New Hampshire soldiers before the Antietam. One German Yankee exclaimed, "Mein Gott! We shall have a blacksmith's shop to come next."[1]

After the bloody repulse of the 2nd Maryland and 6th New Hampshire, the 9th New Hampshire and the 48th Pennsylvania and other IX Corps units, continued to blast away at the stubborn Georgians. One captain of the 48th Pennsylvania described in his diary the continuous exchanges of musketry across the Antietam. "It was a Desperate struggle," he wrote, "who should have Controal [sic] of the entrance." More than in any of his previous engagements, the captain realized that "it's victory or death hear [sic]."[2]

Lt. Colonel Herbert Bradwell Titus of the 9th New Hampshire suffered what appeared initially to be a mortal wound when hit during the duel of musketry that roared across Antietam Creek, and by now so many 9th New Hampshire leaders were down that Colonel Fellows, wearing a wide-brimmed palm-leaf hat for protection against the scorching sun and to disguise his rank, was the only remaining field officer left standing.[3]

Unknown to Toombs, several thousand Yankees meanwhile were attempting to gain his flank and rear. The farther Rodman's regiments struggled southward down the Antietam, the closer they came to the two vital fords on the Snavely farm. The Yankees still lost time in struggling through underbrush and saplings bordering the creek, and all along the length of the difficult route, the blueclads felt the plunging fire from the 50th Georgia's skirmish line. Leading the way for Rodman's division, two companies of 8th Connecticut skirmishers hunted for the elusive ford, pushing southward as the sound of the firing around the Rohrbach Bridge grew more distant and the day hotter. At the main Snavely's Ford—farther west of the smaller ford on the Snavely Farm after the creek turned west— the handful of Palmetto Sharpshooters on the right flank of the 50th Georgia prepared for the worst, fearing they were too few in numbers to make a difference today. Still their fire slowed the bluecoats' relentless advance, buying time. General Rodman's artillery and ammunition wagons also slowed the advance, and the 11th Connecticut became separated from the main column.[4]

The long rows of Federal artillery meanwhile continued to pound Toombs's position without receiving much return artillery fire. Even Lieutenant Benjamin, commanding the 2nd United States Artillery, was surprised at how little they were fired at throughout the day, although Union artillery fire became more concentrated as Burnside, in his own words, "directed the batteries on the left to concentrate their fire on the woods above the bridge." A rain of shells consequently hit Georgians behind the stone wall, trees, or in rifle pits, as others screamed over the defenders' heads to slam into the haystacks on the high ground behind Toombs's line. Here, some Georgia wounded had been laid by comrades, and Federal soldiers later would be horrified to discover "in the ashes of some hay-ricks which had been fired by our shells the charred remains of several Confederates."[5]

By noon General McClellan dispatched his inspector general, Col. Delos B. Sackett, to remind Burnside of the importance of taking the bridge. Burnside ordered Sturgis to try again, and Sturgis ordered his second brigade, under the newly commissioned brigadier general Edward Ferrero, to storm the bridge and finally push the Georgians off the hill "at all hazards." A dapper urbanite, born in Spain of Italian parents, and a lover of New York City life, Ferrero now took the toughest assignment of his career. Without exaggeration he called the Rohrbach a "bridge naturally almost impregnable, and very strongly fortified by the enemy."

To storm the triple-arched bridge, Ferrero picked his two finest regiments, the 51st Pennsylvania and the 51st New York, the last his own regiment that he had led as a colonel at the war's beginning. After the bloody repulse of the 2nd Maryland and the 6th New Hampshire, Cox was anxious about that murderous flank fire, which so punished those troops. He went back, therefore, to launching a direct frontal assault, but with some tactical modifications to enhance his chances for success. When the attack came, the two regiments would charge straight west off the twin knolls, while advancing side by side in a formidable attack column. After crossing the bridge on the run, the regiment on the left would turn left, and then both commands would surge up the high ground together. The New York and Pennsylvania regiments would be supported by the concentrated fire of the survivors of the 2nd Maryland, 6th and 9th New Hampshire, and the 21st and 35th Massachusetts. Then, once the foremost attackers broke through the Georgians' defense, these regiments would advance to exploit the advantage.[6] Two more IX Corps batteries were placed in new positions to aid in clearing the wood on the opposite bank.[7]

The 51st New York was commanded by Col. Robert Brown Potter and had already tasted success during General Burnside's North Carolina expedition. Ferrero had organized the regiment in New York City during the fall of 1861, drawing from militia units such as the Scott Rifles, Empire Zouaves, Union Rifles, Mechanic Rifles, Yates Rifles, United States Rangers, and Shepard Rifles.[8] The 51st Pennsylvania, under Col. John Frederick Hartranft, who raised the regiment, were even tougher than Colonel Ferrero's New Yorkers. The Pennsylvanians' well-deserved reputation for rowdiness began in the early days at Camp Curtin in Harrisburg, Pennsylvania, the largest instructional camp and rendezvous site in the North. According to one historian, "If Camp Curtin had been a schoolroom the 51st might have been the incorrigible student." Considering themselves more as westerners than easterners, these rough-and-tumble Pennsylvanians were unruly farmers and woodsmen, teachers, merchants, and clerks. More than half the regiment simply deserted their encampment on impulse in 1861 to enjoy a wild fling in Harrisburg before departing for the seat of war. Guards dispatched to bring them back to camp joined the spree. Not all of these Pennsylvania boys were rowdy, however. Among them marched Sgt. George Washington Whitman, brother of poet Walt Whitman. Most companies hailed from Norristown, Pennsylvania, as strong a contributor of men to the 51st Pennsylvania as was Columbus, Georgia, to Toombs's Brigade. Norristown eventually boasted of five Union generals, including Colonel Hartranft. The final struggle for possession of the Rohrbach Bridge was destined in many ways to become a showdown between Columbus Rebels and Norristown Yankees.[9]

The high-spirited nature of the 51st Pennsylvania was evident when Company A's Pvt. Levi Bolton, on a guard detail at Annapolis, Maryland, in December 1861, actually arrested General Burnside when he could not give a password. The good-natured general finally remembered the countersign as Private Bolton was marching him off to the guardhouse and was then released, much to the amusement of the general, who thereafter praised Bolton "for his resolution and vigilance."[10]

Colonel Hartranft could handle such men. Educated at Treemount Seminary, Marshall College, and Union College, he was an engineer for a Pennsylvania railroad before the war, and became a deputy sheriff of Montgomery County before taking up law. He then became the captain of the Norris Rifles of Norristown, and in 1859, served as a lieutenant colonel in the Pennsylvania state militia. Like many of his Pennsylvania Yankees, he spoke with a German accent. When the colonel was not around, the boys called him "Black John" because of his dark features. But a more frequently used nickname for the colonel was "Old Johnnie." As a colonel of the 4th Pennsylvania at the beginning of the war, he yet felt the shame of seeing his soldiers walk off the field of first Manassas on the morning of 21 July, 1861, because their ninety-day enlistments had expired. The Bull Run humiliation haunted the young colonel, who was now determined to wipe the black mark from his record. "I cannot think for one moment of returning home from the field until this war is ended," he told his wife. His perseverance eventually earned him a Medal of Honor and a major general's rank.[11]

The 21st Massachusetts consisted of volunteers from Boston and small towns like Amherst and Springfield, where the rifled muskets that they now carried were manufactured. These Massachusetts boys had fought well in Burnside's North Carolina expedition, whereas the 35th Massachusetts was a fresh regiment, having been mustered into service just the previous month. The recent fighting at South Mountain was its first. These Massachusetts men had earlier believed that the struggle to gain possession of the bridge across the Antietam would be easy. One officer, for example, mistakenly wrote in a letter, that "the appearance in the morning was that it would be an Artillery fight" today, and nothing more.

The Pennsylvania and New England soldiers now ordered to capture the bridge would never forget the sight of the yet unattainable stone bridge, the high ground rising up like a wall, and the piles of bluecoat bodies. "It would be impossible for any one to convey the idea of our feelings," wrote one Massachusetts soldier upon first viewing the field ahead of them.[12]

Following the same route taken by Nagle's ill-fated soldiers through the dusty cornfield and then up the road leading to the bridge, General Ferrero shifted his troops, east and toward the bridge. In disciplined step, like veterans, these Yankees marched by the left flank opposite the big looping bend in the Antietam. By this time, all that Ferrero knew about the tactical situation was that "there was a bridge to be taken 'at once.'" Upon reaching the edge of the corn, Ferrero and his soldiers finally obtained their first good look at their objective.[13] "Here we again halt, the enemy hurling at us shells and solid shots, which whistle fiercely over our heads, and raise great clouds of dust as they strike the ground in the fields beyond," recalled Maj. Edwin Schall, 51st Pennsylvania. He would never forget the "music of the terrible cannonading and musketry fire."[14]

Almost 700 Federals of the two 51sts pushed through the Rohrbach cornfield. The Pennsylvania boys made last minute preparations for the attack. "Again we halt," wrote a frustrated Major Schall. "Now comes the order to each company to unsling knapsacks and pile them on a heap, and place a guard over them. In a moment this is done, each man re-grasping his piece knowing full well that ere many minutes he would be in the midst of the terrible struggle going on." A young aide to Colonel Ferrero, Lt. John Williams Hudson, looked ahead and saw the bridge. "The bridge, which was of stone," he recalled, "with three arches, & itself curved up from either end toward us, about 10 to 12 feet wide between the stone parapet (covered with weatherboard) which rose 3 feet, inside, above the hard earth-covered carriage-way. The outter [sic] parapet of the curve which just began upon the bridge . . . was 7, 8, or 9 feet above the ground beneath it on our side."[15]

Upon nearing the body-strewn road leading to the bridge, Colonel Ferrero was astounded by the extent of the carnage that lay before him. It was now obvious that attacking straight ahead up the Rohrersville road was suicidal.[16]    Seeing this, Ferrero delayed in obeying his orders to attack. He rested his men while contemplating how best to deal with the most formidable obstacle that he had ever seen. Ferrero then dispatched a messenger to General Sturgis, asking him what to do.[17] An impatient General Sturgis sent back his final directive: "Immediately . . . take the bridge there must be no delay. General Burnside is waiting for that to be done now."[18]

After delaying as long as possible, Ferrero finally began to take action. Mounted before his two regiments, he first ordered them forward. Nothing happened. Even though Ferrero finally acquiesced to obeying his orders, Hartranft and Potter, self-made soldiers with little respect for Ferrero, chose to ignore the instructions. Ferrero rode away thinking that the two 51sts were about to leap forward as ordered, whereas neither colonel was willing to take the lead. Noting the inactivity, Ferrero galloped back to Hartranft and demanded, "Why in the hell don't you go forward?" Hartranft snapped back: "Who do you want to go forward?" Ferrero angrily repeated his orders. Knowing that many of his men were about to be slaughtered, Hartranft replied bitterly, "Why don't you say what you mean when you want me to move?" Pvt. Henry Groff wrote that "an air of sadness overshadowed our Colonel Hartranft's countenance for a time when the 51st was ordered to take the lead, as if conscious of the sacrifice to be made of his fine large regiment." Duryea had warned Colonel Hartranft, "Don't go up the road," and one Pennsylvania private recalled that "as we look down the line, we wonder how many will be with us at the rising of tomorrow's sun! Some must fall in the fearful contest in which we are about to engage. 'Who will it be?' is the question that rises on our lips. But time alone can tell."[19]

As Ferrero prepared to attack the bridge, not all of the regiments of his brigade were to be participants. The Massachusetts regiments would play only secondary roles. The 35th Massachusetts lost Ferrero's confidence after these inexperienced soldiers fired into the 51st Pennsylvania's rear during the confused fighting on South Mountain at Fox's Gap. In fact, both of the 51sts were hit by the fire of these jumpy New Englanders, causing the New Yorkers to threaten to open fire on the 35th if they failed to stop shooting at them. The 21st Massachusetts, meanwhile, took position near the fence below the bridge to lay a covering fire from the south. Col. William S. Clark's regiment, which had first seen action during Burnside's North Carolina expedition, was rudely awakened early that morning when a shell exploded in its front ranks, "blowing colors and guards in all directions."[20]

Ferrero would get excellent fire support from the Union artillery. Two well-positioned guns of Capt. Seth J. Simmond's Kentucky Light Artillery, supported by half of the 28th Ohio, blasted away from the northernmost knoll before the bridge. With the aim of seasoned artillerymen, the Kentucky cannoneers concentrated their fire upon the heights above the far end of the bridge, whereas the Georgians' artillery support was insufficient to knock out these advanced guns. Lt. Benjamin's Company E, 2nd United States Artillery also continued to fire from its commanding hilltop position, while half a dozen IX Corps support batteries blanketed the Georgia Rebels with a converging fire.[21]

Ferrero turned to his men, in neat attack formations with fixed bayonets. He shouted to them: "It is General Burnside's especial request that the two 51st's take that bridge! Will you do it?" Angry that their whiskey ration was cut off because of past breaches of discipline, Corp. Lewis Patterson, the 51st Pennsylvania, shouted back, "Will you give us our whiskey, Colonel, if we take it?" "Yes, by God! You shall have as much as you want, if you take the bridge," the colonel responded. "Will you take it?" In response the Keystone State soldiers cheered.

Determined not to have his boys slaughtered by an attack straight up the road, Hartranft prepared to push northeastward away from the creek to redeploy on the high ground opposite the bridge. By doing so, the Pennsylvania and New York troops would have to cover a shorter distance in launching a direct attack from the east rather than up the road from the south. As they moved forward to redeploy, Ferrero reminded them of their valor at Roanoke, and New Bern, and promised them "a treat" if they succeeded in taking the bridge. They would get their whiskey.

The New York and Pennsylvania bluecoats pushed onward in an effort to gain the relative safety of the rear of the twin knolls. In the words of Major Schall, "quickly we move along, pass over the road, and through the columns of the troops just repulsed." Before reaching the twin knolls, the assault column could be seen by the Georgians, who blasted away at them until the blueclads reached the east side of the knolls. Major Schall later wrote home of how "we are just now moving under the musketry fire of the enemy. Several have already fallen. But we stop not."

Now, the timber screened the redeploying troops from Rebel eyes, concealing their movements to get in position to strike from a new direction. Then, after shifting behind the high ground for protection, the two 51sts began to scale the knolls from which they would launch their attack. In one Pennsylvanian's words, "All this time the regiment was receiving volley after volley of musketry, grape and shell from the rebel forces, on the opposite side of the creek."[22] "Up the steep hill we go, and wheel into close column of companies as we descend," wrote a Pennsylvania officer. "There, in the deep ravine, in full view, is the bridge."

In overall tactical terms, yet another attack by the IX Corps right wing on the bridge continued to be necessary because Rodman's flanking movement had not only not yet struck the Georgians but also had yet to cross the Antietam. Largely forgotten, the struggle for two fords and their defense by the handful of Palmetto Sharpshooters, the 50th Georgia infantrymen, and a few Virginia troopers under Col. Thomas Taylor Munford, was vital to Toombs's main bridge defense.

Munford was a Virginia Military Institute graduate from Richmond, Virginia, and his cavalrymen guarded the line beyond General Lee's right. Directly west of the main Snavely's Ford and southwest of the 50th Georgia's right, a scattered handful of Virginians held a commanding hilltop position overlooking Myer's Ford. From this perch, the Virginians could fire down on any bluecoats crossing at the main Snavely's Ford. Along with the men on the 2nd Georgia's right, the 50th Georgia defenders could also play a key role in thwarting a IX Corps crossing at the two Snavely's Fords. "We had a great deal of skirmishing at the fords," Munford would say, "and but for the splendid marksmen of my old Regiment it would have been impossible for me to have held my line on the Antietam. I had a great many mountaineers that could kill a running deer with their fires or cut off a wild turkey's head and it was not safe for any man, especially an officer, to come within range of their rifles[;] I had some superior sharpshooters . . . and they were dangerous fellows."

The Virginians unleashed a flank fire from the west, ripping into Rodman's left as it descended off the high ground and into the creek valley toward Snavely's Ford, proper. Just to the northeast, the half company of South Carolina skirmishers along the bank and the 50th Georgia defenders above them hit the bluecoats with a two-tier frontal fire.

Despite the defenders' fire, thousands of Rodman's Federals would not be stopped from crossing the Antietam. In desperation, Toombs continued to request artillery and at least one regiment to bolster his thin line of defenders around the main Snavely's Ford, but nothing came from Lee, Longstreet, or Jones.[23]

As if to formally announce the opening of the most powerful infantry attack of the day, around 12:30 P.M., the 12-pounder howitzer and one Parrott rifle of the Kentucky battery now delivered more severe punishment upon the Georgians. Switching from shell, these Kentucky cannoneers pounded the Georgians with double loads of canister, spraying the west end of the stone bridge with the iron hail. Taking the worst artillery punishment of the day, Benning described how "a battery was placed in position from which it could command at almost an enfilade the whole face of the hill occupied by our troops."[24]

From the smoke-ringed southernmost knoll opposite the bridge, some Yankees could see the tattered battle flags of the Georgians lying limp in the heat of midday, barely distinguishable amid the drifting smoke. Impressed by the sight of the high ground bristling with Rebel marksmen, one Pennsylvanian noted how the defenders "were snugly ensconced in their rude but substantial breastworks, in quarry holes, behind high ranks of cordwood, logs, stone piles, etc."

Meanwhile, surviving company commanders in gray went along these ranks, moving among the rifle pits to inspire confidence. Preparing their boys for the day's heaviest attack, young but experienced Georgia officers hurriedly passed along the slope, reemphasizing the need to aim low and make every shot count because ammunition was desperately low. A pile of wounded Yankees lying in the narrow bridge would be an effective obstacle, clogging the stone avenue to effectively impede the attackers.[25] By now, Toombs had bought time for Lee to utilize the tactical option of allowing Stonewall Jackson to counterattack on the left. All the while, the Georgians were prepared to "go down like Napoleon at Waterloo, in a blaze of glory."[26]

As he waited in the 51st Pennsylvania's line, an uneasy Major Schall, who had five brothers wearing blue, took out an incomplete letter. Haunted by a premonition of death, he hastily recorded some final thoughts:

> This is a fearful moment. The First Brigade has just been repulsed in the attempt to carry the bridge. The road is strewn with their dead and wounded, and the living have fallen back. The Second Brigade must now do what the 1st failed to accomplish. The task is a

desperate one. The enemy fight bravely and the repulse of our troops has only inspired them with renewed confidence, and they will fight all the harder. But we cannot calculate the chances. The Bridge must be carried. It is essential for the safety of the army and what are lives of men in comparison to the safety of the Republic.[27]

Only a few minutes before, General Sturgis had cheered the Pennsylvania troops forward with the inspiring cry, "If you take that bridge, you will accomplish one of the greatest feats of the war, and your name will be recorded in History!" Here, along the Antietam, this was not hyperbole. The Keystone State veterans responded with their own spirited cries of "We will do it!"[28]

Finally about 12:30, the moment for the attack came. With a cheer, nearly 700 soldiers of the 51st Pennsylvania on the right, with the 51st New York on the left, surged forward with determination. The dense assault column of Yankees rolled down the southernmost knoll opposite the bridge like a blue avalanche. The Pennsylvania and New York bluecoats charged westward with flags waving and bayonets glistening in the bright sunlight of midday. Almost immediately they discovered that this assault would not be a repeat of their successful charges against less experienced Rebels in North Carolina.

Hardly had they surged over the crest of the high ground when Pennsylvania and New York soldiers began falling to a torrent of minié balls. Then, suddenly, a solid sheet of flame exploded from the hillside above the Antietam, sweeping the blue formations with a sheet of bullets. Private Groff described the horror, writing how the gallant Pennsylvanians charged forward, while "cheering and dropping at every step as [we] descended the plowed hill in full view of the enemy. The gravel struck up by the bullets stinging the hand and face . . . we charged in regular order, but some of the boys could not be restrained from firing at the enemy . . . the shrieks of the wounded and the moans of the dying could only be faintly heard amid the din of noise and confusion."

Major Schall described the scene: "The hill on the opposite side boldly confronts us [and] we move onward at a double quick, in the face of a murderous fire . . . and the enemy, from their concealed position are strewing the hill-side with our dead and wounded." Sickened by the slaughter, Colonel Hartranft watched helplessly as his regiment was destroyed by the "close, continued and deadly fire." One dazed survivor of the carnage described in horror how the first section of the attack column "seemed to melt away like a thread of solder before a blowtorch."[29]

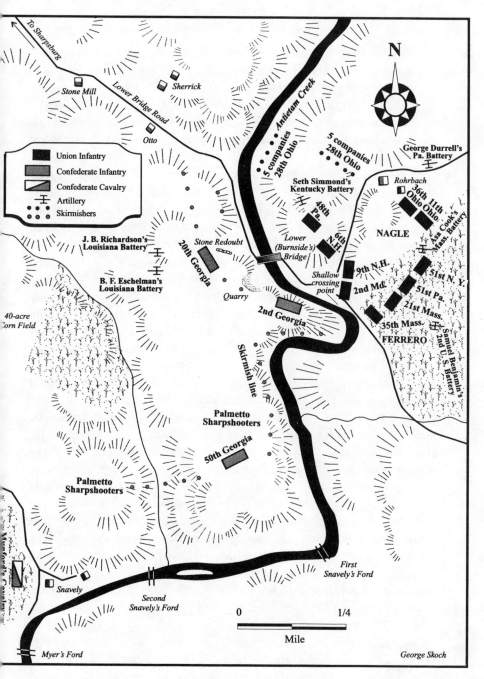

To Sharpsburg

Stone Mill

Sherrick

Lower Bridge Road

Otto

Antietam Creek

N

**Union Infantry**
**Confederate Infantry**
**Confederate Cavalry**
**Artillery**
**Skirmishers**

5 companies 28th Ohio

5 companies 28th Ohio

George Durrell's Pa. Battery

Seth Simmond's Kentucky Battery

Rohrbach

36th Ohio

11th Ohio

48th Pa.

6th N.H.

NAGLE

Asa Cook's Mass. Battery

J. B. Richardson's Louisiana Battery

20th Georgia

Stone Redoubt

Lower (Burnside's) Bridge

Shallow crossing point

9th N.H.

51st N.Y.

B. F. Eschelman's Louisiana Battery

Quarry

2nd Md.

51st Pa.

21st Mass.

2nd Georgia

35th Mass.

FERRERO

Samuel Benjamin's 2nd U.S. Battery

40-acre Corn Field

Skirmish line

Palmetto Sharpshooters

50th Georgia

Palmetto Sharpshooters

Snavely

Second Snavely's Ford

First Snavely's Ford

Myer's Ford

0                    1/4
Mile

George Skoch

*Situation at noon*

With soldiers dropping in piles, natural instincts rose, and simple survival became the attackers' main concern. The foremost Yankees rushed onward more to gain the protection of the stone wall beside the bridge and seek shelter against the storm than to overwhelm the bridge defenders.[30]

On the heights opposite, Colonel Holmes himself wielded an Enfield now, and with his first shot neatly cut down the color-bearer of the 51st Pennsylvania. With the fall of the flag, a cheer echoed across the smoke-covered hillside above the Antietam. A new wave of encouragement surged through the defenders' ranks, fueling the resolve among the surviving Georgia Rebels to stand firm. Holmes yelled to his Burke County boys that "he would not take five hundred dollars for that shot." It was well that Colonel Holmes could briefly take pride in his marksmanship, because he had tested his skill with the rifle for the last time.[31]

Casualties mounted when the attackers finally reached the rail fence, about halfway between the knolls and the creek, along the country lane that led to the Rohrbach house where the bullet-riddled Colonel Kingsbury was now dying. The Pennsylvanians began dismantling the fence, which stalled what remained of the charge's momentum. Nevertheless, the bluecoats passed through the fence, then continued onward.[32]

After taking heavy losses, passing over the fence, and running the gauntlet, the surviving Pennsylvanians finally reached the creek. They took cover behind the stone wall along the east bank above and around the mouth of the bridge. All thoughts of storming across had vanished. "The bridge is reached and here there is a pause," wrote Schall. "The men can no longer resist the temptation, and now they open fire upon the enemy."

With battle flags waving, the cheering New Yorkers charged down the slope hoping to steamroll across the bridge, following on the Pennsylvanians' heels. Suffering an identical fate to the Pennsylvania regiment, the New Yorkers lost many men in surging across the open ground and especially at the rail fence before entering the plowed field. They nevertheless continued onward, swarming off the high ground toward the fence and road immediately below the bridge.[33] As for the Pennsylvanians, as Colonel Hartranft wrote: "While the men replied to the fire of the enemy I was at the end of the upper wing wall and had the two panels of fence nearest the bridge torn down. In the meantime Colonel Potter came up with his regiment . . . and formed to the left of the bridge. . . . Part of the command climbed over the fence and took possession of the lower wing-wall, which turned sufficiently down stream to afford some protection."[34]

The hard-hit New Yorkers, under Colonel Potter, took cover around the bridge, fanning out to the left of the stone structure along the split-rail fence.

Potter somehow managed to keep the regiment intact under the murderous fire. To the left, or south, of the stone bridge, the fence afforded little or no protection and the 51st New York was losing heavily. Hartranft, as well, could only watch helplessly as the best men and officers of the 51st Pennsylvania were slaughtered around him. More bluecoat bodies continued to accumulate around both of the two wooden fences on each side of the road below the bridge and along the stone wall north of the bridge. Still, despite being in serious trouble, the two 51sts had gained a precarious toehold next to the bridge, the most significant gain of the day for the IX Corps.[35]

Witnessing the damage dealt to the two 51sts, the colonel of the advancing 21st Massachusetts sought to avoid their fate by charging straight up the road. After double-quicking his regiment north, he hurriedly formed his survivors to the left of the pinned down New Yorkers. Some Massachusetts soldiers likewise surged forward to gain an advanced position near the bridge, sensibly taking cover along the east bank. From the twin knolls, meanwhile, other 35th Massachusetts Yankees blazed away, firing about twenty rounds.

Now these foremost Union regiments fired at short range, across the smoke-covered Antietam, concentrating principally on the quarry and the far end of the bridge. The poet's brother, Sergeant Whitman, wrote with pride that "the way we showered the lead across that creek was nobody's business." Despite the close, incoming fire from four Union regiments now occupying the east bank of the Antietam, and almost double that number of Yankee regiments firing from the cover of the twin knolls, the Georgians withstood the punishment, spiritedly returning fire.[36]

Against the odds, a relative handful of tough Georgia Rebels had stopped the fifth bloody attack of the day. One amazed Southerner wrote: "A furious artillery fire rained down upon them, a not less formidable fire of musketry came from every part of the opposite [hills] and bank and from greatly superior numbers; column after column of assault dashed up to the very bridge; but still Toombs and his Georgians held on,—held on with no means of replying to the terrible artillery fire, held on after Eubank's guns had been forced from the face of the hill, held till one half of their muskets were silenced by wound or death."[37]

Private Groff recorded the extent of the punishment now delivered to the Georgians at close range: "Forming along a post fence on this side and on the bridge, [we] kept up a continual fire at the enemy, when they could be seen firing from their rifle pits and trees along the side of the steep hill opposite of the bridge, and the stone fence at the top. They were so completely concealed that they could scarcely be distinguished through the leaves from the dark back ground and objects around except by the smoke of their discharged guns, even at the distance of about one hundred yards."[38] On the smoke-covered hillside above the creek, Colonel Cumming, commanding the 20th Georgia, could hardly believe the vast number of adversaries who had been hurled against the bridge during this last great attack. Indeed, he now counted seven Union flags near the bridge.

Members of Ferrero's staff were shocked to discover the plight of the men holding their ground before the bridge. They seemed to have no desire to attempt to cross the bridge under such a fire. Among the best and hardest fighting regiments of the IX Corps, the two veteran 51sts were now not only repulsed but also beaten.[39] All the while the Georgians hurriedly reloaded their Enfields and smoothbores, then took careful aim to steadily drop more prone Yankees around the bridge. Colonel Hartranft swore that the decision to hold their ground around the bridge, and so close to the Georgians, was "the most fatal act of the regiment." Not even well-sheltered hardened veterans could long withstand such punishment.

From behind the knoll's shelter and remote from the slaughter, General Ferrero felt betrayed after witnessing the repulse of his attack, especially with the realization that he had now lost the flower of his veteran brigade for no gain. Ferrero demanded that a staff officer, Lieutenant Hudson, immediately go down to the bridge and ask Hartranft "why he didn't cross the bridge at once."[40]

At this time, the foremost Pennsylvania soldiers were practically on the bridge, many lying down under the cover of the rising roadway in front, and others kneeling at the sides of the bridge's parapets for shelter, and a few others standing—"all vigorously and effectively, firing at the rebs," observed Lt. John Williams Hudson.[41] "Never before had the [51st Pennsylvania] been exposed to so fearful a fire, and never will we forget it," wrote Major Schall. No one on either side ever would, especially the families of one lieutenant colonel, two lieutenants, four sergeants, five corporals, and fourteen privates, a total of 26 men killed, along with nearly 110 wounded from the 51st Pennsylvania alone.[42]

Now finally doing what should have been done earlier, instead of repeatedly attacking the bridge, General Crook dispatched five companies of the 28th Ohio on the double to ford the creek north of the bridge and above the sharp turn in the road leading to Sharpsburg. Here the ground on the west bank was more suitable for a crossing of the Antietam, where the Georgians' bluff suddenly dropped off a short distance above the bridge. Around 250 yards north of the bridge, a long line of Ohio soldiers poured across the creek to become the first bluecoats in this sector finally to reach the west bank.[43] If the Federals now turned south to gain the top of the bluff in the Georgians' rear, then Union volleys would overwhelm the defenders, offering the Georgians no choice but to surrender.

At last, for the first and only time all day, a belated and insufficient effort was finally made to send General Toombs some support. Around noon, General Lee ordered a Washington Artillery officer to "Go to Gen. D. R. Jones, and tell him I wish that battery moved farther to the right, to cover the lower ford, where the enemy will soon endeavor to cross. Let it be done at once." Four Louisiana guns were soon repositioned on the high ground southeast of the bridge to the right of Captain Richardson's Washington Artillery, to overlook the main Snavely's Ford. Once unlimbered on the high ground, these Louisiana cannon had immediately opened fire on General Rodman's soldiers, as they converged on the creek. Initially, this shellfire provided assistance for the skirmishers of the Palmetto Sharpshooters and the 50th Georgia, but nothing could now stop the Yankees from pouring across the Antietam to the south.

In contrast to the Georgians' lack of artillery support, the massed fire of the IX Corps batteries easily outgunned Captain Richardson's two Napoleons and his Louisiana cannoneers. Lieutenant Benjamin's battery on the knoll before the bridge was especially effective. All the while, the powerful batteries of the IX Corps continued to roar from the heights opposite the bridge. In total, four 20-pounders and two 10-pounder Parrotts of Lieutenant Benjamin's battery; Lt. Charles P. Muhlenberg's six 3-inch ordnance guns; Capt. Jacob Roemer's six 3-inch ordnance guns; Capt. Asa M. Cook's six 12-pounder howitzers; the six 10-pounder Parrotts of Capt. George Washington Durell; Capt. Joseph C. Clark's four 10-pounder Parrotts; Capt. Simmonds's four 10-pounder Parrotts, two 20-pounder Parrotts, and one 12-pounder howitzer; and Capt. James R. McMullin's six 10-pounder Parrotts from Ohio were positioned roughly in a semicircle along the high ground overlooking the eastern approaches to the bridge.[44]

Dozens of artillery pieces roared like thunder, pouring a solid stream of shot and shell into the high ground above the creek. After raking the belt of woods around the bridge with a heavy fire for two hours, Lieutenant Muhlenberg, commanding Battery A, Fifth United States Artillery, directed his efforts toward destroying the bridge defenders. Muhlenberg wrote that, "I again opened upon the woods, with shell and spherical case, directing my fire entirely upon those points around the bridge, in which I supposed the enemy to be concealed." Other Union artillery commanders on the heights opposite the bridge, and only around 400 to 500 yards distant, likewise concentrated their fire, pounding the Georgians' advanced position. By this time, too, a section of Parrotts of Captain Simmond's battery on the knoll north of Lieutenant Benjamin's guns also enfiladed the Georgians' lines around the bridge.

The superior firepower of the IX Corps batteries was turned to overwhelm Captain Eshleman's guns poised atop the high ground southwest of the bridge. "A long range battery of the enemy on the opposite bank of the stream opened upon and enfiladed [Captain Eshleman's] guns, and he was compelled to retire, not, however, before he had driven the enemy back from the ford," proudly wrote Colonel Walton. But more important, Eshelman unlimbered his Washington Artillery guns on high ground closer to the main Snavely's Ford. Here, from the new position, the Louisiana cannoneers under cover of a hill that protected them from the enemy's battery, opened fire upon Rodman's troops at the ford with case and shell.[45]

Around the bridge, the Georgians still held their ground with their few remaining rounds. A Union officer recalled that "the rebels were posted behind trees & natural projections of the rocky, wood covered slope, behind little curious shelters made of rails, in the form of small lunettes & provided with loopholes (the rails couldn't be laid close you know) and in a few cases up in the trees—all acting like riflemen." The losses along the Antietam caused Cox to lament that "the proportion of casualties to the number engaged was much greater than common." All the while, however, Toombs's soldiers emptied a growing number of cartridge boxes. Additional defenders were hit, falling to musketry and artillery fire pounding the Georgians' position, the most devastating punishment coming from the blasts of double-shot canister, which swept the hillside with a deadly hail.[46]

South along Antietam Creek, Southern artillery and musket fire rippled off the high ground above the ford, spraying Rodman's soldiers. In marching across country, backtracking, and following the rough ground along the meandering course of the Antietam, General Rodman's men had pushed two miles along the creek to reach finally the main Snavely's Ford. Apparently the 3,000 infantrymen had been forced to continue farther westward and beyond the main ford so that they could descend a less steep slope to the creek, thus reaching the westernmost ford from the west instead of from the east. This difficult maneuver, with artillery and ammunition wagons, across more rough, wooded terrain resulted in the loss of more time. After gaining their objective just before 1:00 P.M., Rodman's troops continued to pour across the main Snavely's Ford. Finally crossing the Antietam, wet to the waist, bluecoats gained the muddy shelf of land before the north-south ravine that cut down from the bluffs. Then, after reforming in line, they moved northward up the brushy draw with fixed bayonets. After leading the way across the main Snavely's Ford, the 9th New York pushed straight up the commanding hill, some 180 feet high, marching toward its peak. Captain Eshleman's battery, after conducting an unflinching defense of the ford was about to be brushed aside easily after being enfiladed by the concentrated firepower of Union artillery.

Splashing through the clear waters, larger numbers of General Rodman's troops continued swarming over the main ford. General Cox realized that the presence of General Rodman's and Colonel Ewing's ten regiments on that side of the stream now threatened the Georgians' rear.

But as throughout the day and like everyone else, General Cox underestimated Toombs's soldiers. Indeed, the Georgia Rebels continued to stand their ground, despite being flanked from not one but two sides, north and south.[47] With thousands of New York, Connecticut, and Rhode Island soldiers of Rodman's division surging through the shallow waters of the Antietam, the handful of Palmetto Sharpshooters continued to pick off bluecoats. Colonel Ewing described the stubborn resistance, writing that "we crossed the ford of the Antietam under a shower of grape" from Eshelman's cannon before they retired. The remaining band of 50th Georgia defenders, meanwhile, unleashed a ragged volley from behind a stone wall at the head of a ravine from which the tributary flowed south into the Antietam. As bluecoats fell into the fast-moving currents of the Antietam, some gray-clad skirmishers banded together to attempt to launch a counterattack, after being driven from their defensive positions. Colonel Fairchild described how a handful of Georgians advanced beyond the safety of their stone wall, and "the enemy then advanced their skirmishers, and were forced to retire by the timely" fire of Rodman's artillery positioned on the high ground to the south. By advancing north to gain the crest, the bluecoats drove a wedge between the 50th Georgia defenders on the 2nd Georgia's right and the 50th Georgia's right flank.

Nothing could halt the surge of the blue tide across the Antietam. After boldly buying time, the young South Carolina lieutenant ordered his Palmetto soldiers to withdraw before it was too late. After the capture of the two Snavely's Fords, General Toombs had to be warned of the danger on his right flank, and a messenger raced northeastward for the bridge to bring the news of disaster. After the soldiers on the 50th Georgia's left fired their last remaining shots, they also pulled back. When the last South Carolina and 50th Georgia defenders on the far right finally departed and headed north toward the bridge, it was only a matter of time before the 2nd Georgia defenders now holding General Toombs's right flank immediately below the bridge were rolled up. Meanwhile, Toombs continued to dispatch couriers to General Jones to request help.

From the Snavely farm, the dirt road led northwestward up the bluff to Toombs's rear, an avenue now devoid of Rebel defenders, providing an open door to Sharpsburg and decisive victory. Despite their right flank having been turned far to the south, the 2nd and 20th Georgia soldiers continued to maintain their defensive positions around the bridge, holding out as long as possible. Colonel Benning never forgave the 50th Georgia for abandoning its assigned positions without orders, leaving his right flank exposed in spite of its spirited stand.[48] It led to the most severe crisis of the day for the 2nd Georgia defenders below the bridge, where casualties were nearing 50 percent and depletion of ammunition was nearly complete. Private Fogle wrote that "so many of the men were shot down that the officers filled their places & loaded & fired their guns." "Our loss . . . was small in comparison with that of the enemy," said Private Terrill, 2nd Georgia, "yet in valuable officers our loss was severe . . . we had, by this time, been marked by the enemy's sharp shooters and the many bullets fell thick and fast." General Toombs had already made preparations for the worst. He was prepared "to fall back when it should become necessary, by my right flank, and to hold a hill about 400 yards below the bridge and immediately on the [creek], as long as it might be practicable, and then to fall back and take position on [Jones's] right in line of battle, with four other brigades of [Jones's] command, about 600 or 800 yards in rear of the bridge."[49]

Suddenly made aware of the crisis to the south by the first returning survivors of the 50th Georgia, 2nd Georgia soldiers around the bridge reacted quickly. "Old Rock" Benning was forced to develop a tactical solution to save his right flank while facing the bulk of the IX Corps before him. To hold the regiment's flank south of the bridge, either Benning or Holmes quickly dispatched a party of sharpshooters to the far right. The 2nd Georgia marksmen and other soldiers took a new defensive position in the open at the high point to the south, known today as the "Georgia overlook." They immediately ran into the middle of a blue assault wave sweeping forward from the south. The flank defenders fell back a short distance and made their stand on what was now the Georgians' extreme right flank, after forming an "L" alignment, probably in the wooded edge of the high ground, to fight on two fronts. Acting on instinct and without an order spoken, they began firing at targets too close to miss.

The right flank of the bridge defenders was now momentarily secure after already having been rolled up for hundreds of yards from the south. Private Fogle was now on the 2nd Georgia's right below the bridge and told of the heroics of one of these men: "Armstrong Bailey was as cool as if he was shooting squirrels, he was some sixty or seventy yards on my right in charge of a party of sharp shooters & nobly they did their duty." Most likely a non-commissioned officer or perhaps an officer commanded the sharpshooters.

As if the collapse of the 50th Georgia was not enough to compromise the bridge's defense, the crippled battery of Captain Richardson retired to Sharpsburg around 1:00 P.M., after the disabling of one of his two Napoleons and with no rounds remaining. Beaten and battered, two Louisiana caissons, limbers, and guns retired to Sharpsburg, concluding their already limited resistance against the odds. This isolated Toombs and Benning even more.

A 35th Massachusetts soldier soon wrote in a letter that he and his comrades were "in front of probably one of the heaviest field batteries in use in our army, the concussion of the reports of which was almost enough to take your breath away [and] more continuous than any thunder you ever heard." The long rows of Federal artillery could not overshoot in aiming low to blast straight into the bluff, where the wide swaths of double-shot canister continued to deal serious damage upon the Georgians. One 21st Massachusetts soldier described that "the bank opposite the 21st was covered from the water's edge with a thicket of brush and trees, presenting a mass of foliage impenetrable to the eye [so we continued] firing from twenty to thirty rounds into the wall of shining leaves, into which six pieces of artillery were at the same time pouring canister over our heads."

Meanwhile, the 21st Massachusetts eased closer to the bridge, reaching the pinned-down survivors of the two 51sts. Pennsylvania, New York, and Massachusetts Yankees now fought as one, united against the stubborn men from a single Deep South state. This same New Englander described the horror as the Massachusetts soldiers faced "a withering fire from the rebel sharp-shooters, secure in their entrenchments, which dotted the field around us with little puffs of dust as the hissing bullets entered the ground; and the pierced bodies of more than twenty of our little band marked the path by which we had made it."[50] George C. Parker of the 21st Massachusetts acquired considerable respect for the Georgia soldiers, writing in a letter, "I only wish you could have seen them . . . a ragged tribe that had just whipped us so handsomely."[51]

Major Schall, described the lengthy exchange of musketry that roared unceasingly across the Antietam: "For nearly an hour an uninterrupted fire of musketry prevailed; but still they maintained their ground, and were inflicting more injury upon us than we did upon them."[52]

A Pennsylvania captain, James Wren, engaged in his own personal duel to the death, probably with a Burke County Sharpshooter, and recorded it in his diary:

I Came near losing my life with 3 difrent musket Balls Coming right over whear I was firing with the musket & the men said, "Captain they have range on you," & watched Closly & saw a Soldier on the other side of the Crick, alongside of the Bridge, step to the one side from behind a tree & fire & the Bullet whistled over my head & [I] secured a safe place & had my gun at a rest & lined [up] for the tree & when he Came out to fire again, I fired but was too slow & I loaded again & Kept my gun lined on the tree & Just as he moved I drew tricker & I saw him Double up at the root of the tree & that Ball Ceased Coming over my head.[53]

Hard-hit Company C, 20th Georgia, was a good example of the extent of the casualties. A journalist of the *Atlanta Southern Confederacy* reported that they had done "their share of the work of death among the enemies of our country, where the heaps of dead Yankees at the bridge attested the valor of the 2d and 20th Ga regiments." One of these Fulton County soldiers wrote that after "their ammunition gave out, they took the cartridges from their dead and wounded comrades and shot it all away at the enemy, and then were clamorous for more."[54] On the 20th Georgia's right, Company F was especially cut to pieces by early afternoon, suffering more than 50 percent casualties, including Lt. John B. Richards. Pvt. George Washington Floyd was killed when a bullet smashed through his head. Sgt. John S. Slight took either a minié ball or shell fragment in the hip that shattered bone and crippled him. In total, ten Company F soldiers were cut down, but in return the Atlanta soldiers of Company F exacted a high toll, some men firing as many as sixty rounds.[55]

Colonel Benning kept his men loading and firing, urging that each shot count. Toombs would never forget the key role played by the colonel today: "Benning stood by his brigade on the Antietam, guiding, directing, and animating his officers and men with distinguished coolness, courage, and skill."[56] Major Schall of the 51st Pennsylvania wrote home that the Georgia Rebels were "inflicting more injury upon us than we did upon them[,] the moment is critical! Our falling comrades admonish us." But the volume of Georgia fire inevitably diminished around one o'clock. For the first time that day, the Yankees were encouraged by hope for success. The Yankees moreover now caught a glimpse of defenders inexplicably leaving their dug-in positions and retiring uphill through the timber as they gradually ran out of ammunition. Rodman's advance north from both of Snavely's Fords was now also beginning to apply increasing pressure on

General Toombs's vulnerable right. Soon even more defenders, with no rounds left, started to head uphill.

But by now the Georgians had accomplished their mission. Toombs and Benning had successfully kept the IX Corps at bay all morning and into the early afternoon. Their success in holding the army's right flank before Sharpsburg helped to ensure that General Lee's lines on both the left and the center would not break, while guaranteeing that General McClellan would not unleash his reserves to attack across the Middle Bridge. Throughout the day, repeated Union assaults failed to penetrate Toombs's front. Private Fogle described the achievement in eloquent understatement: "We just used up their infantry." One lethal Georgia marksman cut down almost a score of attackers, shooting at least eighteen Yankees along the Antietam. Few struggles of the war saw so few men deliver so much punishment for so long as Toombs's and Benning's Georgians.[57]

A Southern journalist soon wrote the first of many tributes to the hard-fighting Georgians, relating how fewer than 300 soldiers "have been especial subjects of comment, because of the splendid manner in which they successively met and defeat[ed] seven regiments of enemy . . . they fought until they were cut to pieces, and then retreated only because they had fired their last round." In only a few hours, Lt. Charles W. Squires would inform General Toombs that the accomplishment of the Georgia Rebels "was the talk of the army . . . he had held the whole of Burnside's corps in check all day—and that with only two regiments."[58]

Colonel Holmes's example had fortified the defenders' resolve during the worst of the day. Private Terrill believed that in this army, there was not "a braver man[,] he was insensible to fear, bombs and bullets were to him a pastime. I verily believe that it was a matter of perfect indifference with him whether he was killed or not. He would not take care when he could. It may be said of him that he was foolishing brave." Benning paid a higher compliment to his top subordinate, writing that Holmes was "a good officer, and as gallant a man, I think, as my eyes ever beheld."[59]

A frustrated Toombs lamented that he could not hold the stone bridge any longer. "After these repeated disastrous repulses, the enemy, despairing of wresting the bridge from the grasp of its heroic defenders, and thus forcing his passage across the river at this point, turned his attention to the fords," reported Toombs, "and commenced moving fresh troops in that direction by his left flank. The old road, by the upper of the two fords . . . led over a hill on my right and in my rear, which completely commanded my position and all ingress and egress to and from it below the bridge. My communications with the rear above the bridge were beset with other, but scarcely less, difficulties. This approach could have been very successfully defended by a comparatively small force, and it was for this purpose that I so often and urgently asked the aid of a regiment on the day of the battle, not having another man available for that purpose."[60]

For nearly an hour, meanwhile, hundreds of Yankees along the stone wall and the east bank below the bridge continued to rain fire onto the surviving Georgians on the high ground. Encouraged by the defenders' diminishing fire and seeing additional Rebels withdrawing uphill through the layers of smoke, Colonel Potter determined to exploit the situation. He dashed over to Colonel Hartranft, and there proposed that now was the time to make a rush on the bridge. But Hartranft, the senior colonel of the two, yelled to Potter above the roar of crackling rifles, that the Georgians' fire was still too heavy for a renewed effort. Potter, still confident that now was the time to strike with the fading Rebel gunfire, requested permission to storm the bridge with his New Yorkers, and Colonel Hartranft reluctantly consented.[61]

As throughout the day, General McClellan remained at his headquarters, effectively unaware of the situation at the Rohrbach Bridge. At 1:25 P.M., he sent yet another telegram to Washington describing the tactical situation. "We are in the midst of the most terrible battle of the war, perhaps of history," he wrote. "I have thrown the mass of the Army on their left flank. Burnside is now attacking their right & I hold my small reserve consisting of Porters (5th Corps) ready to attack the center as soon as the flank movements are developed." The Georgians' defense of the Rohrbach Bridge was not only preserving Lee's right flank, but also delaying the opportunity for McClellan to unleash his massed reserves in his center. The struggle for possession of the little stone bridge was still controlling the outcome of what, to date, was the most decisive battle of the war.[62]

CHAPTER 8

"Hold the Bridge
or Die in the Ditch!"

*The Federals Advance Again to Capture Burnside's Bridge*

THE FINAL UNION EFFORT TO CAPTURE THE ROHRBACH BRIDGE ON THE war's bloodiest day was anticlimactic, one of the most lackluster charges of the war. Benning described his hopeless situation: "The enemy about 1:00 P.M. advanced a very long line, with its centre about opposite the bridge and the flanks far beyond ours. These flanks, having nothing to oppose them in their front, waded the creek, which, though wide, was shallow, and came around to envelop the Second and Twentieth [after] their ammunition was exhausted." Those Georgians without ammunition were slowly pulling back, hesitant to leave so many of their dead and wounded comrades on their high ground and bridge. "I had fired sixty rounds with my old Enfield rifle in this fight and my right shoulder was kicked blue," wrote one private. "I came out of the fight without a scratch[,] the closest call I had was when a bullet passed through the left sleeve of my coat." Those defenders with a few remaining cartridges kept up a steady fire that helped to conceal the withdrawal.[1] General Ferrero once again ordered the commanders around the bridge to resume the attack, and Potter received consent from Hartranft, the 51st New York at last prepared to reluctantly push forward. These veterans knew that the narrow bridge had bottlenecked them together as compact targets for the Georgians. But now for the first time all day, the IX Corps timing was perfect, catching the defenders at their most vulnerable, without artillery or infantry support, with little ammunition, and with many comrades killed and wounded. The Georgians' defensive effort had never been more precarious than now.[2]

With comrades lying dead and wounded around them, the New Yorkers sprang from their protective cover and surged forward after Colonel

127

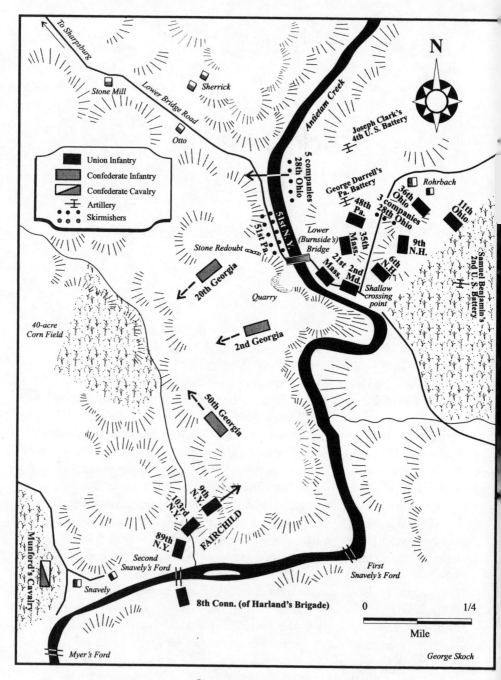

Situation at 1:30 P.M.

Potter dashed before them with upraised saber. "Forward!" he shouted just before a Georgia sharpshooter cut him down. When the New Yorkers came within several feet of the bridge, the sight of the rejuvenated attack inspired Hartranft and his Pennsylvanians. Major Schall never forgot the sight of Hartranft holding his hat high above him, and waving it with his sword, as he ordered the charge. The color-bearers with their standards rushed to the front, and in the face of "that leaden rain of balls" they began to push toward the stone bridge.

The 51st Pennsylvania soon advanced side by side with their New York comrades. Heartened by the sight of more Georgians retreating through the smoke, a number of bluecoats began shouting, "Remember Reno!" above the rifle fire, recalling Gen. Jesse Reno, killed at South Mountain a few days before.[3]

Still, the Rebel bullets and the bloody lessons of the morning made the advance cautious and tentative. The bloodied veterans moved slowly with heads low, and the final offensive effort began to bog down before it fairly began, especially as the dead and wounded Federals impeded progress on the narrow roadway, as did the blood-covered stones of the bridge. The renewed effort of the two regiments was a gradual and methodical advance.

Most resistance among the battered Georgians had already collapsed. A shocked Yankee lieutenant marveled that "those in the advance saw they had nothing to rush upon and overwhelm, and naturally desire, in self-defense and for the purpose of doing what service they could, to load and fire as often as any single enemy was to be seen—for nothing like an uncovered rank of rebels was discernible, or indeed, existed. Those of our troops not in the advance crossed upon those in front—and the whole column while on the bridge appeared like an irregular mob moving nervously, but at a snail's pace, toward the enemy."[4]

The close-range fire of Benning's defenders continued, though diminished, from three levels, the bank, the slope, and the crest. The 20th Georgia soldiers, north of the bridge and along the slope and level ledge along the bank, turned to the right to cut down bluecoats who, by moving so slowly across the bridge, presented ideal targets. A frontal and two enfilade fires simultaneously ripped into the Union troops crossing the bridge. From the top of the bluff, meanwhile, the Georgians on the high ground above the Antietam now fired almost straight down upon the bridge. Lt. Farquhard McCrimmon's soldiers and Capt. Thomas E. Dickerson's Burke County Sharpshooters were especially deadly, the 2nd Georgia Rebels unleashing "buck and ball" at nearly point-blank range. Unable to escape, some wounded Georgians remained in position, loading and firing from their rifle pits as long as they could.[5]

Into the Georgians' fire, the 51st Pennsylvania survivors were led forward by the color guard soldiers of Company C, with Colonel Hartranft beside them. Noncommissioned leaders inspired other Pennsylvania soldiers to cross, stepping over bodies and firing up into the trees, where at least a couple of Georgia snipers were shot out of the treetops.

After leaving the shelter of the stone wall, the Pennsylvania regiment suffered. "The ground . . . was strewn with the heroic dead and wounded, the whole thing not occupying above twelve minutes after leaving the wall, yet in that time no less than twenty-nine were killed outright, and ninety-six wounded," wrote one. Now, those Georgians with a few remaining rounds, centered their fire on the head of the mob of advancing Federals, where two United States flags and the regimental colors of the 51st Pennsylvania were clumped.[6] Loading and firing with newfound speed, desperate Georgians picked off the foremost bluecoats. Even easier targets for Benning's marksmen appeared when the mass of slow-moving Yankees reached the center of the bridge, the highest point of the 125-foot span. There on the hump of the bridge's center the Federals presented elevated targets. Private Fogle was among the bridge defenders. "I fired . . . at a bunch of six or seven Yankees," he wrote home. "The musket was a smooth bore & loaded with a ball & three buckshot. I wont say whether I hit my mark or not. Mother, I'll give you the benefit of the doubt."[7]

Despite close-range punishment, the Federals continued to inch across the bridge, loading and firing along the way. A final rush would have minimized losses, but physical exhaustion, fallen bodies impeding the advance, the irresistible temptation to return fire, and the volume of incoming fire, all combined to slow them. The attack's slowness gave the Georgians more time to kill. At times, the jumbled mass of Union soldiers practically stopped in the face of the fire. Finally, after swarming down from the elevated midway point of the bridge, the Yankees pushed toward the bridgehead and neared the foremost Georgia defenders, Captain Dickerson's and Lieutenant McCrimmon's soldiers, who continued to hold firm with the attackers only a few yards distant.

One Pennsylvania soldier recorded that now "our troops press them harder across the stone bridge, with nothing to protect them from the enemies['] bullets, but the parapets at the sides about three foot high which was a slight shelter against the fire from an oblique direction." The 12-foot width of the bridge continued to bottleneck the advancing men, crowding them together in the face of a concentrated fire. In a foremost group of

51st Pennsylvania attackers, Lt. Gilbert Beaver toppled over dead when a load of "buck and ball" hit him square in the face.[8]

The two 51sts, reinforced by the onrushing 21st Massachusetts, nevertheless, continued across the bridge. Colonel Hartranft waved his hat, imploring his soldiers to cross the bridge.[9]

On the heights directly above, the Georgians fired straight down now into the blue swarm inching across the bridge. Because of the high parapet on each side, Yankees piled up on the bridge, further impeding progress. But near the west bank, the bridge widened again, releasing the compacted ranks of blue. This opening finally freed the Northerners.

Colonel Fellows led his 9th New Hampshire forward, waving his palm hat and shouting, "Follow the old palm leaf!" The onrushing regiments now raced each other to be the first to cross the Antietam. Commanding Company C, Capt. William Allebaugh, of Norristown, the first Yankee to step off the bridge, became the pride of the 51st Pennsylvania.[10] The Federals began to pour onto the west bank. As if this breakthrough was not enough to doom the Georgians, it was not long before McCrimmon and Dickerson's Confederates saw a swarm of Yankees descend from the high ground behind Companies D and H at the quarry and around the bridgehead. These were 51st New York soldiers who splashed across the creek immediately below the bridge after reaching a level shelf on the west bank, and then ascending a deep ravine to the elevation just to the south. With the 50th Georgia long gone from the rapidly collapsing battle line, the 2nd Georgia's right was easily flanked from the south and east. After reaching the top of the bluff immediately above the bridge, the New York Yankees turned downhill to strike the defenders from behind.

Benning recorded the fate of some of his best soldiers during the combat around the bridge. "Lieutenant McCrimmon, of the Twentieth Georgia, with sixteen men, not all under him, was captured at the mouth of the bridge, the enemy who had waded the creek above coming in behind them to their surprise, while occupied with the enemy in front."[11] Lieutenant McCrimmon's band had no time to fix bayonets; and without ammunition, they threw down their muskets and gave themselves up.[12] Colonel Benning described the tense situation: "When the seventeen men surrendered, the enemy enraged were about to massacre them, saying they had fought too long against such odds."[13] Lt. Col. Thomas Bell "rode upon the bridge and remonstrated with the men and mollified them, and then sent the prisoners under guard to General Burnside's headquarters. As they marched off, this colonel later rode down to the water's edge to let his horse drink; whilst there a shell from one of our guns burst near him and killed him."[14]

Behind the 51st Pennsylvania, the 51st New York, and the 21st Massachusetts, a soldier of the advancing 35th Massachusetts described the combat on the west side of the Antietam in the Georgians' sector. The Yankees found "the enemy posted behind trees, rails and stones, upon the rocky acclivity across the stream; dead and wounded men in blue lay about tossing and writhing in their agony." But a solid stream of elated Federals continued to flood across the bridge.[15]

More Rebels now began to give up. Some desperate Georgians stuck newspapers on the end of bayonets and muskets to signal submission. In the confusion, both fighting and surrendering took place simultaneously amid the smoke and noise. Other Georgians fell back but remained defiant, if only in gesture after their ammunition was expended. An amazed Pennsylvania soldier saw that "occasionally one would retreat over the hill, leisurely, as if aware of another strong force not far off . . . some sneaking out of their hiding places from behind the cover of the leaves and trees almost unobserved. A number were taken prisoner, either having delayed their retreat too long, or not having dared to get out of their pits till the firing ceased. Then some walked off as if unwilling to surrender while others gave themselves up willingly." A pair of Georgians hiding under the stone arch of the bridge, meanwhile, had no time to flee up the slope, and decided not to risk running the gauntlet of bullets. With Federals all around them, two found a hiding spot right under the Yankees' noses until taken prisoner.

With McCrimmon's company overwhelmed, the Georgians with rounds atop the bluff and in the treetops had a better field of fire on the bluecoats storming uphill, but there were now too many Yankees to resist. A 35th Massachusetts soldier could hardly believe his eyes, when suddenly "Confederate sharpshooters dropped or slid from the overhanging trees in which they had been hidden." Some Georgia snipers trapped up trees were not taken prisoner on this early afternoon. Some were shot out of their perches by volleys from New York, Pennsylvania, and Massachusetts soldiers. One Georgian was shot out of a large tree near the creek, crashing and dropping through the limbs and leaves until his uniform sleeve caught on a tree branch. The dead or dying Georgia sniper dangled above the Antietam for several seconds before finally plunging into the creek.

One Yankee of the 51st Pennsylvania wrote in a letter of the unusual capture of a clever Georgia sniper, who was trapped high up in a tree. "[He was] hidden behind the fork of two limbs of the tree, that he could hardly be seen—when pointed out to some standing by—at the distance of twenty five yards," he wrote. "He had evidently acted as a sentinel to inform those below of the movements of our forces advancement, but thinking prudence the better part of valor he kept his post."[16]

One Pennsylvanian marveled at the camouflage of the Georgia soldiers. "Whatever may be said of the motley appearance of their dusty grey, and brown linsey suits," he wrote, "it is not so much an indication of want of anything better as a thing chosen on their part, designed to deceive the eyes and evade detection. This was clearly experienced in this battle, for so completely did their dress blend with the yellow soil, and other objects, that they could with difficulty be detected by the keenest eye, as they lay in ditches and behind fences, among the thick and tall corn. Whilst they could see us at once, formed in regular line, take aim and fire before we had a chance of seeing them."[17]

Scattered close-range combat swirled across the slope and the top of the bluff for more than a half hour after the Federals launched their final attack. Surviving Rebels continued to retire up and through the trees amid a hail of bullets. Although the Yankees continued to pour across the bridge, Colonel Holmes refused to accept that he was now forced to relinquish his claim to the Rohrbach Bridge. Earlier he had sworn to Toombs and Benning that "he would hold the Bridge or Die in the ditch," and he meant it. Dressed in a double-breasted Confederate uniform of gray with blue trim and with three gold stars of a colonel on his collar, he wore a fancy shoulder knot. Despite being dirty sweaty and sooty, young Holmes looked the part of a leader in gray. [18]

Many of his 2nd Georgia soldiers were yet inflicting damage. "The men were clamorous for fresh ammunition," said one, "for it had now become a point of honor with them to maintain their ground, even if [it] cost the life of the last one of them."[19] To rally what little remained of his command, Holmes reasoned that the best tactic was to take the offensive. A counterattack sweeping off the high ground just might take the Federals by surprise, buying time or even perhaps hurling them from the bridge.[20]

With the 2nd Georgia now having suffered more than 50 percent casualties, Holmes could perhaps count only twenty soldiers whom he could possibly hope to rally. Perhaps Holmes knew that the other two regiments of Toombs's Brigade, the 15th and 17th Georgia, with full cartridge boxes, had been ordered to reinforce the bridge defenders. Indeed, these Georgians were now marching in a belated effort to reinforce the bridge before it was too late.[21]

Nevertheless, he could not wait.

One 21st Massachusetts soldier never forgot what happened next. The "rebels left their cover and fled," he wrote, "all but the devoted leader of their nearest regiment who ran down to the edge of the bank, and with a cry of defiance shook his sword in the faces of our men for a moment." The incredulous Yankees witnessed a finely uniformed Confederate colonel charging down the hill alone, and now only a few feet away and an easy target. Colonel Holmes made his daring one-man charge just to the right of the quarry, and north of Lieutenant McCrimmon's captured squad. He almost reached the bridgehead and the west bank of the Antietam. Holmes's last act of defiance was short-lived. An estimated twenty to thirty Yankees immediately brought their Springfields to their shoulders and pulled triggers almost simultaneously, unleashing the final volley of the struggle for possession of the Rohrbach Bridge. A good distance ahead of his soldiers, Colonel Holmes stood alone with a drawn saber, when the volley tore into him. Perhaps the last Confederate to die in the bridge's defense, he "fell pierced by a dozen bullets." Ironically, for some time now he had confessed a feeling that he would die in battle. At his fall, one Yankee wrote, "the bridge was won at last."

After killing Colonel Holmes near the bridgehead, the Yankees continued to surge uphill to exploit their success. Leaping over the blood-soaked body of Holmes, the attackers moved on with fixed bayonets. Those few 2nd Georgia Rebels who followed behind their colonel were quickly shot or captured. A handful of Holmes's boys made a daring attempt to retrieve his body, despite the Federals' swarming up the slope. These Georgians racing down the slope were quickly cut down, but the failed rescue only inspired others to make the attempt. "We could not bring his remains off the field," lamented Private Fogle. "Three men tried it & two of them were shot down. I wanted to go with them but I knew it was not right to expose myself in that way. Col. Homes was dead & it was not right for us to risk our lives simply to get his body off the field."

But other soldiers felt more strongly. Lt. Heman Perry and Sgt. James Burton of the Burke County Sharpshooters were quickly shot down trying to reach their dead colonel. Capt. Abner McCoy Lewis, who was destined to command the 2nd Georgia in the days ahead, even made a futile attempt to retrieve Colonel Holmes's body, and then the suicidal efforts to retrieve it ended.

"Our Col. (Col. Holmes of Burke County Ga) was killed about half an hour before," wrote Private Fogle. "He was a[s] brave a man as I ever saw. He was perfectly cool & calm & did not seem to know what the word danger meant, he had won the confidence of the regiment at the battle of Manassas, poor man he was pierced by three balls after he received his death wound."

General Toombs paid tribute to Holmes in his battle report. "Lieutenant-Colonel Holmes, who commanded the Second Georgia Volunteer Regiment, fell near the close of his heroic defense of the passage of the Antietam, and it is due to him to say that, in my judgment, he has not left in the armies of the republic a truer or braver soldier, and I have never known a cooler, more efficient, or more skillful field officer."[22] Fulfilling the colonel's last wish, a soldier led Colonel Holmes's bay rearward for the horse's return to Burke County, Georgia.[23]

Captain Wren of the 48th Pennsylvania, noted that day in his diary: "We also saw a rebel Colnal [*sic*] who was Killed Laying in a ditch who told he would hold the Bridge or Die in the ditch, as we was informed by a prisoner that was taken at the Bridge & sure enough, he died in a ditch. He was in full uniform & had a fine gold watch which one of our troops relieved him of & a good pair of Boots which was taken possession of by 2 of our troops, each man a boot. They then tossed up who should have boath [*sic*]. Captain Gilmour, of Co. H of our regiment, got a shoulder knot & the Buttons off his Coat was all Cut off by the men as relics of the event."

Colonel Holmes's body never went home, though family erected a monument in Georgia. He lies in an unmarked grave at an unknown location not far from the triple-arched stone bridge for which he gave his life. His real memorial, however, is the Rohrbach Bridge.[24]

After Holmes's death, command of the 2nd Georgia went to North Carolina-born Maj. Skidmore Harris, as the command pulled itself together amid the Yankee avalanche. Harris, a hard-fighting Methodist, continued to lead his soldiers with skill during the confused last minutes of combat in the bridge's defense. In Toombs's words, "Skid" Harris, "though suffering from a painful wound, stood firmly and gallantly by his command during the whole day."[25] By this time, the situation for Toombs's men was critical. Toombs described his dilemma in his report of the battle:

> Not being able to get any re-enforcements for the defense of these two fords, and seeing that the enemy was moving upon them to cross, thus enabling him to attack my small force in front, right flank, and rear, and my two regiments having been constantly engaged from early in the morning up to 1 o'clock with a vastly superior force of the enemy, aided by three heavy batteries, the commanding officer, Lieutenant-Colonel Holmes, of the Second, having been killed in the action, and the only remaining field officer, Major Harris, being painfully wounded, and fully one half of this regiment being killed and wounded, and the Twentieth having also suffered severely in killed and wounded, and the ammunition of both regiments being nearly exhausted, and Eubank's battery having been withdrawn to the rear nearly two hours before, I deemed it my duty, in pursuance of your original order, to withdraw my command.[26]

Benning now ordered the remaining soldiers to fall back to General Jones's line. Two companies of the 20th that had a few rounds of ammunition left, stayed behind as a rear guard, delaying the Yankees' advance as long as cartridges remained.[27] General Toombs reflected with pride that the five assaults "were gallantly met and successfully repulsed" before the sixth resulted in the bridge's capture.[28] The Georgians readily obeyed the order to withdraw, retiring by the left flank in good order. As many of the wounded as possible were helped to escape. Other defenders had to be left behind. In a letter, Private Fogle described the fate of one: "Poor [Pvt. John C.] Spivey was shot through the knee & could not walk. We had to leave him[,] we had to double quick to save ourselves from being taken prisoner." Young Spivey would fall captive to the victorious IX Corps, only to die in a Yankee prison in 1864.[29]

Saddest of all were the few killed in the final moments. "Poor Johnnie Slade, he was a splendid soldier. He did his duty well before he fell," wrote Fogle. "He had nearly shot away all his cartridges & was standing up watching the effect of his last shot when a ball passed through the third finger of his right hand & into his stomach & liver. It came out at his back, he was carried off to a safe place."[30]

Like the boys in gray and butternut, the advancing Yankees were hungry after battling the Georgians for most of the day. Some Yankees took provisions from the haversacks of the Georgia dead. One Pennsylvanian upon "seeing a rebel soldier's Haversack, Rather large, overhauled it & found it full of Johnny Cakes & emptied them into his & was eating them, when [one] of our men said he Could not eat anything out of a dead man's haversack & replied, 'Damn 'em man, the Johnny is dead, but the Johnnycakes is no Dead' & he Continued eating ahead."[31]

With cartridge boxes empty, all that now remained to defend the high ground above the bridge were bayonets, rocks, and musket butts. In final acts of resistance, even after Colonel Benning ordered his men to fall back, some defenders greeted the foremost Union attackers with these weapons. The thick foliage and drifting smoke kept some soldiers of Company D, the color company of the 2nd Georgia, from seeing the gradual withdrawal, or receiving the order. These men of the Burke County Sharpshooters withdrew only belatedly, barely escaping the encircling Yankees.

The day after the battle, one Southerner summarized the inevitable conclusion of the stubborn stand along the Antietam: The Georgians "were very much reduced, but they discharged their duty most heroically—Regiment after regiment, and even brigades, were brought up against them; and yet they held their ground, and the bridge too, until they had fired their last cartridge." At long last the IX Corps could now call the Rohrbach Bridge its own. "We did terrible work there, the Yankees acknowledge a loss of 500 killed at that bridge alone & there is no telling what their loss in wounded was," In a letter, Private Fogle wrote. "I know the field & road in front of us was black with their bodies . . . we had driven back seven full Yankee regiments in succession & then they came by Brigades & our ammunition was exhausted & we had to leave, but only then after the Yankees had crossed the river [creek] and were advancing in line on our right. They were also in front of us in overwhelming numbers." Another Southerner wrote that "the enemy lay in heaps in front of the bridge," estimating the next day "that the 2d and 20th regiments killed dead on the field twice their whole number engaged in the fight." Colonel Benning thought "the loss of the enemy was heavy near the bridge that lay in heaps. Their own estimate, as a paroled sergeant of ours taken at the bridge told me, was at from 500 to 1,000 killed." Colonel Cumming would write in his battle report that the Georgians "inflicted a heavy loss to the enemy, killing and wounding . . . nearly 1,000."

In fact, losses among the IX Corps's twelve regiments engaged at the bridge were probably closer to 900 soldiers. Colonel Ferrero's brigade alone lost 469 men, and General Nagle more than 204, totaling 673 casualties. In his Ohio brigade, General Crook lost 67 and the 11th Connecticut could count almost 140 casualties, a total of at least 879 men lost in those units that attacked the bridge. Losses in other units at the bridge that saw heavy fighting later that day cannot be segregated from later casualties. Still, the total losses among the attacking twelve regiments, and the IX Corps batteries, at the bridge must reach 900, perhaps even more, well above traditional estimates of around 500 during the attacks to capture the bridge.

There would be a few more casualties. The 51st New York pushed up the hill to the left, or south, of the bridge, and burst through what little was left of the 2nd Georgia's line during their surge uphill and then continued onward. The bluecoats continued to blast away while rolling up the steep slope. This brought out Potter on top of the bluff behind the small Georgia rear guard. Potter halted his men and gave the Georgians a close and well-aimed volley. "I saw them afterwards, lying there in regular rank, the commanding officer five paces behind the color guard," penned a triumphant Federal. It was what was left of the rear guard defenders of the Burke County Sharpshooters of Company D, 2nd Georgia. One man escaped with the company's colors.

Casualties among the Georgians were equally high. The dead and wounded lay scattered all across the hillside overlooking the Antietam.

After bleeding to death, one Georgia soldier was found clutching a photograph of his children. Other defenders lay slumped over fallen logs, behind rocks, and crumpled at the bottom of rifle pits and behind the rail and log lunettes.

Colonel Benning estimated that the 2nd Georgia lost forty-two killed and wounded, nearly half of its number. The loss of the 20th Georgia in killed, wounded, and missing was sixty-eight, more than a third. But Benning underestimated the 2nd Georgia's casualties, which in fact were higher. Other sources indicate a loss as high as 160 killed and wounded, including those soldiers lost in the fighting after the bridge's capture, when General Toombs and his Georgians spearheaded the attack of A. P. Hill's recently arrived division, hurling the IX Corps back to Antietam Creek.

Toombs and Benning withdrew their last remaining soldiers from the heights above the bridge around 1:30 P.M. Then, at Jones's order, Toombs took position on the high ground opposite the two lower fords, some half a mile to the right and front of Jones's line of battle. Benning described that "the men of both regiments, though retreating different ways, were exposed for a long distance to the shells of the enemy . . . we were driven from the bridge, but we had held it long enough to enable the advance troops of General A. P. Hill to [eventually] reach their position in the line of battle; and this, I suppose, was attaining the great object." Indeed it was. Lee had been waiting all day for Hill's Division to arrive on his right flank, after marching hard from Harpers Ferry.[32] In an audacious performance, fewer than 300 Georgians bought time for their army's survival by holding their advanced position, while thwarting McClellan's plan for winning a decisive victory. McClellan had paid a high price for his earlier belief that "one Southerner is not equal to more than 3 Northern men!" McClellan and Burnside and almost all levels of IX Corps leadership deserve censure for the costly failures at the bridge.

Benning penned a simple tribute to his men: "No words of mine in praise of officers and men are needed[,] the simple story is eulogy enough," he wrote. "During that long and terrible fire not a man except a wounded one, fell out and went to the rear—not a man." General Toombs likewise grasped for words to describe what his Georgians accomplished: "The conduct of the officers and men generally under my command in the battle of Sharpsburg was so strongly marked with the noble virtues of the patriot soldier that a narrative of this day's deeds performed by them, however simple and unadorned, if truthful, would seem like the language of extravagant and unmerited eulogy." As Toombs had said, "This brigade knows how to die, but not yield to the foe."[33]

CHAPTER 9

# "Reversing the Tide
at Antietam"

## *The Final Counterattack*

DESPITE SUFFERING HEAVY LOSSES IN DEFENDING THE ROHRBACH BRIDGE, General Toombs and Colonel Benning were not finished fighting that day. The crisis on General Lee's right flank was destined to become more severe. Soon Benning's and Toomb's Georgians and three small brigades of General Jones's division stood between the might of the victorious IX Corps and Sharpsburg.[1]

With the Yankees preparing to advance beyond the bridge toward Sharpsburg, the Georgians continued to retire westward. The soot-covered Rebels marched through the hot grain and clover fields heading up rising ground toward the Harpers Ferry Road. General Toombs wrote that "this change of position was made to my entire satisfaction, and with but small loss, in the face of greatly superior numbers," although one Rebel found that "they seem inordinately cheerful as they passed rearward." At the forty-acre cornfield roughly half way between the Harpers Ferry Road and the Rohrbach Bridge, Benning's 2nd and 20th Georgia finally linked with the 50th Georgia and the Palmetto Sharpshooters companies retiring from the Snavely's Ford area. This spot, 650 yards west of the bridge and poised on high ground, served as a natural rallying point. Finding good cover, Toombs and Benning now made their stand at the western edge of the field to provide a defensive anchor on the far right of General Lee's line.

A chorus of cheers soon erupted down the 2nd and 20th Georgia ranks when the remaining two regiments of Toombs's Brigade, the 15th and 17th Georgia, arrived. Merely reaching the field in a timely manner had been costly for these reinforcing regiments. Private Duggan, 15th

139

Georgia, wrote that "as we entered the field the enemy did not fail to salute us with well directed shells [and] a shell burst in our midst, tore our flag, flag bearer, and one other man all to pieces. Another was so mangled that he died soon. A more horrid sight I have never seen." Weariness, empty cartridge boxes, and high casualties lessened the effectiveness of the 2nd and 20th Georgia soldiers. Private Duggan was unnerved at his first sight of the thinned ranks of the defenders. He described in a letter that "already the 2nd and 20th had suffered severely [and] Col. Holmes of the 2nd had fallen." Relieved for the first time that day, Col. Jonathan B. Cumming's 2nd Georgia and Maj. William Terrill Harris's 20th Georgia regiments began to trudge north toward Sharpsburg for rest.

Finally receiving the first reinforcements of the day, Colonel Benning wrote that "the other two regiments and the five companies returned from their pursuit of the [Union] cavalry, worn down by marching day and night. I took command of them, and was ordered by Toombs to place them behind a stone fence far to the right of the road from the bridge, and stay there till relieved." The Georgia reinforcements, nearly as exhausted as the bridge defenders, lay down to rest.

These infantrymen, meanwhile, kept out of sight of Federal guns, covered by a stone wall that ran along a small country lane at the western edge of the cornfield. Both Toombs and Benning realized that this was a good defensive position to make a stand against the IX Corps. The Georgians' new position, moreover, was situated on high ground between the main Snavely's Ford to the south and Sharpsburg to the north. Several companies of 11th Georgia skirmishers went forward, descending the sloping ground toward the valley of the Antietam and easing ever closer to Burnside's advancing corps. The first shots rang out as skirmishing became brisk on the Georgians' right, promising yet more hard fighting ahead for the Georgia Rebels on General Lee's far right.[2] But some of the best men and officers of Toombs's brigade now lay dead or wounded. A Pennsylvania captain wrote that "we came to a hay stack whear [sic] the enemy laid thear [sic] wounded [but they] did not get them away in time."[3]

General Jones, meanwhile, withdrew his brigades closer to Sharpsburg, taking better defensive positions amid the concealing shelter of a cornfield north of Toombs's new position below the town. Here, near the Avery Magraw house, which stood about halfway between the Harpers Ferry Road and the road that led up from the Rohrbach Bridge, General Jones's troops were poised to contest the Yankee advance up either road that led to Sharpsburg. On the east side of Sharpsburg, meanwhile, General Garnett's Virginia brigade stood astride the Boonsboro Road to face the tentative forward movements of General McClellan's cavalry reserve, which continued to cross the Middle Bridge.

It seemed as if nothing could impede McClellan and Burnside from sweeping over Sharpsburg to gain the Army of Northern Virginia's rear. Hundreds of bluecoats poured across the Rohrbach Bridge, swinging past the dead and wounded Rebels of the 2nd and 20th Georgia. If the IX Corps gained the high ground below Sharpsburg, then McClellan and Burnside would be closer to decisive victory than ever before.[4]

But the IX Corps's right wing, nearest to Sharpsburg, had paid a high price by hurling itself for hours against the flaming wall of Georgia rifle fire. The battered IX Corps was no longer the formidable fighting machine that it had been that sunrise. Burnside's corps was in poor shape for a renewal of offensive operations, suffering from heavy casualties, especially among leading officers; lacking in confidence after taking its worst physical and psychological beating to date; low on ammunition, morale, energy, and momentum; and having lost much of its fighting instinct in its earlier success in North Carolina. The IX Corps regiments now acted as much like beaten troops as victors—frustrated, humbled, and deflated by defeat for most of the day. It was after 3:00 P.M. when the IX Corps finally surged forward beyond the bridge.[5]

Before the Harpers Ferry Road just southeast of Sharpsburg, Colonel Benning galloped down his thin line. With General Toombs now conferring with General Jones at Sharpsburg, "Old Rock" held immediate command. Knowing that more hard fighting lay ahead, he shouted words of encouragement to prepare his men for action. The 15th Georgia was poised on the right, the 17th Georgia held the center, and the five unbloodied companies of the 11th Georgia anchored the left flank.[6]

Despite Colonel Holmes's death and the wounding of Major Harris, Toombs and Benning could count on a number of lieutenants. The thirty-nine-year-old colonel William T. Millican now led the 15th Georgia. Another product of the University of Georgia, Millican, a Jackson County lawyer and family man, had a reputation as a fighter. Captain McGregor, who had long served as Colonel Benning's subordinate, now commanded the 17th Georgia. Another dependable officer was Maj. Frank Little, leading the five companies of the 11th Georgia, just back from their assignment in guarding Gen. D. H. Hill's commisary train at Martinsburg.

Also strengthening the Georgians' thinned ranks at the last moment was the return of Colonel Cumming and a number of his men of the 20th Georgia, who had been relieved and sent to Sharpsburg. The colonel was not under order to march back and rejoin the Georgia battle line, but these

20th Georgia soldiers could not be kept out of the fight. Some of Colonel Holmes's grimy 2nd Georgia likewise joined the battle line, but with full cartridge boxes and a fighting spirit.[7] Both the 15th and 17th Georgia were now stronger than either the 2nd or 20th had been before the struggle for the bridge, the 15th Georgia numbering about 125 to 130 soldiers, still a small number. The veteran leadership of General Toombs's brigade would have to make up for the disparity in numbers.[8]

Attempting to link up after crossing Antietam Creek, General Burnside's two wings swung forward on the west side of the Antietam. Pushing north toward Sharpsburg, General Rodman's division, with General Sturgis's division close behind after crossing Snavely's Ford, attempted to unite with the northwest-moving units of Willcox's division for a combined surge to overwhelm Sharpsburg. Immediately south of town, the remainder of Jones's division met the onslaught, opening fire on the bluecoats. Private Duggan wrote later that "the battle raged severely on our left [and more Federal units] endeavored to press us vigorously on the right. We were not engaged, except in skirmishing, until late in the evening." With rifle fire roaring to the north, the Georgians felt anxious about both their exposed position and their fate. Colonel Benning's troops, nevertheless, remained in position awaiting developments to unfold in conjunction with General Jones's recent order to take position on his right, as soon as Gen. Maxcy Gregg's South Carolina brigade, the first of A. P. Hill's infantry expected to reach the field, could relieve them. General Jones's hard-hit battle lines initially withstood heavy pressure from the IX Corps but not for long. His weak defense began to falter until collapse seemed only a matter of time. In an eerie replay of the bridge confrontation, soon Toombs's and Benning's Georgians were the only organized body of infantry on General Lee's right.[9]

By 4:00 P.M., General Lee was experiencing a small measure of relief, after Gregg's South Carolina soldiers finally reached the field. After marching seventeen miles in seven hours, these foremost of A. P. Hill's infantrymen were broken down by the race through heat and dust. Not surprisingly, therefore, the first of General Hill's regiments to reach Antietam were mere skeleton commands, as hundreds yet straggled and lined the road from Harpers Ferry for miles. Thanks to the two-hour respite, Benning's and Toomb's Georgians by this time were in better shape than Hill's soldiers.

Finally relieved for the first time all day, the worn Georgians pushed northwest through the hot clover fields, marching toward Cemetery Hill and the vital Harpers Ferry Road leading north to Sharpsburg. This key road was becoming increasingly vital in determining the fate of the Army of Northern Virginia. In a short time, it would again be up to Toombs and Benning to help ensure that General Lee's army would live.[10]

The first of Hill's batteries to reach the field was Capt. David McIntosh's Pee Dee Artillery of South Carolina. In a swirl of dust, the guns advanced to unlimber ahead of General Toombs's redeploying Georgians just east of the Harpers Ferry Road, where they filled a key gap in the Confederate lines.[11]

After more hard fighting in approaching the town, meanwhile, the right of the IX Corps's advance steadily pushed Jones's brigades northward and toward Sharpsburg. By 4:00 P.M., the IX Corps swept closer to the outskirts of town. Punished by both musketry and artillery fire, General Jones's soldiers continued to retire under the pounding, giving up more ground. Gen. James Kemper's Virginia brigade sullenly withdrew toward Sharpsburg. Then, Generals Drayton's, Evans's, and Garnett's brigades withdrew after taking a beating at the hands of the IX Corps. When Kemper's regiments fell back, the three fieldpieces of the Pee Dee Battery on his right were overrun. General Jones dispatched urgent orders for help not long after 4:00 P.M.

Colonel Benning and his men were now ordered by Toombs to double-quick toward Sharpsburg to bolster the collapsing defensive line and to link with the retiring beaten brigades. Colonel Benning never forgot how the messenger made a most "startling addition that the enemy had broken our line and were nearly up to the [Harpers Ferry] road with not a soldier of ours in their front!"[12] Soon Toombs was attempting to rally hundreds of Jones's panicked Rebels. Obeying this order to redeploy to link with Jones's troops was a difficult challenge for exhausted soldiers. The news that the thin defensive line of Jones's Division around Sharpsburg had collapsed shocked the Georgia soldiers, but they shouldered muskets and hastened northward to rejoin what was left of Jones's brigades. On the run up the Harpers Ferry Road, the Georgians were reinforced by Colonel Kearse's band now resupplied with ammunition as they hurried to rejoin "Old Rock" Benning and his boys.

The Georgians raced past a cornfield on the high ground of Cemetery Hill just below Sharpsburg only to find a strong line of Federals occupying General Jones's former line, about one hundred yards distant, and now atop Cemetery Hill and in the rear of the three captured guns of McIntosh's battery. The Yankees were in the exact position Jones had ordered Toombs to occupy. The victorious Yankees held all the ground from the cornfield down to the Antietam Bridge Road, including the eastern outskirts of Sharpsburg itself. In this most vital of sectors, Colonel Benning's force was the only intact unit remaining on the right of General Lee's battle line below Sharpsburg and in a position to meet the threat.

The demise of the Pee Dee Artillery had been quick, after withdrawing the guns became impossible with so many horses killed. A young South Carolina cannoneer of the Pee Dee Artillery recalled that at this moment, "Toombs came up at double-quick and formed a line of battle in the ditch behind the fence about one hundred yards in our rear." After quickly forming his panting men, Benning was stunned to see the shortness of his command line. Toombs and Benning, nevertheless, now formulated plans to do what was least expected. They would attack.

They would strike a blow in a desperate attempt to save the Army of Northern Virginia until General Hill's main van arrived by hitting the advancing Federals before they gained the vital Harpers Ferry Road.[13]

General Lee's peril around Sharpsburg was the greatest of his career. Almost all resistance on the right had collapsed. After a stubborn fight, Kemper's and Drayton's brigades had been hurled off Cemetery Hill and pushed through Sharpsburg by the Federal juggernaut. General Garnett's Virginia brigade, immediately south of the Boonsboro Pike on the east side of town, also had been forced to retire west through Sharpsburg to redeploy to the north. Jenkins's South Carolina brigade, to Drayton's left, likewise had been pushed back before the onrushing IX Corps. In frustration, General Lee watched almost helplessly as confusion engulfed his collapsing right.

Never before had he seen his army so battered. Generals Kemper, Drayton, and Garnett had desperately attempted to rally their troops as they streamed through town, and Lee himself rode to the fleeing throng, trying to stem the rout. He also hurried forward as much artillery as he could find below Sharpsburg in a bid to bolster his line. All the while, the Virginian peered southward in hope to spy the arrival of General Hill's division. Worse, Lee's only route of withdrawal across the Potomac to Virginia was now threatened by the advance of General Burnside's divisions. At this critical moment, only the small remnant of General Toomb's brigade, and those Georgia troops now attached to it, remained intact and ready to strike back.

"Under this state of facts, I had instantly to determine either to retreat or fight," Toombs wrote later. "A retreat would have left the town of Sharpsburg and General Longstreet's rear open to the enemy, and was inadmissible. I, therefore, with less than one-fifth of the enemy's numbers, determined to give him battle." Most importantly, the Georgians were determined that the Federals would not gain the Harpers Ferry Road, by which General Hill sought to reach Lee in time. Fortunately, off to the left lay an unexpected opportunity. Rodman's advance had fragmented during the success of routing Jones's brigades in the final surge to overrun Sharpsburg, and now a gap opened between Col. Harrison S. Fairchild's 1st Brigade on General Rodman's right, and Col. Edward Harland's 2nd Brigade. Colonel Fairchilds's advancing left flank was thus vulnerable, even as the onrushing New York brigade swarmed through the open fields southeast of Sharpsburg with victory cheers. Even more, the overall IX Corps advance was hampered because yet another gap—between Willcox on the right and Rodman on the left—opened up. Toombs was intact and close enough to strike.

Gregg's South Carolinians, meanwhile, in the forty-acre cornfield southeast of the Georgians, were once more aligned in a defensive position and prepared to occupy the bulk of Colonel Harland's brigade. Toombs huriedly formed his 15th and 17th Georgia, some remnants of the 2nd and 20th Georgia, a few 15th Georgia soldiers, and the five 11th Georgia companies, into a battle line within barely a hundred paces of the advancing enemy's lines, though concealed by the rows of high-standing corn. He also hid some of his men in the northwestern edge of the cornfield bordering the Harpers Ferry Road to cover his flank.

Meanwhile, the foremost regiment of the IX Corps in the Harpers Ferry Road sector, the 8th Connecticut, pushed west almost to the Harpers Ferry Road. Advancing on its own beyond its brigade, under Colonel Harland, on the left flank, or south, of Fairchild's brigade, the 8th Connecticut had endured a hard day so far. Two companies had led the way for Rodman's advance south down Antietam Creek to hunt for a fording point, only to feel the 50th Georgia's sting. Now, as they neared the Harpers Ferry Road, their commander, Lt. Col. Hiram Appleman, lay behind them, cut down by a Rebel bullet. It was just about 4:30 P.M., and Toombs and Benning were ready for them.[14]

The Georgians planned to charge out of the corn by the right flank and fire by twos from the rear rank. This swift and unexpected forward movement from the concealment of the green cornfield was sure to catch the advancing Federals by surprise, perhaps giving the illusion of a larger unseen force behind them in the corn. Toombs and Benning were gambling that their audacity might make up for numbers to take the Yankees unprepared. The band of Georgia soldiers stood in formation with fixed bayonets amid the field of sweet corn. Colonel Benning and a handful of surviving Georgia officers quickly drew their sabers and Colt and Navy revolvers, preparing for what seemed like a suicidal attack.[15]

Without a cheer or a shout to betray them, the Georgia column sud-denly surged out of the sea of green stalks. The foremost Georgians advanced on the run, swung swiftly into firing positions, then unleashed a close-range volley into the advancing ranks of the 8th Connecticut, and also hitting the exposed left flank of Colonel Fairchilds's brigade, immedi-ately north of the Connecticut regiment. Then Toombs' Rebels surged onward into the gap, where the right flank of the Connecticut troops and left flank of Fairchilds's brigade were vulnerable. Quickly the Georgians' musketry swept the flanks of both advancing units, inflicting some damage and much surprise.

Then Little's battalion, followed by the 17th, 15th, and 20th Georgia, emerged from the corn. Colonel Benning described the offensive effort, which was every bit as desperate as the defense of the Rohrbach Bridge:

> The men fired as each came up, and by the rear rank. No time to form. The fire on both sides was very spirited but not effective—they shooting over us, we under them. Very soon our fire improved and became deadly. In ten or fifteen minutes their line showed signs of wavering. At this moment a shot or two from a gun went quartering over us and struck near them . . . they broke and run under the hill, and were out of sight in less than a minute.

Leading the 17th Georgia, Captain McGregor reported that "I . . . ordered my men to open fire upon them, at the same time to be cool and aim well, which they did [and soon] the enemy gave way."[16]

Toombs and Benning knew that they had to exploit the tactical advan-tage while they could. Dismounted at the head of his men, Toombs shouted to them that they must retake the lost guns of McIntosh's South Carolina battery and told them to follow him. Follow him they did. "I immediately ordered a charge," said Toombs, "which, being brilliantly and energetically executed by my whole line, the enemy broke in confusion and fled." The shouting Georgians continued to surge forward, as the Rebel yell split the air in the first successful offensive thrust of the day on General Lee's right. Private Duggan later wrote proudly that the enemy

> advanced in great numbers, and were already in good range of our trusty Enfields. The order to fire was obeyed with the greatest alacrity. For some time the enemy preserved an admirable line, but at length it began to waver, we leaped the fence, raised a yell, and pushed the scattered fugitives over ground strewn with their own

fallen. New lines of reinforcements were met in the same manner. . . . [W]e had no reinforcements [but] chivalry [was] displayed on this occasion, while our little regiment loaded itself with laurels, [which] challenges admiration beyond anything I have ever witnessed. I have never seen it equalled before! I never expect to see it again.

All three cannon of the Pee Dee Artillery were recaptured by the onrushing Georgians, who continued to charge past the guns with victory cheers. Most importantly, the counterattack by the Georgia Rebels reversed the tide, for the IX Corps advance had reached its high-water mark. Their success also ensured that the two advancing wings of the IX Corps—those of Wilcox and Rodman—would not unite, guaranteeing a crucial gap between the advance on Sharpsburg and the Harpers Ferry Road to the south.

During the bitter fighting General Rodman tumbled off his horse after a Georgia bullet tore through his chest. Evidently a lone sharpshooter who had been sent out to cover the flanks of General Toombs's advance shot the general. The obstinate men in gray, who had thwarted Rodman's efforts in crossing the Antietam below the bridge for most of the day, inflicted a mortal wound upon the Quaker general. General Toombs reported that within less than thirty minutes after the commencement of this attack, the enemy had fled in confusion toward the bridge, "making two or three efforts to rally, which were soon defeated by the vigorous charges of our troops."

Two guns of the Washington Artillery, ordered forward by Toombs, also played a role in driving the Yankees back. Meanwhile, to the southeast and below the Georgians' right, Gregg's South Carolina brigade was significantly inspired by the success of Toombs's counterattack, which had halted the Federals' advance and regained the initiative. With a shout, the Palmetto soldiers advanced and surged eastward to hit the far left flank of Rodman's advance. Even those Southern troops who had been mauled by the IX Corps's right wing were likewise brought back to life by the success of the Georgians' charge. Garnett's brigade rallied upon hearing of Toombs's success, and these Virginians returned to fight once more, linked with some of Drayton's and Kemper's rallied soldiers north of the attacking Georgians. In fact, General Toombs and his staff officers had earlier rallied some of Kemper's troops to protect their left. These Virginia Rebels aligned along the road and fence line bordering the road to Toombs's left rear, and also delivered fire upon Colonel Fairchilds's troops. By doing so, this band of Jones's troops aided the Georgians in flanking Fairchilds's brigade and then joined the Georgia Rebels' advance to Toombs's left, increasing the momentum that was first gained by Toombs's counterattack.

Led by Toombs and Benning, the Georgians continued to advance downhill through the body-strewn fields and east toward the Rohrbach Bridge. Now several batteries of General Hill's arriving division were sent by General Lee and hurriedly deployed on the high ground just west of the Harpers Ferry Road to open fire. The Palmetto regiments of General Gregg continued to batter Harland's brigade on Rodman's left. Gregg was cut down during this bitter struggle, but the South Carolina advance relieved pressure on the Georgians' right, helping to clear the way for additional gains. Both Georgians and South Carolinians continued to hurl bluecoats across farmer Otto's fields. Meanwhile, more and more of General Hill's units were reaching the field, bolstering General Lee's right.

To exploit the advantage won by the Georgians, Hill sent Gen. James Archer's brigade forward south of the Georgia attackers. Moving forward from the Harpers Ferry Road, this small brigade of less than 400 Virginia, Alabama, and Tennessee soldiers attacked General Toombs's right rear.

Another one of General Hill's "Light Division" units, under Irish-born Brig. Gen. Lawrence O'Brien Branch, likewise advanced to Archer's right and Gregg's left. Branch would soon be killed near Otto's field toward the end of the day.[17] The hard-hit units of Jones's Division began to re-form now. These once-routed Rebels joined the Georgians in the chain reaction begun by Benning's and Toombs's attack, which ensured that the Harpers Ferry Road would not be captured and paved the way for Hill's arrival and counterstroke. Describing how the Georgians' counterattack turned the tide, Virginian Pvt. John Dooley wrote in his diary that "we met Toombs' brigade of Georgians advancing in line of battle to our relief. Hastily forming in their rear we returned to our former line which by this time a well directed volley from this little brigade of Georgians had restored again to our possession. . . . General Toombs rides up and down the line like one frantic, telling the men to stand firm." Thousands of Rebels now advanced against the IX Corps.

The enemy sent a battery over the bridge to bolster Rodman's stunned brigades, and Toombs countered by ordering Richardson's battery of the Washington Artillery to open upon it, and at the same time ordered the 15th and 20th Georgia forward. They pursued the Yankees so close to their battery that their musketry threatened Yankee cannon. After a few shots, the Union artillery pulled out to retreat across the bridge with the fleeing infantry.[18] Toombs wanted to do more than simply drive the enemy back into the valley of the Antietam. As the opportunity remained, he proposed to push the Yankees back across the Antietam and recapture the bridge itself.

Colonel Benning persuaded Toombs to reconsider:

> We could not see what was below the crest of the hill, but I knew a very large force of the enemy must be somewhere below it, for I had from our late position seen three or four successive long lines of them march out from the bridge. I therefore suggested to General Toombs the propriety of halting the line, as its numbers were so small and it had no supports behind it, just before it reached the crest of the hill, and sending to that crest only the men armed with long-range guns [Enfield rifles]. This suggestion he adopted, and the men armed with those guns quickly advanced to the crest and opened on the retreating enemy. Their other forces under the hill soon commenced falling back also. After getting near the creek, however, a large portion of them [the 35th Massachusetts just west of the bridge] halted and formed behind a fence. On discovering this General Toombs ordered down the greater part of the command to dislodge them, soon following himself. After a very hot fight . . . he succeeded in his object.[19]

A journalist with the army described Toombs's actions on the field a few weeks later: "Toombs, cool in the hour of danger, but impetuous in the charge, seemed to court death by the exposure of his person and the intreped manner in which he rushed at the head of the column, apparently, into the very jaws of death."[20]

Surprisingly, the losses among the Georgia soldiers were relatively light during the counterattack. The surprise of the unexpected assault saved a good many Georgia lives, along with the gathering darkness of the late afternoon attack. The most severe loss among the Georgians was the fall of the commander of the 15th Georgia, Colonel Mullican. During the final clash of the day, just west of Rohrbach's Bridge with the 35th Massachusetts, the promising Georgia colonel was cut down "while gallantly leading his regiment in the final charge."

Despite the loss of Colonel Mullican and more good soldiers, General Toombs had only been convinced to halt his attack to recapture the Rohrbach Bridge at the last moment. The combination of Colonel Benning's counsel, General Jones's order to halt the attack, the uncertainty of the enemy's positions, strengths, and locations, and the setting sun, finally brought an end to his burning ambition to hurl the IX Corps to the east side of the Antietam to reclaim "his" bridge.[21]

Toombs might have been able to drive the Yankees back across the Antietam, had General Jones not called a halt to the advance. General Jones had lost his fighting spirit on this day. He ordered his victorious men, including A. P. Hill's newly arrived attackers, to consolidate their gains by taking defensive positions on the high ground southeast of Sharpsburg.[22] More than Jones's orders stopped Toombs, however. Benning and Toombs also discovered now that the enemy had unlimbered batteries on their left.[23]

Summarizing the closing scenes of the battle on General Lee's right, Benning placed the Georgians' role in what he thought a proper perspective: "A. P. Hill's troops came up before night, but none of them had much part in the fight." But more correctly he said that "none of [Hill's troops] had any part in first breaking the line." Casualties among Hill's division, less than 350 soldiers, supported Colonel Benning's claim. He was correct, moreover, in emphasizing that the Georgia Rebels were the first Confederates to deliver a counterblow on General Lee's right, spearheading the offensive effort that opened the door for Hill's troops to later counterstrike. As almost the sole guardians of Sharpsburg at the decisive moment, it had been Toombs's and Bennings' soldiers who had delivered the initial decisive blow at the most critical time, as almost all of General Hill's troops were still on the road and marching toward Sharpsburg.

For his performance this day, Toombs received more than the compliments of General Lee and the Army of Northern Virginia. During a hot skirmish with a squadron of reconnoitering Yankee cavalry about 8:30 that evening, Toombs was shot in the hand by a blue-clad trooper. The political general finally had a badge of bravery to silence his critics.[24] Some of the finest tributes to the Georgians came from the Yankees. An incredulous Captain Wren watched as his men were driven back to Antietam Creek, and a Maj. William N. Merserve now worried that "there was imminent danger of losing the bridge."[25]

Despite two improbable successes on the same day, Toombs, Benning, and their Georgians would not receive their due recognition in the postwar years. Colonel Benning explained after the war, "I have understood that the credit of retaking Sharpsburg was perhaps claimed for General A. P. Hill. Toombs is the man, however."[26] The misconception that General Hill alone saved the day at Antietam during the late afternoon of 17 September would go unchallenged in Civil War historiography for generations. Modern works continue to promote the popular General Hill as the solitary hero of Antietam, overshadowing the success of the Georgians' dual defensive and offensive roles on both sides of the creek.

Ironically, Toombs, Benning, and their Georgia soldiers were widely recognized as the saviors of the Army of Northern Virginia at the time. Indeed, across the Confederacy, Southern newspapers such as Atlanta's *Southern Confederacy* told readers how the 2nd and 20th Georgia "have received the highest commendations from the commanders and in the public journals of the day."

In addition, the newspaper emphasized how "the gallant conduct of Toombs' brigade at Sharpsburg was the theme of both sides [and] the country rang with its exploits and the fiery Georgia brigadier became the toast of the army." A Charleston, South Carolina, newspaperman recorded the "glowing accounts of the excellent behavior of . . . the Second and Twentieth Georgia . . . the last two regiments have been especial subjects of comments, because of the splendid manner in which they successively met and defeated seven regiments of the enemy." A Savannah journalist concluded that "to Toombs we are indebted for saving the afternoon on the right."

Benning proudly claimed that no comparable fighting "had been done by any two regiments in this war, equal to that done by the 2d and 20th on the bloody field of Sharpsburg." Even as the guns of Antietam were yet thundering on this late summer evening, General Lee's headquarters was abuzz with glowing reports of how the fighting of the 2nd and 20th "had kept an entire Federal Corps at bay" at the bridge for most of the day.[27]

General A. P. Hill's division suffered, by the Virginian's own estimate, fewer than 350 casualties at Antietam. In fact, out of General Hill's 2,000 soldiers, only 63 were killed, which hardly suggests the most dominant role in a counterattack that hurled the IX Corps from the outskirts of Sharpsburg and back to the Rohrbach Bridge. Even Hill's biographers have found Hill's losses inexplicably small compared with the impact of his attack. The explanation for this paradox is simple. Toombs and Benning's counterattack played a much more significant role in reversing the tide than has been recognized by generations of historians. By the end of 17 September, General Toombs, Colonel Benning, and their Georgia Rebels had once again won a victory as dramatic as their earlier success in delaying the IX Corps at the Rohrbach Bridge. In contrast to Hill's light losses, Toombs's regiments suffered terribly, yet inflicted almost 2,500 casualties on the IX Corps, with the assistance of Jones and others.[28]

Certainly Toombs did not minimize the magnitude of what they had accomplished. Unpromoted after Antietam, an angry Toombs resigned "with honor" from the Army of Northern Virginia in March 1863 to return to Georgia. The news of Toombs's sudden resignation was another public relations reversal for the Davis administration, raising a storm of protest from some Southerners.

A journalist from the *Richmond Enquirer* opined on 7 March 1863, that "there will be a general feeling of regret that this distinguished statesman and soldier has resigned his command."

Considering his important role at Sharpsburg, General Toombs might well have deserved promotion for leading his men with such distinction. Among other Southern leaders, Gen. P. G. T. Beauregard certainly thought so, urging Tombs's promotion to major general. The problem was that Toombs's proponents were, like Toombs himself, opponents of the Davis administration.

Toombs's legacy, however, lived on despite his resignation. It endured throughout 1863 to 1865 in the battlefield accomplishments of the soldiers of the "Old Rock Brigade" as they continued to fight across the South with the Army of Northern Virginia under Colonel, and later Brigadier General, Benning. The names of Gettysburg, Chickamauga, the Wilderness, Spotsylvania, and Petersburg would adorn the tattered banners of Toombs's old Georgia regiments before the war's end. The Georgians were and remained one of the best combat brigades of the Army of Northern Virginia. But their finest day was at Antietam.

In contrast with the continued legacy of his old brigade, Toombs endured a steady decline in the years following Antietam. In the end, embittered by both his personal and professional life, lonely, diseased, and alcoholic, he died a pitifiul death in 1885 at his stately mansion at Washington, Georgia. Because of his commitment to the Confederate dream of nationhood, Toombs lost almost everything during the war years: fortune, respect, position, family, nation, and most of all, dreams and promises of the future.

But even at the end, Toombs, Benning, and their soldiers always remembered what everyone else seemed to have forgotten—the remarkable battlefield accomplishments they achieved in western Maryland on 17 September 1862, when a relative handful of ragged Georgia soldiers repulsed five attacks in five hours and stood firm for most of the day, defying a tenacious Federal corps and spearheading a successful counterattack to reverse the day's fortunes, when the life of the Army of Northern Virginia was at stake.[29]

# EPILOGUE

DURING HIS PREWAR MILLEDGEVILLE SPEECH, "OLD ROCK" BENNING HAD promised that the men of the South would fight with the spirit of Leonidas when he and his Spartan warriors defended the pass of Thermopylae against the Persian hordes. Hardly could Colonel Benning have realized that he and General Toombs would channel the spirit of Leonidas when they defended the Rohrbach Bridge.

Fewer than 300 Georgia defenders preserved General Lee's vulnerable right flank and rear for most of the day, held onto Lee's right so that General McClellan would not unleash his reserves in the Middle Bridge sector, and bought time for Lee to reposition troops from his right to his left and for Hill to arrive.[1] The price of emulating the Spartans was high, but the sacrifice was not in vain. The Georgians, by repeatedly rebuffing the IX Corps, spearheaded the counterattack of A. P. Hill's division, which drove the IX Corps back to the Antietam. Burnside was devastated by the damage to his fine corps. "Our loss at this place was fearful, the enemy being posted in rifle-pits and behind barricades, within easy musket range of our men, and almost entirely concealed and covered from our shots. We lost at this point some of our most valuable officers." One IX Corps soldier wrote that the struggle for possession of the bridge was a "great blood-bath." The episode deepened the ill feeling between Burnside and McClellan.

General Lee in his battle report offered his own tribute to his Georgians at the stone bridge. "General Toombs's small command repulsed five different assaults made by greatly superior forces, and maintained its position with distinguished gallantry." Colonel Alexander would write that the

Georgians' efforts accomplished much and actually "save[d] the battle." In the days after Antietam, another Southerner described how the 2nd and 20th Georgia's defense of Rohrbach's Bridge was performed "with a coolness and tenacity unsurpassed in history." Private Duggan of Toombs's Brigade attested soon afterward that only a "few remaining strings of our battle flag" were all that remained of his regiment's colors.[2]

Perhaps never again would so few Confederate soldiers play so large a role in saving the Army of Northern Virginia from possible destruction. In the months ahead, General Lee would come to view the battlefield accomplishments of his outnumbered troops at Antietam as his army's finest hour, because the common soldiers in the ranks repeatedly rose to the challenge. At Antietam a relative handful of ragged and barefoot 2nd and 20th Georgia soldiers performed one of the most important military feats of the war by holding Rohrbach's Bridge for most of 17 September 1862. These Georgians were truly Spartans in gray, who fought against impossible odds to achieve the Thermopylae of the Civil War.[3]

# NOTES

## CHAPTER ONE

1. John J. Hennessy, *Return to Bull Run: The Campaign and Battle of Second Manassas* (New York: Simon and Schuster, 1993), 454–72; Emory M. Thomas, *Robert E. Lee: A Biography* (New York: W. W. Norton, 1995), 256–57; Clement Eaton, *Jefferson Davis* (New York: Free Press, 1977), 159–60; William C. Davis, *Jefferson Davis: The Man and His Hour* (New York: HarperCollins, 1991), 469–71; James I. Robertson Jr., *Stonewall Jackson: The Man, the Soldier, the Legend* (New York: Simon and Schuster, 1997), 575.

2. Robertson, *Stonewall Jackson,* 32, 454–72, 575; Grady McWhiney and Perry D. Jamieson, *Attack and Die: Civil War Military Tactics and the Southern Heritage* (Tuscaloosa: University of Alabama Press, 1982), 6–7; Clifford Dowdey and Louis H. Manarin, eds., *The Wartime Papers of R. E. Lee* (New York: Bramhall House, n.d.), 292; E. M. Thomas, *Robert E. Lee,* 256–57; Richard B. Harwell, ed., *The Confederate Reader* (New York: Dorset Press, 1992), 131–32; W. C. Davis, *Jefferson Davis,* 469.

3. Dowdey and Manarin, *Wartime Papers of R. E. Lee,* 284–85; E. M. Thomas, *Robert E. Lee,* 256–57; Harwell, *Confederate Reader,* 131; James M. McPherson, *Battle Cry of Freedom: The Civil War Era* (New York: Oxford University Press, 1988), 534; Robertson, *Stonewall Jackson,* 575.

4. E. M. Thomas, *Robert E. Lee,* 256–57; Harwell, *Confederate Reader,* 131–33; Michael C. C. Adams, *Fighting for Defeat: Union Military Failure in the East, 1861–1865* (Lincoln: University of Nebraska Press, 1992), 98–101; John B. Gordon, *Reminiscences of the Civil War* (New York: Charles Scribner's Sons, 1904), 66; Dowdey and Manarin, *Wartime Papers of R. E. Lee,* 293–95; Ulrich Bonnell Phillips, *The Correspondence of Robert Toombs, Alexander H. Stephens, and Howell Cobb* (New York: Da Capo Press, 1970), 2:604–5; William W. Hassler, ed., *The General to His Lady: The Civil War Letters of William Dorsey Pender to Fanny Pender* (Gaithersburg, Md.: Ron R. Van Sickle, 1988), 159, 171–72; James A. Kegel, *North with Lee and Jackson: The Lost Story of Gettysburg* (Mechanicsburg, Pa.: Stackpole Books, 1996), 11–31; Robertson, *Stonewall Jackson,* 576, 581.

5. Adams, *Fighting for Defeat,* 125; Burke Davis, *Gray Fox: Robert E. Lee and the Civil War* (New York: Fairfax Press, 1981), 132; E. M. Thomas, *Robert E. Lee,* 256–57; Charles P. Roland, *The Confederacy* (Chicago: University of Chicago Press, 1960),

158–61; Richard E. Beringer et al., *The Elements of Confederate Defeat: Nationalism, War Aims, and Religion* (Athens: University of Georgia Press, 1988), 32–43.

6. Stephen W. Sears, *To the Gates of Richmond: The Peninsula Campaign* (New York: Ticknor and Fields, 1992), xi–xii, 343; Thomas L. Connelly, *The Marble Man: Robert E. Lee and His Image in American Society* (Baton Rouge: Louisiana State University Press, 1977), 206–8.

7. Gary W. Gallagher, ed., *Fighting for the Confederacy: The Personal Recollections of General Edward Porter Alexander* (Chapel Hill: University of North Carolina Press, 1989), 113; Dowdey and Manarin, *Wartime Papers of R. E. Lee*, 285; Robert A. Toombs to Mrs. Julia Toombs, 19 May 1862, Robert A. Toombs Papers, Manuscripts Collection, University of Georgia Library (cited hereafter as UGL), Athens; Connelly, *The Marble Man*, 206–8; Mills Lane ed., *"Dear Mother: Don't Grieve about Me. If I Get Killed, I'll Only Be Dead": Letters from Georgia Soldiers in the Civil War* (Savannah: Beehive Press, 1977), xxii, xxvii, 148, 153, 157, 185; William R. Houghton and Milton B. Houghton, *Two Boys in the Civil War and After* (Montgomery, Ala.: Paragon Press, 1912), 72.

8. Hennessy, Return to Bull Run, 456; Dowdey and Manarin, *Wartime Papers of R. E. Lee*, 287–88, 295; Connelly, *The Marble Man*, 202-3; Alexander Hunter, "The Battle of Antietam," *Southern Historical Society Papers* 31 (1903): 38; Jennings Cropper Wise, *The Long Arm of Lee*, vol. 1, *Bull Run to Fredericksburg* (Lincoln: University of Nebraska Press, 1991), 274–79; E. M. Thomas, *Robert E. Lee*, 256–57; R. Lockwood Tower, ed., *Lee's Adjutant: The Wartime Letters of Colonel Walter Herron Taylor, 1862–1865* (Columbia: University of South Carolina Press, 1995), 39; Robertson, *Stonewall Jackson*, 581–82.

9. Ivy W. Duggan to *Central Georgian*, 14 Oct. 1862, Duggan Letters, University of Georgia Libraries, Athens; Aurelia Austin, *Georgia Boys with "Stonewall" Jackson* (Athens: University of Georgia Press, 1967), 50; George Washington Hall Diary, Manuscript Division, Library of Congress, Washington, D.C. (cited hereafter as LC); Robertson, Stonewall Jackson, 582; Byron Farwell, *Stonewall: A Biography of General Thomas J. Jackson* (New York: W. W. Norton, 1992), 418.

10. Dowdey and Manarin, *Wartime Papers of R. E. Lee*, 298; Daniel Carroll Toomey, *The Civil War in Maryland* (Baltimore: Toomey Press, 1988), 5–6; Harry Wright Newman, *Maryland and the Confederacy* (Annapolis: privately printed, 1976), 290; Duggan to *Central Georgian*, 14 Oct. 1862; G. W. Hall Diary; Gary W. Gallagher, ed., *Antietam: Essays on the 1862 Maryland Campaign* (Kent, Ohio: Kent State University Press, 1989), 11–12; Hassler, *The General to His Lady*, 254; Robertson, *Stonewall Jackson*, 582.

11. Duggan to *Central Georgian*, 14 Oct. 1862; Judson Harvey Hightower to family, 9 Sept. 1862, Hightower Letters, Robert L. Rodgers Collection, Georgia Department of Archives and History, Atlanta; R. B. Wilson to Ezra A. Carmen, Carmen Battle of Antietam Manuscript, Box 3, LC, Washington, D.C.; Theodore Fogle to parents, 13 Oct. 1862, Fogle Letters, Robert W. Woodruff Library, Emory University, Atlanta, (cited hereafter as EUL); *Weekly Columbus Enquirer*, 20 Jan. 1863; Hightower to sister, 11 Nov. 1862; G. W. Hall Diary; James D. Waddell to wife, 20 Oct. 1862, James D. Waddell Papers, EUL; William E. Spear, *The North and the South* (Boston: privately printed, 1908), 18; Lane, *"Dear Mother"*, 10, 135.

12. Duggan to *Central Georgian*; Fogle to parents; Spencer B. King, *Sound of Drums: Selected Writings of Spencer B. King from His Civil War Centennial Columns Appearing in the Macon (Ga.) Telegraph-News, 1960–1965* (Macon, Ga.: Mercer University

Press, 1984), 93; Lane, *"Dear Mother",* xii, 4, 84, 139; Robertson, *Stonewall Jackson,* 582.

13. Robert Manson Myers, ed., *The Children of Pride: A True Story of Georgia and the Civil War* (New York: Popular Library, 1977), 4:207–8; Lane, *"Dear Mother,"* xii.

14. Duggan to *Central Georgian;* Austin, *Georgia Boys,* 52; Fogle to parents, 23 June 1861; Hall Diary; Daily Columbus *(Ga.) Enquirer,* 5 Jan. 1864; J. Cutler Andrews, *The South Reports the Civil War* (Princeton: Princeton University Press, 1970), 199; John William Lokey Typescript, 20th Georgia Infantry File, Antietam National Military Park Archives (cited hereafter as ANMPA), Antietam, Md.

15. Lane, *"Dear Mother,"* 14; Robertson, Stonewall Jackson, 581–82.


## CHAPTER TWO

1. William C. Davis, "A Government of Our Own," in *The Making of the Confederacy* (Baton Rouge: Louisiana State University Press, 1994), 158–59; *Columbus (Ga.) Weekly Sun,* 23 Nov. 1860; Etta B. Worsley, *Columbus on the Chattahoochee* (Columbus, Ga.: Office Supply, 1951), 277; James Cooper Nisbet, ed., *Four Years on the Firing Line* (Jackson, Tenn.: McCowat-Mercer Press, 1963), 18; Houghton and Houghton, *Two Boys,* 8, 11, 57; Compiled Service Records of Confederate Soldiers Who Served in Organizations from the State of Georgia (cited hereafter as CSRG), National Archives, Washington, D.C. (cited hereafter as NA); Webb Garrison, *Civil War Curiosities: Strange Stories, Oddities, Events, and Coincidences* (Nashville: Rutledge Hill Press, 1994), 108; Lane, *"Dear Mother,"* xiii, 13; Diffee William Standard, *Columbus, Georgia: Georgia in the Confederacy: The Social and Industrial Life of the Chattahoochee River Port* (New York: William-Frederick Press, 1954), 11, 21–24, 33; Thomas E. Blanchard Diary, Simon Schwab Memorial Library, Columbus College, Columbus, Ga.

2. *Augusta (Ga.) Daily Constitutionalist,* 15 Aug. 1861; Joseph T. Derry, "Georgia," in *Confederate Military History* (Wilmington, N.C.: Broadfoot Publishing, 1987), 25–26, 172–73, 549–50, 709–10, 968; C. A. Richardson, "Incidents of Sharpsburg," *Confederate Veteran* 15 (1907): 380; Nisbet, *Four Years,* 18; Fogle to parents, 29 May, 23 June, and 29 Sept. 1861; "The Burke County Sharpshooters," *Confederate Veteran* 32 (1924): 464–66; Paul J. Semmes Papers, Manuscripts Division, William R. Perkins Library, Duke University, Durham, N.C.; William Jones Memoirs, Georgia State Archives, Atlanta; Edward Porter Alexander, *Fighting for the Confederacy* (Chapel Hill: University of North Carolina Press, 1989). 79–80, 137; 2nd Georgia Infantry File, ANMPA; Standard, *Columbus, Georgia,* 11, 21–23, 33.

3. Derry, "Georgia," 596–97, 968–69; Lokey Typescript; Houghton and Houghton, *Two Boys,* 182; James Lee Conrad, *The Young Lions: Confederate Cadets at War* (Mechanicsburg, Pa.: Stackpole Books, 1997), viii; 9–11, 17, 33–34, 114–15.

4. Duggan to *Central Georgian;* Derry, "Georgia," 982; Houghton and Houghton, *Two Boys,* 180.

5. Derry, "Georgia," 435–38; 20th Georgia Infantry File.

6. *Weekly Sun,* 29 May, 11 June, and 12 June 1861; Robert K. Krick, *Lee's Colonels: A Biographical Register of the Field Officers of the Army of Northern Virginia* (Dayton, Ohio: Morningside Bookshop, 1992), 215.

7. *Weekly Sun,* 13 Aug. 1861; Derry, "Georgia," 41; 20th Georgia Infantry File; Krick, *Lee's Colonels,* 95, 103, 150.

8. Houghton and Houghton, *Two Boys,* 60, 185–89.

9.   Derry, "Georgia," 596–97, 968, 1016; Krick, *Lee's Colonels*, 341; Conrad, *Young Lions*, viii, 9–11, 14, 17.

10.  James C. Bonner, *Milledgeville: Georgia's Antebellum Capital* (Macon, Ga.: Mercer University Press, 1985), 145–48; Derry, "Georgia," 437–38; James L. Conrad, "Training in Treason," *Civil War Times Illustrated* 30 (Sept–Oct 1991): 23–24, 26, 28–29, 62–64; Krick, *Lee's Colonels*, 20; Conrad, *Young Lions*, 14, 17, 25.

11.  Derry, "Georgia," 395–96, 915, 968, 1016; Joseph Pryor Fuller Diary, Manuscript Division, LC; William Y. Thompson, *Robert Toombs of Georgia* (Baton Rouge: Louisiana State University Press, 1966), 7; Krick, *Lee's Colonels*, 20, 84, 108, 184, 215, 254, 272, 380; Waddell Papers; Houghton and Houghton, *Two Boys*, 58, 79.

12.  *Weekly Sun*, 20 Aug. 1861; Houghton and Houghton, *Two Boys*, 57; Derry, "Georgia," 968.

13.  Derry, "Georgia," 435–36; *Weekly Sun*, 17 Apr. 1861.

14.  Fogle to parents, 29 Sept. 1861; Lane, *"Dear Mother,"* 19.

15.  Derry, "Georgia," 437–38, 549–50; Krick, *Lee's Colonels*, 337–38.

16.  John K. Mahon, *History of the Second Seminole War, 1835–1842* (Gainesville: University Presses of Florida, 1967), 196; Stephen B. Oates, *To Purge This Land with Blood: The Biography of John Brown* (New York: Harper and Row, 1970), 320–24, 334, 359–61; Avery Craven, *The Coming of the Civil War* (Chicago: University of Chicago Press, 1974), 407–12; Phillips, *Correspondence of Toombs, Stephens, and Cobb*, 449–50; Robert T. Stiles, *Four Years under Marse Robert* (New York: Neale Publishing, 1910), 26; Gilbert Moxley Sorrell, *Recollections of a Confederate Staff Officer* (Dayton, Ohio: Morningside Bookshop, 1978), ii–iv; Ulrich B. Phillips, *The Life of Robert Toombs* (New York: Burt Franklin, 1968), 182–83; Lokey Typescript; Houghton and Houghton, *Two Boys*, 15, 80–81; Maury Klein, *Days of Defiance: Sumter, Secession, and the Coming of the Civil War* (New York: Alfred A. Knopf, 1997), 60.

17.  Fogle to parents, 15 Oct. 1861; *Daily Enquirer*, 22 Sept. 1862 and 5 Jan. 1864; G. W. Hall Diary.

18.  Gerald J. Smith, *Smite Them Hip and Thigh!: Georgia Methodist Ministers in the Confederate Military* (N.p.: privately printed, 1993), 118–19, 124; Hightower to sister, 8 Aug. 1862; G. W. Hall Diary; Houghton and Houghton, *Two Boys*, 58, 77, 83–84.

19.  William H. Andrews, *Footprints of a Regiment: A Recollection of the 1st Georgia Regulars, 1861–1865* (Marietta, Ga.: Longstreet Press, 1992), 4, 8; Houghton and Houghton, *Two Boys*, 58, 183, 203–4, 208.

20.  Houghton and Houghton, *Two Boys*, 88.

## CHAPTER THREE

1.   W. C. Davis, "A Government of Our Own," 155–56, 203, 379–80; Thompson, *Robert Toombs*, ix, 3–6, 9, 14; Dubose Lewis Toombs Jr. to author, 27 Sept. 1990 and 19 Oct. 1990; Benjamin A. Williams, ed., *A Diary from Dixie by Mary Chesnut* (Boston: Houghton, Mifflin, 1949), 230; Pleasant A. Stovell, *Robert Toombs: Statesman, Speaker, Soldier, Sage* (New York: Cassell Publishing, 1892), 1–2, 4, 7; Charles C. Jones Jr., "Brigadier-General Robert Toombs," *Southern Historical Society Papers* 14 (Jan. 1886): 301; Jai S. Cochran, "The Contentious Robert Toombs," *Civil War Magazine* 11 (Mar.- Apr. 1993): 32–33, 45–50; Alexander, *Fighting for the Confederacy*, 73.

2.   Thompson, *Robert Toombs*, 8–14, 16, 22–23, 46–47; Varina Howell Davis, *Jefferson Davis, Ex-President of the Confederate States of America: A Memoir by His Wife* vol. 1

(1890; reprint, Freeport, N.Y.: Books for Libraries Press, 1971), 409–12; Richard Taylor, *Destruction and Reconstruction: Personal Experiences of the Late War* (New York: Longmans, Green, 1955), 259, 261; Kenneth Coleman and Charles Stephen Gurr, *Dictionary of Georgia Biography* vol. 2 (Athens: University of Georgia Press, 1983), 989; Jack Bauer, *Zachary Taylor* (Baton Rouge: Louisiana State University Press, 1985), 218–19.

3. Thompson, *Robert Toombs*, 52–55, 65, 146, 151; Henry Whitney Cleveland, "Robert Toombs," *The Southern Bivouac* 1 (Jan. 1886): 450; Spencer B. King Jr., *Georgia Voices: A Documentary History to 1872* (Athens: University of Georgia Press, 1966), 272; William W. Freehling and Craig M. Simpson, *Secession Debated: Georgia's Showdown in 1860* (New York: Oxford University Press, 1992), xv, 31–32, 48–49; W. C. Davis, "A Government of Our Own," 55.

4. *Milledgeville (Ga.) Southern Federal Union*, 15 Jan. 1861; Thompson, *Robert Toombs*, 154; Burton J. Hendrick, *Statesman of the Lost Cause* (New York: Literary Guild, 1939), 69–75; C. C. Jones, "Brigadier-General Robert Toombs," 297; Klein, *Days of Defiance*, 190.

5. Thompson, *Robert Toombs*, 159–63; Cass Canfield, *The Iron Will of Jefferson Davis* (New York: Fairfax Press, 1978), 52; C. C. Jones, "Brigadier-General Robert Toombs," 299; John B. Jones, *A Rebel War Clerk's Diary* (Baton Rouge: Louisiana State University Press, 1993), 175; Robert Leckie, *None Died in Vain* (New York, Harper Perennial, 1991), 383; W.C. Davis, "A Government of Our Own," 91–93, 118–20.

6. W.C. Davis, "A Government of Our Own," 116–17, 172–73, 177, 184, 239, 301–2, 365, 376; Thompson, *Robert Toombs*, 156–75; Canfield, *Iron Will*, 57; *Daily Constitutionalist*, 17 June 1861; Diary and Reminiscences of Stephen R. Mallory, Manuscript Division, LC; Phillips, *Life of Robert Toombs*, 236–37; William Y. Thompson, "Robert Toombs: Confederate Soldier," *Civil War History* 7 (Dec. 1961): 406–7; E. Merton Coulter, *Georgia: A Short History* (Chapel Hill: University of North Carolina Press, 1947), 327–28; Klein, *Days of Defiance*, 293, 399.

7. Thompson, *Robert Toombs*, 12; Coleman and Gurr, *Dictionary of Georgia Biography*, 990; Phillips, *Life of Robert Toombs*, 238; Houghton and Houghton, *Two Boys*, 68, 120; W. C. Davis, "A Government of Our Own," 55, 187.

8. W.C. Davis, "A Government of Our Own," 142.

9. Ibid., 187, 410; Robert A. Toombs Papers, Manuscripts Division, EUL; Nisbet, *Four Years*, 96–97; Clifford Dowdey, *The Seven Days: The Emergence of Lee* (Boston: Little, Brown, 1964) 170; Douglas Southall Freeman, *Lee's Lieutenants: A Study in Command*, (New York: Charles Scribner's Sons, 1942–44), 1:621–25; *Augusta (Ga.) Weekly Chronicle and Sentinel*, 24 June 1862; *Milledgeville (Ga.) Southern Federal Union*, 3 June 1862; Thompson, *Robert Toombs*, 409.

10. *Daily Constitutionalist*, 29 Nov. 1861; Robert A. Toombs Papers, Special Collections, William R. Perkins Library, Duke University (cited hereafter as DUL), Durham, N.C.; Toombs Papers, UGL.

11. W. C. Davis, "A Government of Our Own," 92; Robert A. Toombs to Jefferson Davis, 1 Sept. 1861, Toombs Papers, DUL; William Garrett Piston, *Lee's Tarnished Lieutenant: James Longstreet and His Place in Southern History* (Athens: University of Georgia Press, 1987), 29; G. Moxley Sorrell, *Recollections of a Staff Officer* (1905; reprint, Wilmington, N.C.: Broadfoot Publishing, 1995), 95, 101; Cleveland, "Robert Toombs," 453; Phillips, *Life of Robert Toombs*, 237–38; Thompson, *Robert Toombs*, 414; Lane, *"Dear Mother,"* xvii.

12. Phillips, *Correspondence of Toombs, Stephens, and Cobb*, 576–77; *Savannah Republican*, 13 May 1862; Joseph P. Cullen, *The Peninsula Campaign, 1862: McClellan and*

*Lee Struggle for Richmond* (New York: Bonanza Books, n.d.), 66; Robert A. Toombs to Mrs. Julia Toombs, 13 May 1862, Toombs Papers, UGL; Phillips, *Life of Robert Toombs*, 243; Connelly, *The Marble Man*, 203.

13. Cleveland, "Robert Toombs," 452–53.

14. W. H. Andrews, *Footprints of a Regiment*, 15, 37–38; *Weekly Sun*, 10 Dec. 1861; Captions and Records of Events, Company D, 15th Georgia, Georgia Department of Archives, Atlanta; Duggan to *Central Georgian*, 14 Oct. 1862.

15. Nisbet, *Four Years*, 96; Cullen, *Peninsula Campaign, 1862*, 119; Sears, *Gates of Richmond*, 166, 247, 258–59; James Longstreet, *From Manassas to Appomattox: The Memoirs of the Civil War in America.* (1896; reprint, Bloomington: Indiana University Press, 1960), 113; Piston, *Lee's Tarnished Lieutenant*, 21; Dowdey, *Seven Days*, 264–66; John H. McIntosh, *The Official History of Elbert County, Georgia* (Elberton, Ga.: Daughters of the American Revolution, Stephen Hear Chapter, 1940), 115; W. H. Andrews, *Footprints of a Regiment*, 39–40; Freeman, *Lee's Lieutenants*, 1:625–26; Mark M. Boatner III, *The Civil War Dictionary* (New York: David McKay, 1959), 325; Thompson, *Robert Toombs*, 187–91; Stovall, *Robert Toombs*, 238–39, 250–51; Burke Davis, *The Civil War: Strange and Fascinating Facts* (New York: Fairfax Press, 1982), 59; Lane, *"Dear Mother,"* 149; Krick, *Lee's Colonels*, 254; Richard Seker, "Fighting under the Influence," *America's Civil War* (Jan. 1998): 41.

16. Sears, *Gates of Richmond*, 329, 333; *Savannah Republican*, 19 July 1862; Thomas L. Ware Diary, Southern Historical Collection, University of North Carolina, Chapel Hill; Freeman, *Lee's Lieutenants*, 1:626–28; *Daily Constitutionalist*, 19 July 1862; U.S. War Department, *The War of the Rebellion: A Compilation of the Official Records of the Union and Confederate Armies* (Washington, D.C.: Government Printing Office, 1880–1901), vol. XII, ser. I, pt. 2: 629, 701–5 (cited hereafter as *O.R.*); Craig L. Symonds, introduction to *Jubal Early's Memoirs: Autobiography Sketch and Narrative of the War between the States* (Baltimore: Nautical and Aviation Publishing, 1989), 81–82; Thompson, *Robert Toombs*, 192–94; Stovall, *Robert Toombs*, 1, 252–53; Phillips, *Life of Robert Toombs*, 244; Alexander, *Fighting for the Confederacy*, 113; Charles W. Squires Transcripts, Miscellaneous Manuscript Collection, no. 224, Manuscript Division, LC; Hal Bridges, *Lee's Maverick General: Daniel Harvey Hill* (Lincoln: University of Nebraska Press, 1991), xiii–xix, 49–50, 79–82, 85–87; Frank E. Vandiver, *Ploughshares into Swords: Josiah Gorgas and Confederate Ordnance* (College Station: Texas A&M University Press, 1994), 111–12; Krick, *Lee's Colonels*, 78; Houghton and Houghton, *Two Boys*, 78, 181, 207; W. H. Andrews, *Footprints of a Regiment*, 52; Mark Perry, *Conceived in Liberty: Joshua Chamberlain, William Oates, and the American Civil War* (New York: Viking, 1997), 192.

17. W. H. Andrews, *Footprints of a Regiment*, 37–38.

18. Phillips, *Correspondence of Toombs, Stephens, and Cobb*, 603–4; Freeman, *Lee's Lieutenants*, 2:52–62; Jeffrey D. Wert, *General James Longstreet: The Confederacy's Most Controversial Soldier* (New York: Simon and Schuster, 1994), 393; Fitzhugh Lee, *General Lee* (1894; reprint, New York: Da Capo Press, 1994), vi–vii.

19. Freeman, *Lee's Lieutenants*, 1:628; Stephen W. Sears, ed. *The Civil War Papers of George B. McClellan: Selected Correspondence, 1860–1865* (New York: Ticknor and Fields, 1989), 121 (cited hereafter as *McClellan*).

20. *O.R.*, vol. XII, ser. I, pt. 2: 583–84, 587, 592–93; Hennessy, *Return to Bull Run*, 402–24.

21. Hennessy, *Return to Bull Run*, 423; Sorrell, *Recollections*, 101; Phillips, *Life of Robert Toombs*, 245; Stovall, *Robert Toombs*, 261.

22. W. H. Andrews, *Footprints of a Regiment*, 67.
23. 2nd Georgia File; W. H. Andrews, *Footprints of a Regiment*, 15, 28–29.


## CHAPTER FOUR

1. G. W. Hall Diary; Bell Irvin Wiley, *The Life of Johnny Reb: The Common Soldier of the Confederacy* (Baton Rouge: Louisiana State University Press, 1978), 253–54; Hunter, "Battle of Antietam", 38; Wert, *Longstreet*, 181–82; John W. Schildt, *Drums along the Antietam* (Parsons, W.V.: McClain Printing, 1972), 239; *O.R.*, vol. XIX, ser. I, pt. 2: 596, 602–3, 605; Lane, *"Dear Mother,"* xviii, 87, 121; Robertson, *Stonewall Jackson*, 582, 586–88.
2. William Allen, *The Army of Northern Virginia in 1862* (New York: Houghton Mifflin, 1892), 324–25; W. H. Andrews, *Footprints of a Regiment*, 78; Gallagher, *Antietam: Essays*, 42–43; Joseph G. Dawson III, "The Confederacy Revisited: Encyclopedia of the Confederacy," *Civil War History* 40 (Dec. 1994): 314; J. Cutter Andrews, *The South Reports the War*, 198; *Daily Columbus Enquirer*, 22 Sept. 1862; Lane, *"Dear Mother,"* 217; Houghton and Houghton *Two Boys*, 121; Hassler, *The General to His Lady*, 175; Robertson, *Stonewall Jackson*, 586.
3. Phillips, *Correspondence of Toombs, Stephens, and Cobb*, 612–13.
4. Hightower to family, 24 Sept. 1862, 3 Aug. and 25 Sept. 1863; Mamie Yeary, ed., *Reminiscences of the Boys in Gray, 1861–1865* (Dallas: Press of Wilkinson Printing, 1912), 740; Lane, *"Dear Mother,"* 121; Houghton and Houghton, *Two Boys*, 75.
5. Wiley, *Life of Johnny Reb*, 120; David R. Rice Diary, Manuscript Collection, LC; W. H. Andrews, *Footprints of a Regiment*, 77–78; John G. Barrett, ed., *Yankee Rebel: The Civil War Journal of Edmund DeWitt Patterson* (Chapel Hill: University of North Carolina Press, 1966), 64–65; King, *Sound of Drums*, 93; J. C. Andrews, *The South Reports the War*, 199; *Charleston (S.C.) Daily Courier*, 3 Sept. 1862; W. H. Andrews, "Tige Anderson's Brigade at Sharpsburg," *Confederate Veteran* 16 (1908): 578; Piston, *Lee's Tarnished Lieutenant*, 27–28; Fogle to parents, 28 Sept. 1862; Standard, *Columbus, Georgia*, 32; Helen Elize Terrill, *History of Stewart County, Georgia* (Columbus, Ga.: Columbus Supply, 1958): 276; Houghton, *Two Boys*, 66, 164–65; Thomas W. Cutrer, ed., *Longstreet's Aide: The Civil War Letters of Major Thomas J. Goree* (Charlottesville: University Press of Virginia, 1995), 98; Robertson, *Stonewall Jackson*, 586; E. M. Thomas, *Robert E. Lee*, 259.
6. Fogle to parents, 28 Sept. 1862.
7. *O.R.*, vol. XIX, ser. I, pt. 2: 597.
8. Dowdey and Manarin, *Wartime Papers of R. E. Lee*, 288–89; J. C. Andrews, *The South Reports the War*, 206; Wert, *Longstreet*, 182–83, 187–88; Lane, *"Dear Mother,"* 181; Robertson, *Stonewall Jackson*, 479–84, 591–95; Piston, *Lee's Tarnished Lieutenant*, 24–25; E. M. Thomas, *Robert E. Lee*, 258.
9. Robertson, *Stonewall Jackson*, 593.
10. Dowdey and Manarin, *Wartime Papers of R. E. Lee*, 289; Stephen W. Sears, *George B. McClellan: The Young Napoleon* (New York: Ticknor and Fields, 1988), 111, 294, 449–51, 453–57, 461; Wert, *Longstreet*, 183–84, 190–93, 201; Lee Barron and Barbara Barron, *The History of Sharpsburg* (Sharpsburg, Md.: privately printed, 1972), 47, 58; Schildt, *Drums along the Antietam*, 39; Bridges, *Lee's Maverick General*, 115–16; Lee, *General Lee*, 207–10; E. M. Thomas, *Robert E. Lee*, 258–59; Perry, *Conceived in Liberty*, 131.

11.    Sears, *McClellan,* 302–3; Wert, *Longstreet,* 184–88, 201; Barbara W. Tuchman, *The March of Folly: From Troy to Vietnam* (New York: Alfred A. Knopf, 1984), 25; *O.R.,* vol. XIX, ser. I, pt. 2: 281.

12.    Lee, *General Lee,* 207.

13.    Bridges, *Lee's Maverick General,* 91–93; Lokey Typescript; Albert B. Ross Diary, Manuscript Department, New York Historical Society, New York (cited hereafter as NYHS); Krick, *Lee's Colonels,* 326; E. M. Thomas, *Robert E. Lee,* 258.

14.    Duggan to *Central Georgian,* 14 Oct. 1862; Henry L. Benning, "Notes by General H. L. Benning on the Battle of Sharpsburg," (cited hereafter as "Notes on Sharpsburg") *Southern Historical Society Papers* 16 (1888): 393; Wert, *Longstreet,* 181–83; B. Davis, *Gray Fox,* 136; *O.R.,* vol. XIX, ser. I, pt. 1: 888; Bridges, *Lee's Maverick General,* 91–93; *O.R.,* vol LI, ser. I, pt. 1: 161; Ross Diary; E. M. Thomas, *Robert E. Lee,* 258, 261.

15.    Dowdey and Manarin, *Wartime Papers of R. E. Lee,* 289–90; Sears, *McClellan,* 116–17, 463; Wert, *Longstreet,* 182–84; Bridges, *Lee's Maverick General,* 100–114.

16.    Waddell to Sarah, 1 Oct. 1862.

17.    File of Dispositions of Toombs's Georgia Brigade, ANMPA; Carmen Battle of Antietam Manuscript; John M. Priest, *Antietam: The Soldiers' Battle* (Shippensburg, Pa.: White Mane Publishing, 1989), 218–19; Freeman, *Lee's Lieutenants,* 2: 217; Sears, *McClellan,* 296–97, 463–66; 20th Georgia Infantry File; B. Davis, *Gray Fox,* 141; *O.R.,* vol. XIX, ser. I, pt. 1: 888–89; Alexander, *Fighting for the Confederacy,* 146–47; James I. Robertson Jr., *General A. P. Hill: The Story of a Confederate Warrior* (New York: Vintage Books, 1992), 140–41; Terrill, *History of Stewart County,* 1: 276; *O.R.,* vol. LI, ser. I, pt. 1: 161–62; Ezra A. Carmen Collection of Antietam Battlefield Maps, ANMPA; Waddell Papers; Lokey Typescript; *O.R.,* vol. LI, ser. I, pt. 1: 161, 168; Ross Diary; A. Wilson Greene, "The Bridge and Beyond: Ambrose Burnside and the Ninth Corps at Antietam," *Civil War: The Magazine of the Civil War Society* 9 (June 1987): 66–67; Houghton and Houghton, *Two Boys,* 58, 70, 78–79, 124–25; Lee, *General Lee,* 208.

18.    Isaac W. Heysinger, *Antietam and the Maryland and Virginia Campaigns of 1862* (New York: Neale Publishing, 1912) 106.

19.    *O.R.,* vol. LI, ser. I, pt. 1: 160–61.

20.    Ibid., vol. XIX, ser. I, pt. 1: 889; Carmen Battlefield Maps.

21.    Benning, "Notes on Sharpsburg," 393; Houghton and Houghton, *Two Boys,* 76, 78; Carmen Battle of Antietam Manuscript; Lane, *"Dear Mother,"* 177; Krick, *Lee's Colonels,* 197; Terrill, *History of Stewart County,* 1: 277–78; Carmen Battlefield Maps; William R. Holmes File, Bruce S. Allardice Collection, Des Plaines, Il.; John William Hudson Map, Letter to Sophy, 15 Oct. 1862, Western Maryland Room, Washington County Free Library, Hagerstown, Md.

22.    Derry, "Georgia," 395–96; Jon L. Wakelyn, *Biographical Dictionary of the Confederacy* (Westport, Conn.: Greenwood Press, 1977), 98; Allen Johnson, ed., *Dictionary of American Biography* (New York: Charles Scribner's Sons, 1985), 1: 202–3; Phillips, *Life of Robert Toombs,* 53; Henry L. Benning File, U.S. Army Infantry Center and Museum, Fort Benning, Ga.; Standard, *Columbus, Georgia,* 21–22; Houghton and Houghton, *Two Boys,* 60, 79.

23.    Emory M. Thomas, *The Confederate Nation, 1861–1865* (New York: Harper and Row, 1979), 152; Robertson, *A. P. Hill,* 95.

24.    Derry, "Georgia," 396–97; A. J. Johnson, *Dictionary of American Biography,* 1: 203; Lokey Typescript; W. H. Andrews, *Footprints of a Regiment,* 61; Allen D. Candler,

*The Confederate Records of the State of Georgia* (Atlanta: Charles P. Byrd, State Printer, 1909), 1: 212–13, 216–17, 286–89, 330–31; Benning File; W. A. Flanagan, "Account of How Some Flags Were Captured," *Confederate Veteran* 13 (1905): 250; *Daily Constitutionalist,* 15 Oct. 1862; *O.R.,* vol. XII, ser. I, pt. 2: 580–81; Wert, *Longstreet,* 164–66; Standard, *Columbus, Georgia,* 21–22; Houghton and Houghton, *Two Boys,* 122–23, 180–81; Freehling, *Secession Debated,* xx–xxi, 115–16, 120, 126, 132, 144; Gordon C. Rhea, *The Battle of the Wilderness, May 5–6, 1864* (Baton Rouge: Louisiana State University Press, 1994), 303–4; Klein, *Days of Defiance,* 24.

25. Henry McCauley to George W. Randolph, 23 June 1862, Henry L. Benning Papers, Southern Historical Collection, University of North Carolina Library (cited hereafter as UNCL), Chapel Hill; Carmen Battle of Antietam Manuscript; Chris M. Calkins, *The Battles of Appomattox Station and Appomattox Court House, April 8–9, 1865* (Lynchburg, Va.: Howard Publishing, 1987), 106.

26. Calkins, *Appomattox Station,* 106; Robert E. Lee to Robert Toombs, 13 July 1862, Benning Papers; Waddell to Sarah, 1 Oct. 1862, Waddell Papers.

27. Waddell Papers; Glenn Tucker, *High Tide at Gettysburg: The Campaign in Pennsylvania* (New York: Bobbs-Merrill, 1958), 390.

28. Tucker, *High Tide at Gettysburg,* 390; Waddell to Sarah, 26 Jan. and 12 Feb. 1862, Waddell Papers.

29. Carmen Battle of Antietam Manuscript; Priest, *Antietam,* 218; "New Commander of the Georgia Division," *Confederate Veteran* 12 (April 1904): 150–51; Derry, "Georgia," 123–24; Carmen Battlefield Maps; William Walker and Robert Houston, *The War in Nicaragua* (Tucson: University of Arizona Press, 1985), 1–12; Constance Pendleton, ed., *Confederate Memoirs: Early Life and Family History: William Frederic Pendleton* (Bryn Athyn, Pa.: privately printed, 1957), 7, 11–28, 31, 33, 35, 39, 66; *O.R.,* vol. XIX, ser. I, pt. 1: 889; Derry, "Georgia," 190; Krick, *Lee's Colonels,* 219, 252, 303; *O.R.,* vol. LI, ser. I, pt. 1: 167; Rossiter Johnson, *Campfires and Battlefields: A Pictorial Narrative of the Civil War* (New York: Civil War Press, 1967), 180; *O.R.,* vol. LI, ser. I, pt. 1: 166.

30. *O.R.,* vol. XIX, ser. I, pt. 1: 889; "The Burke Sharpshooters," 464; Emory M. Thomas, *Bold Dragon: The Life of J. E. B. Stuart* (New York: Vintage Books, 1988), 219–31, 236.

31. Priest, *Antietam,* 218; Miscellaneous Papers, Micah Jenkins Papers, South Caroliniana Library, Columbia; William James Rivers, *Rivers' Account of the Raising of Troops in South Carolina for State and Confederate Service, 1861–1865* (Columbia, S.C.: Bryan Printing, State Printers, 1899), 36–37; Burke Davis, *Our Incredible Civil War* (New York: Ballantine Books, 1974), 148; John P. Thomas, *Career and Character of General Micah Jenkins, C.S.A.* (Columbia, S.C.: State, 1908), 3–17; Compiled Service Records of Soldiers Who Served in Organizations from the State of South Carolina (cited hereafter as CSRSC), NA; Derry, "South Carolina," in *Confederate Military History,* 51–54, 63, 70–72, 134, 430–31, 531–32, 579, 914; James A. Hoyt, *The Palmetto Riflemen: Historical Sketch* (Greenville, S.C.: Hoyt and Keys, 1886), 29–30, 37, 59; Jenkins to wife, 18 June, 11, July, 7, 13, 24 Aug. 1862, Jenkins Papers; Palmetto Sharpshooters File, ANMPA; W. H. Andrews, *Footprints of a Regiment,* 58; Krick, *Lee's Colonels,* 35, 223; *O.R.,* vol. LI, ser. I, pt. 1: 166; James K. Swisher, *Prince of Edisto: Brigadier General Micah Jenkins, C.S.A.* (Berryville: Rockbridge Publishing, 1996), 1, 4, 10–14, 34–40, 43, 48–55, 67–69, 74–75; James T. Baldwin III, *The Eagle Struck: A Biography of Brigadier General Micah Jenkins: A History of the Fifth South Carolina Volunteers and the Palmetto*

*Sharpshooters* (Shippensburg, Pa.: White Mane Publishing, 1996), 25, 90–145, 154–60, 174, 236.

32.  Benning, "Notes on Sharpsburg," 393; Theodore Fogle to parents, 28 Sept. 1862; John W. Hudson to Sophy, 15 Oct. 1862, Western Maryland Room, Washington County Free Library, Hagerstown, Md. (cited hereafter WCFL); Henry Kyd Douglas, *I Rode With Stonewall* (Greenwich, Conn.: Fawcett Publications, 1961). 13, 170; Carmen Battlefield Maps; Gallagher, *Antietam: Essays*, 42–44; *O.R.*, vol. XIX, ser. I pt.I: 888–89; Hunter, "Battle of Antietam," 40; CSRG; Lane, *"Dear Mother,"* xxiii; Thomas Munford to E. Carmen, Ezra A. Carmen Letters, Carmen Collection, Manuscript and Rare Book Section, 10 Dec. 1894, New York Public Library, (cited hereafter as NYPL); *O.R.* vol. LI, ser. I, pt. I: 162, 168; Houghton and Houghton, *Two Boys*, 165.

33.  Carmen Battle of Antietam Manuscript; CSRSC; Priest, *Antietam*, 218; King, *Georgia Voices* 273; Allen, *The Army of Northern Virginia*, 428; "The Burke Sharpshooters," 464–66; *O.R.*, vol. XIX, ser. I, pt. I: 273, 889; Heysinger, *Antietam*, 106; Lane, *"Dear Mother,"* 273; *O.R.*, vol. LI, ser. I, pt. I: 162.

34.  Wise, *The Long Arm of Lee*, 1: 278–81; Herman Hattaway, *General Stephen D. Lee* (Jackson: University Press of Mississippi, 1976), 51.

35.  Wise, *The Long Army of Lee*, 1: 93–94; Compiled Service Records of Confederate Soldiers Who Served in Organizations from the State of Louisiana (cited hereafter as CSRL), NA; William M. Owen, *In Camp and Battle with the Washington Artillery of New Orleans* (Boston: Griffith-Stillings Press, 1903), 3–5, 21–22, 27–28, 52, 71–73, 89, 120–26, 135–36; J.C. Andrews, *The South Reports the War*, 71; Squires Transcripts; Washington Artillery File, ANMPA; Alexander, *Fighting for the Confederacy*, 153; Webb Garrison, *A Treasury of Civil War Tales* (New York: Ballantine Books, 1988), 37; Carl Moneyhon and Bobby Roberts, *Portraits of Conflict: A Photographic History of Louisiana in the Civil War* (Fayetteville: University of Arkansas Press, 1990), 24, 79.

36.  Squires Transcripts; *O.R.*, vol. XIX, ser. I, pt. I: 889; Curt Johnson and Richard C. Anderson, Jr., *Artillery Hell: The Employment of Artillery at Antietam* (College Station: Texas A & M University Press, 1995), 5–7. *O.R.*, vol. XIX, ser. I, pt. I: 889.

37.  *O.R.* vol. XIX, ser. I, pt. I: 849–50, 891; CSRL; Moneyhon and Roberts, *Portraits of Conflict*, 46.

38.  Antietam Files, ANMPA; Wise, *The Long Arm of Lee*, l: 281, 285; *O.R.*, vol. XIX, ser. I, pt. I: 889–90; Priest, *Antietam*, 218; John W. Schildt, *The Ninth Corps at Antietam* (Chewsville, Md.: privately printed, 1988), 104; Carmen Battlefield Maps; *O.R.*, vol. XIX, ser. I, pt. I: 889–90; Hattaway, *General Stephen D. Lee*, 46–50.

39.  *O.R.*, vol. XIX, ser. I, pt.I: 889.

40.  David T. Cottingham, *Bridges: Our Legacy in Stone* (Washington County, Md.: Washington County Board of County Commissioners, 1977), 1–5, 16; CSRG; Carmen Battle of Antietam Manuscript; Barron and Barron, *The History of Sharpsburg*, 54–56; John W. Schildt, *Drums along The Antietam*, 20; Helen Ashe Hays, *The Antietam and Its Bridges: The Annals of an Historic Stream* (New York: G. P. Putnam's Sons, 1910), 75.

## CHAPTER FIVE

1.  Wise, *The Long Arm of Lee*, 1: 294; Charles F. Walcott, *History of the 21st Massachusetts Volunteers in the War for the Preservation of the Union* (Boston: Houghton, Mifflin, 1882), 200; Freeman, *Lee's Lieutenants*, 2: 217–218; CSRG; Schildt, *The Ninth*

*Corps at Antietam*, 104; Carmen Battle of Antietam Manuscript; Lokey Typescript; *O.R.*, vol. LI, ser. I, pt. I: 162, 165; Houghton and Houghton, *Two Boys*, 60; Leckie, *None Died in Vain*, 383.

2. Fogle to parents, 24 April 1861; CSRG; *O.R.*, vol. XIX, ser. I, pt. I: 418; Lee, *General Lee*, 208.

3. *O.R.*, vol. XIX, ser. I, pt. I: 418–19, 885–87, 889–90; *O.R.*, vol. LI, ser. I, pt. I: 162, 168; Ross Diary; Houghton and Houghton, *Two Boys*, 78; Cutrer, *Longstreet's Aide*, 95, 100; John Cannan, *The Antietam Campaign: August-September 1862*, (Conshohocken, Pa.: Combined Publishing, 1994), 113–115.

4. Stovall, *Robert Toombs*, 270; Phillips, *The Life of Robert Toombs*, 219; CSRG; Josephine Mellichamp, *Senators From Georgia* (Huntsville, Ala.: Strode Publishers, 1976), 139.

5. Bridges, *Lee's Maverick General*, 85; Toombs Papers, DUL; Toombs Papers, UGL.

6. Alan T. Nolan, *Lee Considered: General Robert E. Lee and Civil War History* (Chapel Hill: University of North Carolina Press, 1991), 81–103; Stovall, *Robert Toombs*, 240–41, 246; John Cannan, *The Antietam Campaign*, 127.

7. *O.R.*, vol. LI, ser. I, pt. I: 162.

8. Schildt, *The Ninth Corps At Antietam*, 98; Carmen Battle of Antietam Manuscript; *O.R.*, vol. LI, ser. I, pt. I, 161–62.

9. Mellichamp, *Senators From Georgia*, 139; Wert, *Longstreet*, 194–95; GCSR, NA; *O.R.*, vol. XIX, ser. I, pt. I, 419, 849–50, 889–90; Carmen Battle of Antietam Manuscript, LC; *O.R.*, vol. LI, ser. I, pt. I, 162; Ross Diary, NYHS; Houghton and Houghton, *Two Boys*, 78.

10. *O.R.*, vol. XIX, ser. I, pt. II, 272, 314; CGSR, NA; *O.R.*, vol. XIX, ser. I, pt. I: 423, 424, 889–90.

11. *O.R.*, vol. XIX, ser. I, pt. I: 423, 424, 889–90.

12. Carmen Battle of Antietam Manuscript; William Marvel, *Burnside* (Chapel Hill: University of North Carolina Press, 1991), 111–12; Robert Underwood Johnson and Clarance C. Buel, eds., *Battles and Leaders of the Civil War*, (New York: Thomas Yoseloff, 1956), 2: 649; Bruce Catton, *The Army of the Potomac: Mr. Lincoln's Army* (Garden City, N.Y.: Doubleday, 1962), 255–57; Sears, *McClellan*, 297–98; Schildt, *The Ninth Corps at Antietam*, 8, 12–14; Priest, *Antietam*, 217; Fogle to parents, 28 Sept. 1862; John Michael Priest, ed., *Captain Wren's Civil War Diary: From New Bern to Fredericksburg* (New York: Berkley Books, 1991), 87; Stephen W. Sears, *Landscrape Turned Red: The Battle of Antietam* (New York: Warner Books, 1983), 258–59; Sears, *McClellan*, 25, 58, 61–62, 85, 133–34, 178, 260, 269–70, 297, 310, 324, 335, 382, 394–95, 397, 407, 436, 461, 520–21; John Michael Priest, *Before Antietam: The Battle of South Mountain* (New York: Oxford University Press, 1996), 215–16; William F. McConnell, *Remember Reno: A Biography of Major General Jesse Lee Reno* (Shippensburg, Pa.: White Mane Publishing, 1996), 81; Ari Hoogenboom, *Rutherford B. Hayes* (Lawrence: University of Kansas Press, 1995), 128.

13. Sears, *McClellan*, 20, 26, 36.

14. Geoffrey Regan, *Great Military Disasters: A Historical Survey of Military Incompetence* (New York: M. Evans and Company, 1987), 26–28; Carmen Battle of Antietam Manuscript; Marvel, *Burnside*, 130–35; Sears, *McClellan*, 69, 244–45, 332.

15. Carmen Battle of Antietam Manuscript; Priest, *Antietam*, 217–18; Schildt, *The Ninth Corps at Antietam*, 98; Wert, *Longstreet*, 194–95; Barron and Barron, *The History of Sharpsburg*, 54; CSRG; *O.R.*, vol. XIX, ser. I, pt. I: 419, 424–25, 890; E. Quinn letter, undated, Carmen Letters; Derry, "Georgia," 967; Marvel, *Burnside*, 135.

16. *O.R.*, vol. XIX, ser. I, pt. I: 890; Carmen Battle of Antietam Manuscript.

17. Carmen Battle of Antietam Manuscript; Priest, *Antietam*, 218.

18. Lokey Typescript.

19. Carmen Battle of Antietam Manuscript; Jay Luvass and Haróld W. Nelson, *The U.S. Army War College Guide to the Battle of Antietam: The Maryland Campaign of 1862* (New York: Harper and Row Publishers, 1987), 222–23; R. U. Johnson and Buel, *Battles and Leaders of the Civil War*, 2: 650; Marvel, *Burnside*, 129, 137–38; Schildt, *The Ninth Corps at Antietam*, 15; *Norristown (Pa.) National Defender*, 18 Nov. 1862; *O.R.*, vol., XIX, ser. I, pt. I: 424; Sears, *Landscape Turned Red*, 259–60; Guy R. Everson and Edward W. Simpson, Jr., *"Far, Far From Home": The Wartime Letters of Dick and Tally Simpson, Third South Carolina Volunteers*, (Oxford: Oxford University Press, 1994), 150; Robertson, *Stonewall Jackson*, 617–18.

20. Greene, "The Bridge and Beyond," 70; Sears, *McClellan*, 302–3, 306–7.

21. Sears, *McClellan*, 296–309; Schildt, *The Ninth Corps at Antietam*, 15, 19; Marvel, *Burnside*, 123–25, 129–30; Dennis Fry, interview by author, National Park Service, 19 Feb. 1991; Carmen Battle of Antietam Manuscript; Mary Elizabeth Sergent, *They Lie Forgotten: The United States Military Academy, 1856–1861*, (Middletown, N.Y.: The Prior King Press, 1986), 152–53; Barron and Barron, *The History of Sharpsburg*, 42; Eleventh Connecticut Infantry File, ANMPA; Schildt, *The Ninth Corps at Antietam*, 42; Martin F. Schmitt, ed., *General George Crook: His Autobiography* (Norman: University of Oklahoma Press, 1986), 96; Wise, *The Long Arm of Lee*, 1: 294; Heysinger, *Antietam*, 106–7; Lokey Typescript; Sears, *Landscape Turned Red*, 258–60.

22. Carmen Battle of Antietam Manuscript; Schildt, *The Ninth Corps at Antietam*, 45–46; CSRG; Edward J. Stackpole, *Drama on the Rappahannock: The Fredericksburg Campaign* (New York, N.Y.: Bonanza Books, n.d.), 61–62; Sergent, *They Lie Forgotten*, 153–54; George Bronson to family, 21 Sept. 1862; John Rouse Diary, ANMPA; R. U. Johnson and Buel, *Battles and Leaders of the Civil War*, 2: 650–51, 675; Allen, *The Army of Northern Virginia*, 429; Barron and Barron, *The History of Sharpsburg*, 31.

23. *O.R.*, vol. LI, ser. I, pt. I: 162–63.

24. Carmen Battle of Antietam Manuscript; Munford to Carmen, 10 Dec. 1894; Marvel, *Burnside*, 137–38; *O.R.*, vol. LI, ser. I, pt. I: 163; Sears, *McClellan*, 291; R. U. Johnson and Buel, *Battles and Leaders*, 2: 628.

## CHAPTER SIX

1. *O.R.*, vol. LI, ser. I, pt. I: 162; R. Johnson, *Campfires and Battlefields*, 179; Lee, *General Lee*, 209.

2. Carmen Battle of Antietam Manuscript; Schildt, *The Ninth Corps at Antietam*, 45–46; Rouse Diary; Marvel, *Burnside*, 135; Derry, "Georgia," 190; Stovall, *Robert Toombs*, 245; Sears, *Landscape Turned Red*, 145.

3. Carmen Battle of Antietam Manuscript; Priest, *Antietam*, 221–22; Schildt, *The Ninth Corps at Antietam*, 45–46, 104–105; Eleventh Connecticut File; Rouse Diary; *O.R.*, vol. LI, ser. I, pt. I: 162.

4. Carmen Battle of Antietam Manuscript; Schildt, *The Ninth Corps at Antietam*, 105–106; *O.R.*, vol. LI, ser. I, pt. I: 162.

5. Carmen Battle of Antietam Manuscript; Schildt, *The Ninth Corps at Antietam*, 45–46; Priest, *Antietam*, 219; Rouse Diary; E. Quinn letter, undated, Box 3, Carmen Letters; *O.R.*, vol. XIX, ser. l, pt. I: 418–19, 473; Marvel, *Burnside*, 130, 135;

*O.R.*, vol. LI, ser. I, pt. I: 162–63; Fogle to parents, 28 Oct. 1862; Martin F. Schmitt, *General George Crook*, 97–98; *National Defender*, 18 Nov. 1862.

6. Carmen Battle of Antietam Manuscript; Priest, *Antietam*, 218–20.

7. Carmen Battle of Antietam Manuscript; Schildt, *The Ninth Corps at Antietam*, 46; Priest, *Antietam*, 220; Sergent, *They Lie Forgotten*, 154–55; Rouse Diary; Stephen W. Sears, "Antietam," *Civil War Times Illustrated* 20 (April 1987): 33; *O.R.*, vol. LI, ser. I, pt. I: 163; Greene, "The Bridge and Beyond," 71.

8. Carmen Battle of Antietam Manuscript; Schildt, *The Ninth Corps at Antietam*, 46–47; Priest, *Antietam*, 220; Sergent, *They Lie Forgotten*, 155–56; 11th Connecticut File; *New Haven Connecticut War Record* Nov. 1864; Rouse Diary; Marvel, *Burnside*, 136; Owen, *In Camp and Battle*, 158; *O.R.*, vol. LI, ser. I, pt. I: 165; Sears, *McClellan*, 473.

9. Carmen Battle of Antietam Manuscript; Priest, *Antietam*, 220; 11th Connecticut File; CSRG; *Augusta (Ga.) Daily Constitutionalist*, 15 Aug. 1861; *The Daily Columbus Enquirer*, 22 Sept. 1862; *Weekly Sun*, 13 Aug. 1861; Benning, "Notes on Sharpsburg," 40; R. T. Mockbee, "Why Sharpsburg Was 'a Drawn Battle,'" *Confederate Veteran*, 16 (1908): 160; *O.R.*, vol. XIX, ser. I, pt. I: 890; *O.R.*, vol. LI, ser. I, pt. I: 163.

10. Carmen Battle of Antietam Manuscript; Hall Diary; Derry, "Georgia," 190; CSRG; Fogle to parents, 28 Sept. 1862; Heysinger, *Antietam*, 105–6; Munford to Carmen, 10 Dec. 1894.

11. Carmen Battle of Antietam Manuscript; 11th, 28th, and 36th Ohio Infantry Files, ANMPA; *O.R.*, vol. XIX, ser. I, pt. I: 416, 419, 816, 823, 914; *Antietam: Report of the Ohio Antietam Battlefield Commission* (Springfield, Ohio: Springfield Publishing, 1904), 71–72, 83; R. U. Johnson and Buel, *Battles and Leaders of the Civil War*, 2: 651; Longstreet, *From Manassas to Appomattox*, 256–58; Schildt, *The Ninth Corps at Antietam*, 17–18, 51–54, 76–77; Sears, *Landscape Turned Red*, 263; Sears, *McClellan*, xii, 5.

12. Carmen Battle of Antietam Manuscript; *O.R.*, vol. XIX, ser. I, pt. I: 450–54, 471–72; Priest, *Antietam*, 220–22; Sears, *Landscape Turned Red*, 291; Schildt, *The Ninth Corps at Antietam*, 103; Munford to Carmen, 10 Dec. 1894.

13. Carmen Battle of Antietam Manuscript; R. U. Johnson and Buel, *Battles and Leaders of the Civil War*, 2: 651–53; Sears, *Landscape Turned Red*, 263, 290–91; CSRG; *O.R.*, vol. XIX, ser. I, pt. I: 424–25, 462–63, 473–74; Marvel, *Burnside*, 135–36.

14. Carmen Battle of Antietam Manuscript; *O.R.*, vol. XIX, ser. I, pt. I: 472; CSRG; James V. Murfin, *The Gleam of Bayonets,* (New York: Curtis Books, 1965), 265–66; George Crook Papers, U. S. Army Military History Institute, Carlisle, Pa.

15. Carmen Battle of Antietam Manuscript; Murfin, *The Gleam of Bayonets* 266; Sears, *Landscape Turned Red*, 263; Sears, *McClellan*, 291–92; Marvel, *Burnside*, 131–32, 136; Schildt, *The Ninth Corps at Antietam*, 14; CSRG; Robertson, *Stonewall Jackson*, 617–18.

16. Carmen Battle of Antietam Manuscript; Carmen Battlefield Maps; Greene, "The Bridge and Beyond," 70; Marvel, *Burnside*, 137–38.

17. Carmen Battle of Antietam Manuscript; Heysinger, *Antietam*, 108; Schildt, *Drums along The Antietam*, 132–33, 208; Murfin, *The Gleam of Bayonets*, 263–65; Sears, *Landscape Turned Red*, 291–92; John W. Schildt, *September Echoes: The Maryland Campaign of 1862: The Places, the Battles, the Results*, (Middletown, Md.: Valley Register Publishers, 1960), 89–91; Marvel, *Burnside*, 132–35; Schildt, *The Ninth Corps at Antietam*, 15–16, 106; Priest, *Captain Wren's Civil War Diary*, 4, 27; *O.R.*, vol.

XIX, ser. I, pt. I: 446; C. Johnson and Anderson, *Artillery Hell*, 114; Marvel, *Burnside*, 137–38; Cannan, *The Antietam Campaign*, 187.

18.  Carmen Battle of Antietam Manuscript; Walcott, *History of the 21st Massachusetts Volunteers*, 200.

19.  Priest, *Captain Wren's Civil War Diary*, 9, 26, 36–37, 42, 68–70.

20.  Ibid., 14, 35.

21.  Carmen Battle of Antietam Manuscript; Compiled Service Records of Union Soldiers Who Served in Organizations from the State of Maryland (cited hereafter as CSRM), NA; Schildt, *The Ninth Corps at Antietam*, 30; Second Maryland Infantry File, ANMPA; Priest, *Antietam*, 221–23; Harold R. Manakee, *Maryland in the Civil War* (Baltimore: Maryland Historical Society, 1968), 110–11; Theodore Dimon, "A Federal Surgeon at Sharpsburg," ed. James I. Robertson, Jr., *Civil War History,* 6 (June 1960): 140; *O.R.*, vol. XIX, ser. I, pt. I: 444.

22.  CSRM; 2nd Maryland Infantry File.

23.  Carmen Battle of Antietam Manuscript; 6th New Hampshire Infantry File, ANMPA; Compiled Service Records of Union Soldiers Who Served in Organizations from the State of New Hampshire (cited hereafter as CSRNH), NA; Schildt, *The Ninth Corps at Antietam*, 30–32; Marvel, *Burnside*, 136; Dimon, "A Federal Surgeon at Sharpsburg," 141; *O.R.*, vol. XIX, ser. I, pt. I: 430.

24.  Carmen Battle of Antietam Manuscript; Priest, *Antietam*, 225; Dimon, "A Federal Surgeon at Sharpsburg," 134–41; Sears, *Landscape Turned Red*, 292; Marvel, *Burnside*, 136.

25.  Carmen Battle of Antietam Manuscript; Priest, *Antietam*, 225; CSRM; 2nd Maryland File; Marvel, *Burnside*, 136–37; John Cannan, *The Antietam Campaign*, 187–88.

26.  Carmen Battle of Antietam Manuscript; Lane, *"Dear Mother,"* 276; Marvel, *Burnside*, 136–37; Cannan, *The Antietam Campaign*, 187–88.

27.  Carmen Battle of Antietam Manuscript; Priest, *Antietam*, 225; 2nd Maryland File; CSRM; Dimon, "A Federal Surgeon at Sharpsburg," 141; Sears, *Landscrape Turned Red*, 292; Lane, *"Dear Mother,"* xiv; Derry, "Georgia," 523–24, 1052–53; Fogle to parents, 28 Sept. 1862; Marvel, *Burnside*, 136–37; Frank Moore, ed., *The Rebellion Record*, (New York: n.p., 1862–68), 5: 473; Dimon, "A Federal Surgeon at Sharpsburg," 143; R. U. Johnson and Buel, *Battles and Leaders of the Civil War*, 2: 652; ; Joseph Mills Hanson, Report on the Employment of the Artillery at the Battle of Antietam, ANMPA, 39–40; *O.R.*, vol. XIX, ser. I, pt. I: 419.

28.  Carmen Battle of Antietam Manuscript; Dimon, "A Federal Surgeon at Antietam," 141; Marvel, *Burnside*, 136–37; Cannan, *The Antietam Campaign*, 187–88.

29.  Cannan, *The Antietam Campaign*, 187–88; Carmen Battle of Antietam Manuscript; Sears, *Landscape Turned Red*, 292–93; Marvel, *Burnside*, 136–37; Cannan, *The Antietam Campaign*, 187–88.

30.  Carmen Battle of Antietam Manuscript; CSRG; Fogle to parents, 28 Sept. 1862; Lyman Jackson, *History of the Sixth New Hampshire Regiment in the War for the Union* (Concord, N.H.: Republican Press Association, 1891), 103–104; William Marvel, *Race of the Soil: The Ninth New Hampshire Regiment in the Civil War* (Wilmington, N. C.: Broadfoot Publishing, 1988), 4–5, 16, 18, 41–43, 90; Cannan, *The Antietam Campaign*, 187–88.

31.  Carmen Battle of Antietam Manuscript; Marvel, *Burnside*, 136–37; Sears, *Landscape Turned Red*, 292–93; Schildt, *The Ninth Corps at Antietam*, 125; Priest, *Antietam*, 227; Marvel, *Race of the Soil*, 53–56.

32. Carmen Battle of Antietam Manuscript; Milo M. Quaife, introduction to *Civil War Letters of General Alpheus S. Williams: From The Cannon's Mouth,* (Detroit: Wayne State University Press and Detroit Historical Society, 1959), 134–35.

33. Henry Pleasants, Jr. *The Tragedy of the Crater,* (Philadelphia: Eastern National Park and Monument Association, 1975), 17.

34. Carmen Battle of Antietam Manuscript; Marvel, *Burnside,* 136–37; Moore, *The Rebellion Record,* 5: 474; Luvass and Nelson, *The U.S. Army War College Guide to the Battle of Antietam,* xi; Perry D. Jamieson, *Death in September: The Antietam Campaign* (Fort Worth: Ryan Place Publishers, 1995), 91; R. U. Johnson and Buel, *Battles and Leaders of the Civil War,* 2: 679; Robertson, *Stonewall Jackson,* 617–18.

35. Robertson, *A. P. Hill,* 141–43; Carmen Battle of Antietam Manuscript.

36. McWhiney and Jamieson, *Attack and Die,* 1–24.

## CHAPTER SEVEN

1. W. H. Andrews, *Footprints of a Regiment,* 61; Levi Bolton Family Papers, Richard A. Plotts, Newtown Square, Pa.; Priest, *Antietam,* 225–27; Murfin, *The Gleam of Bayonets,* 266; Schmitt, *General George Crook,* 97; *Atlanta Southern Confederacy,* 9 Oct. 1862; Carmen Battle of Antietam Manuscript; *O.R.,* vol. LI, ser. I, pt. I: 163; Sears, ed., *McClellan,* 243, 340, 467; Cannan, *The Antietam Campaign,* 188.

2. Carmen Battle of Antietam Manuscript; Priest, *Captain Wren's Civil War Diary,* 89.

3. *O.R.,* vol. XIX, ser. I, pt. I: 446–47; Marvel, *Race of the Soil,* 55–57; Carmen Battle of Antietam Manuscript.

4. Carmen Battle of Antietam Manuscript; Priest, *Antietam,* 225–27; Marvel, *Burnside,* 137–38; *O.R.,* vol. XIX, ser. I, pt. I: 419, 436, 450–53, 455–56.

5. Henry Steele Commager, *The Blue and the Gray* (New York: Fairfax Press, 1982), 1: 226; Carmen Battle of Antietam Manuscript; *National Defender,* 18 Nov. 1862; *O.R.,* vol. XIX, ser. I, pt. I: 419, 437.

6. Marvel, *Burnside,* 139; Priest, *Antietam,* 227; Schildt, *The Ninth Corps at Antietam,* 16; Carmen Battle of Antietam Manuscript; 51st New York Infantry File, ANMPA; Sears, *Landscape Turned Red,* 394; *National Defender,* 18 Nov. 1862; *O.R.,* vol, XIX, ser. I, pt. I: 443–44, 448–49; Cannan, *The Antietam Campaign,* 188–89.

7. *O.R.,* vol. XIX, ser. I, pt. I: 444.

8. Carmen Battle of Antietam Manuscript; Schildt, *The Ninth Corps at Antietam,* 16, 40; 51st New York File; *O.R.,* vol. XIX, ser. I, pt. I: 444–45.

9. A. M. Gambone, *Major-General John Frederick Hartranft: Citizen Soldier and Pennsylvania Statesman* (Baltimore: Butternut and Blue, 1995), ii, 2–3, 37; William J. Miller, *The Training of an Army: Camp Curtin and the North's Civil War* (Shippensburg, Pa.: White Mane Publishing, 1990), 56, 124.

10. Murfin, *The Gleam of Bayonets,* 267; Levi Bolton Family Papers; Thomas H. Parker, *History of the 51st Regiment of Pennsylvania Volunteers* (Philadelphia: King and Baird Printers, 1869), 37; Priest, *Captain Wren's Civil War Diary,* 29; Gambone, *Hartranft,* 2–3; W. J. Miller, *The Training of an Army,* 64–65, 124.

11. Harry Roach, "John F. Hartranft: Defender of the Union," *Military Images* 4 (Jan.-Feb. 1982): 4; Gambone, *Hartranft,* iv, 2–9, 12, 18–33, 37.

12. Carmen Battle of Antietam Manuscript; Murfin, *The Gleam of Bayonets,* 267; 51st New York File; 51st Pennsylvania Infantry File, ANMPA; *O.R.,* vol. XIX, ser. I, pt. I: 444, 886; 21st Massachusetts Infantry File, ANMPA; 35th Massachusetts Infantry File, ANMPA; John W. Hudson to Sophy, Oct. 1862; John B. Stickney to family, 28

Sept. 1862, Clinton H. Haskell Collection, Western Maryland Room, WCFL; Charles Hawes to Maria, 17 Sept. 1892, ANMPA; Greene, "The Bridge and Beyond," 72.

13. John W. Hudson to Sophy, 15 Oct. 1862; Carmen Battle of Antietam Manuscript; Cannan, *The Antietam Campaign*, 189.

14. Cannan, *The Antietam Campaign*, 189; *National Defender*, 18 Nov. 1862.

15. *National Defender*, 18 Nov. 1862.

16. *National Defender*, 18 Nov. 1862; Schildt, *The Ninth Corps at Antietam*, 16; Carmen Battle of Antietam Manuscript; Priest, *Antietam*, 257.

17. Priest, *Antietam*, 257.

18. Priest, *Antietam*, 257.

19. Schildt, *The Ninth Corps at Antietam*, 107; *National Defender*, 14 Oct. and 18 Nov. 1862; Friends of the Pennsylvania 51st Infantry Regiment Veteran Volunteers Collection, Norristown, Pa.; William T. Parsons, ed., *Pennsylvania Soldier Life, 1861–65* (Huntingdon, Pa.: Juniata College, 1986), 58, 66, 70–71, 74, 76; Roach, "Hartranft," 5; Gambone, *Hartranft*, 45–50, 54–55, 63; Cannan, *The Antietam Campaign*, 189.

20. Cannan, *The Antietam Campaign*, 189; Carmen Battle of Antietam Manuscript; *National Defender*, 14 Oct. 1862; Friends of the Pennsylvania 51st Infantry Regiment Veteran Volunteers Collection; John L. Smith to Mary, 29 Sept. 1862; Parsons, *Pennsylvania Soldier Life*, 80.

21. Carmen Battle of Antietam Manuscript; *National Defender*, 18 Nov. 1862.

22. *National Defender*, 18 Nov. 1862.

23. Carmen Battle of Antietam Manuscript; Munford to Carmen, 10 and 16 Dec. 1894; Marvel, *Burnside*, 137–38; *National Defender*, 18 Nov. 1862; *O.R.*, vol., XIX, ser. I, pt. I: 451; Robertson, *Stonewall Jackson*, 115; Freeman, *Lee's Lieutenants*, 2: 4, 127; Cannan, *The Antietam Campaign*, 188–89.

24. Cannan, *The Antietam Campaign*, 188–89; Carmen Battle of Antietam Manuscript; Murfin, *The Gleam of Bayonets*, 267; R. U. Johnson and Buel, *Battles and Leaders of the Civil War*, 2: 651–52; Parker, *History of the 51st Regiment of Pennsylvania Volunteers*, 232–39; *O.R.*, vol. LI, ser. I, pt. I: 163; Cannan, *The Antietam Campaign*, 189.

25. GSRG; Carmen Battle of Antietam Manuscript; Parker, *History of the 51st Regiment of Pennsylvania Volunteers*, 232–39; *Southern Confederacy*, 9 Oct. 1862; Parsons, *Pennsylvania Soldier Life*, 80; Gambone, *Hartranft*, 6–7, 52–53.

26. Toombs Papers, UGL; Sears, *Landscape Turned Red*, 42–52, 294; Carmen Battle of Antietam Manuscript; Houghton and Houghton, *Two Boys*, 79; Robertson, *Stonewall Jackson*, 617–18.

27. *National Defender*, 18 Nov. 1862; Parsons, *Pennsylvania Soldier Life*, 52, 79; Sears, *McClellan*, 5.

28. Sears, *McClellan*, 5.

29. Hudson to Sophy, 15 Oct. 1862; Murfin, *The Gleam of Bayonets*, 267–68; Marvel, *Burnside*, 139; Sears, *Landscape Turned Red*, 294; Carmen Battle of Antietam Manuscript; *National Defender*, 14 Oct. and 18 Nov. 1862.

30. *National Defender*, 14 Oct. and 18 Nov. 1862; Parker, *History of the 51st Regiment of Pennsylvania Volunteers*, 232–39; Fogle to parents, 28 Sept. 1862; Carmen Battle of Antietam Manuscript.

31. Terrill, *History of Stewart County*, 1: 278.

32. Ibid; Murfin, *The Gleam of Bayonets*, 267–68; Parker, *History of the 51st Regiment of Pennsylvania Volunteers*, 232–39; Carmen Battle of Antietam Manuscript; Compiled Service Records of Union Soldiers Who Served in Organizations from the State of

Pennsylvania (cited hereafter as CSRP), NA; *National Defender*, 14 Oct. and 18 Nov. 1862.

33. *National Defender*, 14 Oct. and 18 Nov. 1862; CSRG; Parker, *History of the 51st Regiment of Pennsylvania Volunteers*, 232–39; Fogle to parents, 28 Sept. 1862; Carmen Battle of Antietam Manuscript; Priest, *Antietam*, 236.

34. Gambone, *Hartranft*, 64.

35. Gambone, *Hartranft*, 64; Parker, *History of the 51st Regiment of Pennsylvania Volunteers*, 232–39; Fogle to parents, 28 Sept. 1862; Carmen Battle of Antietam Manuscript; *National Defender*, 14 Oct. and 18 Nov. 1862.

36. Carmen Battle of Antietam Manuscript; Stickney to family, 28 Sept. 1862, WCFL; Sears, *Landscape Turned Red*, 294.

37. Allen, *The Army of Northern Virginia*, 430; Carmen Battle of Antietam Manuscript.

38. Priest, *Captain Wren's Civil War Diary*, 89; Carmen Battle of Antietam Manuscript; *National Defender*, 14 Oct. 1862.

39. *National Defender*, 14 Oct. 1862; Parker, *History of the 51st Regiment of Pennsylvania Volunteers*, 232–39; Carmen Battle of Antietam Manuscript; O.R., vol. LI, ser. I, pt. I: 163.

40. O.R., vol. LI, ser. I, pt. I: 163; Carmen Battle of Antietam Manuscript.

41. O.R., vol. LI, ser. I, pt. I: 163; Carmen Battle of Antietam Manuscript; Priest, *Antietam*, 237; Sears, *Landscape Turned Red*, 294.

42. *National Defender*, 18 Nov. 1862; Gambone, *Hartranft*, 310–15; Sears, *Landscape Turned Red*, 294.

43. Schmitt, *General George Crook*, 98; Richard Wheeler, *Lee's Terrible Swift Sword: From Antietam to Chancellorsville: An Eyewitness History* (New York: HarperCollins, 1992), 131–32; Murfin, *The Gleam of Bayonets*, 268; R. U. Johnson and Buel, *Battles and Leaders of the Civil War*, 2: 651; Marvel, *Burnside*, 138–39; Carmen Battle of Antietam Manuscript.

44. Owen, *In Camp and Battle*, 150–52, 154; Wise, *The Long Arm of Lee*, 1: 309; Heysinger, *Antietam*, 111; Allen, *The Army of Northern Virginia*, 431; Gallagher, *Antietam*, 78; O.R., vol. XIX, ser. I, pt. I: 419, 436–37, 849–50, 889–90, 893; Carmen Battle of Antietam Manuscript; Hanson, Report on Artillery at Antietam, 6–9, 39–40; William A. Frassanito, *Antietam: The Photographic Legacy of America's Bloodiest Day* (New York: Charles Scribner's Sons, 1978), 236; Parsons, *Pennsylvania Soldier Life*, 82; *National Defender*, 18 Nov. 1862; C. Johnson and Anderson, *Artillery Hell*, 59, 114; Sears, *Landscape Turned Red*, 294.

45. O.R., vol. XIX, ser. I, pt. I: 851.

46. Wheeler, *Lee's Terrible Swift Sword*, 131; Fogle to parents, 28 Sept. 1862; *National Defender*, 18 Nov. 1862; Carmen Battle of Antietam Manuscript; R. U. Johnson and Buel, *Battles and Leaders of the Civil War*, 2: 653; Carmen Battle of Antietam Manuscript; Hudson to Sophy, 15 Oct. 1862; *Southern Confederacy*, 9 Oct. 1862; Frassanito, *Antietam*, 240–41; O.R., vol. XIX, ser. I, pt. I: 850–51; Sears, *Landscape Turned Red*, 294.

47. Carmen Battle of Antietam Manuscript; R. U. Johnson and Buel, *Battles and Leaders of the Civil War*, 2: 652–53; Fogle to parents, 28 Sept. 1862; *Southern Confederacy*, 9 Oct. 1862; Hanson, Report on Artillery at Antietam, 51; O.R., vol. XIX, ser. I, pt. I: 451–53, 850–51; Marvel, *Burnside*, 138; Sears, *Landscape Turned Red*, 263–64.

48. Marvel, *Burnside*, 138; CSRG; Fogle to parents, 28 Sept. 1862; Carmen Battle of Antietam Manuscript; Sears, *Landscape Turned Red*, 292; O.R., vol. LI, ser. I, pt. I: 162; Priest, *Antietam*, 242; O.R., vol. XIX, ser. I, pt. I: 451, 456–57, 463, 893.

49. Carmen Battle of Antietam Manuscript; Murfin, *The Gleam of Bayonets*, 269–70; Fogle to parents, 28 Sept. 1862; CSRG; Marvel, *Burnside*, 140; *O.R.*, vol, XIX, ser. I, pt. I: 888–89; Terrill, *History of Stewart County*, 1: 277–78.

50. Walcott, *History of the 21st Massachusetts Volunteers*, 200–203; Carmen Battle of Antietam Manuscript; *National Defender*, 18 Nov. 1862; Sears, *Landscape Turned Red*, 294.

51. George C. Parker, "I Feel . . . Just Like Writing You a Letter. . .," " *Civil War Times Illustrated* 16 (April 1977): 14, 17; Sears, *McClellan*, 436; Sears, *Landscape Turned Red*, 294; Carmen Battle of Antietam Manuscript.

52. *National Defender*, 18 Nov. 1862; Sears, *Landscape Turned Red*, 294; Carmen Battle of Antietam Manuscript.

53. *National Defender*, 18 Nov. 1862; Priest, *Captain Wren's Civil War Diary*, 92; Carmen Battle of Antietam Manuscript; Sears, *Landscape Turned Red*, 294.

54. *Southern Confederacy*, 9 Oct. 1862; Krick, *Lee's Colonels*, 337–38; CSRG.

55. CSRG; *O.R.*, vol. LI, ser. I, pt. I: 163; Krick, *Lee's Colonels*, 337–38.

56. *O.R.*, vol. XIX, ser. I, pt. I: 893; Carmen Battle of Antietam Manuscript.

57. Papers of the Military Historical Society of Massachusetts (Boston: Griffith-Stillings Press, 1903), 3: 66; CSRG; Marvel, *Burnside*, 140; Fogle to parents, 28 Sept. 1862; *National Defender* 18 Nov. 1862; Sears, *Landscape Turned Red*, 294–95; Terrill, *The History of Stewart County*, 1: 277–78; Carmen Battle of Antietam Manuscript.

58. Moore, *The Rebellion Record*, 5: 474; Squires Transcripts; Carmen Battle of Antietam Manuscript.

59. Terrill, *History of Stewart County*, 1: 277–78; *O.R.*, vol. LI, ser. I, pt. I: 163.

60. *O.R.*, vol. XIX, ser. I, pt. I: 890; Carmen Battle of Antietam Manuscript.

61. Carmen Battle of Antietam Manuscript; *National Defender*, 18 Nov. 1862; Sears, *Landscape Turned Red*, 294–95.

62. Sears, *McClellan*, 467.

## CHAPTER EIGHT

1. Sears, *Landscape Turned Red*, 295; Benning, "Notes on Sharpsburg," 393; Schildt, *The Ninth Corps at Antietam*, 111; Carmen Battle of Antietam Manuscript; Lokey Typescript.

2. Hudson to Sophy, 15 Oct. 1862; Carmen Battle of Antietam Manuscript; *National Defender*, 18 Nov. 1862; Sears, *Landscape Turned Red*, pp. 294–95.

3. Carmen Battle of Antietam Manuscript; *National Defender*, 18 Nov. 1862; Sears, *Landscape Turned Red*, 295.

4. Sears, *Landscape Turned Red*, 295; *National Defender*, 18 Nov. 1862; Murfin, *The Gleam of Bayonets*, 271.

5. Bolton Family Papers; Carmen Battle of Antietam Manuscript; Parker, *History of the 51st Regiment of Pennsylvania Volunteers*, 37, 232–39; Richard A. Plotts, letter to author, 11 Feb. 1995; *O.R.*, vol. LI, ser. I, pt. I: 163; Sears, *Landscape Turned Red*, 295.

6. Sears, *Landscape Turned Red*, 295; Parker, *History of the 51st Regiment of Pennsylvania Volunteers*, 232–39; *National Defender*, 18 Nov. 1862; Priest, *Antietam*, 239, 243; Carmen Battle of Antietam Manuscript.

7. Hudson to Sophy, 15 Oct. 1862; Benning, "Notes on Sharpsburg," 393; Parker, *History of the 51st Regiment of Pennsylvania Volunteers*, 232–39; CSRG; Sears, *Landscape Turned Red*, 295; Carmen Battle of Antietam Manuscript; Fogle to parents, 28 Sept. 1862.

8.   Carmen Battle of Antietam Manuscript; CSRP; *National Defender*, 14 Oct. and 18 Nov. 1862; Walcott, *History of the 21st Massachusetts Volunteers*, 200–202; Sears, *Landscape Turned Red*, 295.

9.   Parker, *History of the 51st Regiment of Pennsylvania Volunteers*, 232–35; Carmen Battle of Antietam Manuscript; Sears, *Landscape Turned Red*, 295.

10.  A Committee of the Regimental Association, *History of the Thirty-Fifth Regiment Massachusetts Volunteers, 1862-1865* (Boston: Mills, Knight and Company, 1884), 39–42; Lokey Typescript; Marvel, *Race of the Soil*, 57–58; Sears, *Landscape Turned Red*, 295; Carmen Battle of Antietam Manuscript.

11.  Benning, "Notes on Sharpsburg," 393; CSRG; Schildt, *The Ninth Corps at Antietam*, 109; Priest, *Antietam*, 239; Carmen Battle of Antietam Manuscript; Sears, *Landscape Turned Red*, 295.

12.  Sears, *Landscape Turned Red*, 295.

13.  Benning, "Notes on Sharpsburg," 393.

14.  Ibid; Fogle to parents, 28 Sept. 1862; Priest, *Antietam*, 243–45.

15.  A Committee of the Regimental Association, *History of the Thirty-Fifth Regiment*, 39–42; Carmen Battle of Antietam Manuscript.

16.  Schildt, *The Ninth Corps at Antietam*, 109; Carmen Battle of Antietam Manuscript; *National Defender*, 14 Oct. and 18 Nov. 1862; A Committee of the Regimental Association, *History of the Thirty-Fifth Regiment*, 39–42; Priest, *Antietam*, 243; Sears, *Landscape Turned Red*, 295.

17.  *National Defender*, 14 Oct. 1862; Parker, *History of the 51st Regiment of Pennsylvania Volunteers*, 232–35; Sears, *Landscape Turned Red*, 295; Carmen Manuscript, LC.

18.  Priest, *Captain Wren's Civil War Diary*, 91; Walcott, *History of the 21st Regiment Massachusetts Volunteers*, 200–211; Carmen Battle of Antietam Manuscript; Fogle to parents, 28 Sept. 1862; Sears, *Landscape Turned Red*, 295.

19.  *Southern Confederacy*, 9 Oct. 1862; Carmen Battle of Antietam Manuscript; Sears, *Landscape Turned Red*, 295.

20.  Sears, *Landscape Turned Red*, 295; Walcott, *History of the 21st Regiment Massachusetts Volunteers*, 201; *O.R.*, vol. XIX, ser. I, pt. I: 890; Fogle to parents, 17 and 28 Sept. 1862; Priest, *Antietam*, 239; Sears, *Landscape Turned Red*, 295.

21.  Sears, *Landscape Turned Red*, 295; CSRG; *O.R.*, vol. XIX, ser. I, pt. I: 890–91; *Southern Confederacy*, 5 Oct. 1862; Carmen Battle of Antietam Manuscript.

22.  Sears, *Landscape Turned Red*, 295; Priest, *Captain Wren's Civil War Diary*, 91–92; *O.R.*, vol. XIX, ser. I, pt. I: 892; Fogle to parents, 28 Sept. 1862; "The Burke Sharpshooters," 464; *Southern Confederacy*, 9 Oct. 1862; *O.R.*, vol. LI, ser. I, pt. I: 163; Priest, *Antietam*, 239; Carmen Battle of Antietam Manuscript.

23.  *Southern Confederacy*, 5 Oct. 1862; Sears, *Landscape Turned Red*, 295.

24.  Priest, *Captain Wren's Civil War Diary*, 91–92; Krick, *Lee's Colonels*, 197; Sears, *Landscape Turned Red*, 295.

25.  *O.R.*, vol. XIX, ser. I, pt. I: 890, 893; Fogle to parents, 28 Sept. 1862; Krick, *Lee's Colonels*, 184.

26.  *O.R.*, vol. XIX, ser. I, pt. I: 890; Fogle to parents, 28 Sept. 1862; Edward A. Pollard, *Southern History of the War: The Second Year of the War* (New York: Charles B. Richardson, 1863), 136; *O.R.*, vol. LI, ser. I, pt. I: 163, 165, 168; Hassler, ed., *The General to His Lady*, 178; Carmen Battle of Antietam Manuscript; Sears, *Landscape Turned Red*, 295.

27.  *O.R.*, vol. LI, ser. I, pt. I: 163.

28.  *O.R.*, vol. XIX, ser. I, pt. I: 890; Carmen Batttle of Antietam Manuscript.

29. Fogle to parents, 28 Sept. 1862; *O.R.*, vol. LI, ser. I, pt. I: 165; CSRG; Carmen Batttle of Antietam Manuscript; Sears, *Landscape Turned Red*, 295.

30. Fogle to parents, 17 Sept. 1862; Priest, *Antietam*, 239.

31. Priest, *Captain Wren's Civil War Diary*, 91; Benning Papers; Toombs Papers, DUL; CSRG.

32. Fogle to parents, 28 Sept. 1862; CSRG; Priest, *Captain Wren's Civil War Diary*, 91; *O.R.*, vol. XIX, ser. I, pt. I: 427, 888, 890–91; Benning, "Notes on Sharpsburg," 393–95; "The Burke Sharpshooters," 464–65; A. M. Lewis to Benning, 23 Sept. 1862, Benning Papers; *Southern Confederacy*, 9 Oct. 1862; *O.R.*, vol. LI, ser. I, pt. I: 163, 166, 168; Priest, *Antietam*, 247, 322, 339–43; Houghton and Houghton, *Two Boys*, 235; Carmen Batttle of Antietam Manuscript; Sears, *Landscape Turned Red*, 295.

33. *O.R.*, vol. LI, ser. I, pt. I: 163, 168; Carmen Batttle of Antietam Manuscript; Priest, *Antietam*, 256, 308, 321; Jamieson, *Death in September*, 98–102; *O.R.*, vol. XIX, ser. I, pt. I, 892; William N. Wood, *Reminiscences of Big I* (Wilmington, N.C.: Broadfoot Publishing, 1987), 39; Sears, *McClellan*, 37, 467; Sears, *Landscape Turned Red*, 287–96.

## CHAPTER NINE

1. Allen, *The Army of Northern Virginia*, 431; *O.R.*, vol. XIX, ser. I, pt. I: 890–91.

2. Benning, "Notes on Sharpsburg," 393–94; Allen, *The Army of Northern Virginia*, 431–32; *O.R.*, vol. XIX, ser. I, pt. I: 888–93; Priest, *Antietam*, 250–53, 271, 308; Stovall, *Robert Toombs*, 263–64; Duggan to parents, 14 Oct. 1862.

3. Priest, *Captain Wren's Civil War Diary*, 91; Priest, *Antietam*, 253.

4. Murfin, *The Gleam of Bayonets*, 270.

5. Ibid.; *O.R.*, vol. XIX, ser. I, pt. I: 891; Priest, *Antietam*, 256.

6. H. L. Benning to E. P. Alexander, Toombs Papers, DUL; Fogle to parents, 4 Oct. 1862.

7. Fogle to parents, 4 Oct. 1862; Krick, *Lee's Colonels*, 240, 272; *O.R.*, vol. XIX, ser. I, pt. I: 910–11.

8. *O.R.*, vol. XIX, ser. I, pt. I: 910–11.

9. Robertson, *A. P. Hill*, 143; *O.R.*, vol. XIX, ser. I, pt. I: 891; Duggan to family, 14 Oct. 1862.

10. Duggan to family, 14 Oct. 1862; Priest, *Antietam*, 271–72.

11. Robertson, *A. P. Hill*, 143–44; William W. Hassler, *A. P. Hill: Lee's Forgotten General* (Chapel Hill: University of North Carolina Press, 1962), 105–107; Priest, *Antietam*, 262; "Last Colonel of Artillery, A. N. V.," *Confederate Veteran* 20 (1912): 225; D. G. McIntosh, "McIntosh's Battery at Sharpsburg," *Confederate Veteran* 20 (1912): 204.

12. Benning, "Notes on Sharpsburg," 394; *O.R.*, vol. XIX, ser. I, pt. I: 891; Duggan to family, 14 Oct. 1862; *O.R. Supplement*, III: 672; *O.R.*, vol. LI, ser. I, pt. I: 164; Priest, *Antietam*, 259–68.

13. Priest, *Antietam*, 259–68; *O.R.*, vol. XIX, ser. I, pt. I: 891; Priest, *Antietam*, 271–72; Duggan to family, 14 Oct. 1862; D. J. Napier, "McIntosh's Battery at Sharpsburg," *Confederate Veteran*, 19 (1911): 429; *O.R.*, vol. LI, ser. I, pt. I: 164; Carmen Battlefield Maps.

14. Carmen Battlefield Maps; *O.R.*, vol. XIX, ser. I, pt. I: 891; Marvel, *Race of the Soil*, 59; Priest, *Antietam*, 259–77; Freeman, *Lee's Lieutenants*, 2: 220–22; Murfin, *The Gleam of Bayonets*, 273; Carmen Battlefield Maps.

15. Carmen Battlefield Maps; Priest, *Antietam*, 262–65, 272–73.
16. Carmen Battlefield Maps; *O.R.*, vol. LI, ser. I, pt. I: 164, 168; Priest, *Antietam*, 262, 265.
17. Priest, *Antietam*, 262, 265, 272–77, 284–85; *O.R.*, vol. XIX, ser. I, pt. I: 888–93; Duggan to family, 14 Oct. 1862; Freeman, *Lee's Lieutenants*, 2: 223; Hassler, *A. P. Hill*, 105–107; Moore, *The Rebellion Record*, 5: 474; *O.R.*, vol. LI, ser. I, pt. I: 164; Carmen Battlefield Maps; McIntosh, "McIntosh's Battery at Sharpsburg," 204; "Last Colonel of Artillery, A. N. V.," 225; Douglas Southall Freeman, *R. E. Lee: A Biography* (New York: Charles Scribner's Sons, 1962), 400–401.
18. Freeman, *R. E. Lee*, 400–401; Priest, *Antietam*, 275–84; *O.R.*, vol. XIX, ser. I, pt. I: 892; Joseph T. Durkin, ed., *John Dooley: Confederate Soldier* (Washington, D.C.: Georgetown University Press, 1945), 46–47.
19. *O.R.*, vol. XIX, ser. I, pt. I: 892; *O.R.*, vol. LI, ser. l, pt. I:164–65.
20. *Federal Union*, 14 Oct. 1862; *O.R.*, vol. XIX, ser. I, pt. I: 892.
21. *O.R.*, vol. XIX, ser. I, pt. I: 892; J. F. J. Caldwell, *The History of a Brigade of South Carolinians* (Philadelphia: King and Baird Printers, 1866), 44–48; Priest, *Antietam*, 264–300; Carmen Battle of Antietam Manuscript; Duggan to family, 14 Oct. 1862.
22. Priest, *Antietam*, 284; *O.R.*, vol. XIX, ser. I, pt. I: 892.
23. *O.R.*, vol. LI, ser. I, pt. I: 167.
24. Benning, "Notes on Sharpsburg," 394–95.
25. Priest, *Antietam*, 315.
26. Priest, *Captain Wren's Civil War Diary*, 92; Richard Alden Huebner, *Antietam from the Book: Meserve Civil War Record* (Oak Park, Mich.: RAH Publications, 1987), 3; Walcott, *History of the 21st Regiment Massachusetts Volunteers*, 203.
27. Robertson, *A. P. Hill*, 147–48, 150; Moore, *The Rebellion Record*, 5: 474, 476; *Southern Confederacy*, 9 Oct. 1862; Stovall, *Robert Toombs*, 267–68; Priest, *Antietam*, 308; Benning, "Notes on Sharpsburg," 394–95.
28. Robertson, *A. P. Hill*, 147; Murfin, *The Gleam of Bayonets*, 277; Priest, *Antietam*, 343.
29. Moore, *The Rebellion Record*, 7: 42; Toombs Papers, DUL; *O.R.*, vol. XIV, ser. I, pt. I: 826; Allen, *The Army of Northern Virginia*, 430; Toombs Papers, UGL; *Richmond Enquirer*, 7 March 1863.

## EPILOGUE

1. Allen, *The Army of Northern Virginia*, 432, 439; Freehling and Simpson, *Secession Debated*, 132; Sears, *McClellan*, 467; Paul D. Casdorph, *Lee and Jackson: Confederate Chieftans* (New York: Dell Books, 1992), 334.
2. Hudson to Sophy, 15 Oct. 1862; Sears, *Landscape Turned Red*, 295; Stovall, *Toombs*, 263–69; Fogle to parents, 28 Sept. 1862; Heysinger, *Antietam*, 111–112; Luvass and Nelson, *The U.S. Army War College Guide to the Battle of Antietam*, 302; Allen, *The Army of Northern Virginia*, 430; Schildt, *The Ninth Corps at Antietam*, 127; Alexander, *Fighting for the Confederacy*, 152; Carmen Battle of Antietam Manuscript; *O.R.*, vol. XIX, ser. I, Pt. I: 419–20; Marvel, *Race of the Soil*, 63; Duggan to family, 14 Oct. 1862; Moore, *The Rebellion Record*, 5: 476.
3. Wert, *Longstreet*, 201; Derry, "Georgia," 190; Edgar Warfield, *The Civil War Memoirs of Private Edgar Warfield* (McLean, Va.: EPM Publications, 1996), 97.

# BIBLIOGRAPHY

**MANUSCRIPT SOURCES**

Antietam Files, Antietam National Military Park Archives.

Benning, Henry L. File. U.S. Army Infantry Center and Museum, Fort Benning, Ga.

————. Papers. Southern Historical Collection. University of North Carolina Library, Chapel Hill, N.C.

Blanchard, Thomas E. Diary. Simon Schwab Memorial Library, Columbus College, Columbus, Ga.

Bolton, Levi. Family Papers. Richard A. Plotts, Newtown Square, Pa.

Captions and Records of Events, Company D, 15th Georgia. Georgia Department of Archives, Atlanta, Ga.

Carmen, Ezra A. Battle of Antietam Manuscript. Manuscript Division. Library of Congress, Washington, D.C.

————. Letters. Carmen Collection. Manuscript and Rare Book Section, New York Public Library, New York, NY.

Civil War Collection. Simon Schwob Memorial Library, Columbus College, Columbus, Ga.

Collections of Broadfoot's Supplemental Official Records. Wilmington, N.C.

Compiled Service Records of Confederate Soldiers Who Served in Organizations from the State of Georgia. National Archives, Washington, D.C.

Compiled Service Records of Confederate Soldiers Who Served in Organizations from the State of Louisiana. National Archives, Washington, D.C.

Compiled Service Records of Confederate Soldiers Who Served in Organizations from the State of South Carolina. National Archives, Washington, D.C.

Compiled Service Records of Union Soldiers Who Served in Organizations from the State of Maryland. National Archives, Washington, D.C.

Compiled Service Records of Union Soldiers Who Served in Organizations from the State of New Hampshire. National Archives, Washington, D.C.

Compiled Service Records of Union Soldiers Who Served in Organizations from the State Pennsylvania. National Archives, Washington, D.C.

Crook, George. Papers. U.S. Army Military History Institute, Carlisle, Pa.

Duggan, Ivy W. Letters. Special Collections. University of Georgia Libraries, Athens, Ga.

11th Connecticut Infantry. File. Antietam National Military Park Archives, Antietam, Md.

11th Ohio Infantry. File. Antietam National Military Park Archives, Antietam, Md.

51st New York Infantry. File. Antietam National Military Park Archives, Antietam, Md.

51st Pennsylvania Infantry. File. Antietam National Military Park Archives, Antietam, Md.

File of Dispositions of Toombs's Georgia Brigade, Antietam National Military Park Archives, Antietam, Md.

Fogle, Theodore. Letters. Special Collections. Robert W. Woodruff Library, Emory University, Atlanta, Ga.

48th Pennsylvania Infantry. File. Antietam National Military Park Archives, Antietam, Md.

Friends of the Pennsylvania 51st Infantry Regiment. Veteran Volunteers Collection. Norristown, Pa.

Fuller, Joseph Pryor. Diary. Manuscript Division. Library of Congress, Washington, D.C.

Hall, George Washington. Diary. Manuscript Division. Library of Congress, Washington, D.C.

Hanson, Joseph Mills. Report on the Employment of the Artillery at the Battle of Antietam. Antietam National Military Park Archives, Antietam, Md.

Haskell, Clinton H. Collection. Western Maryland Room. Washington County Free Library, Hagerstown, Md.

Hightower, Judson Harvey. Letters. Robert L. Rodgers Collection. Georgia Department of Archives and History, Atlanta, Ga.

Holmes, William R. File. Bruce S. Allardice Collection. Des Plaines, Ill.

Hudson, John W. Letter to Sophy, 15 Oct. 1862. Western Maryland Room. Washington County Free Library Hagerstown, Md.

Jenkins, Micah. Papers. South Carolina Library, Columbia, S.C.

Jones, William. Memoirs. Georgia State Archives, Atlanta, Ga.

Lokey, John William. Typescript. 20th Georgia File. Antietam National Military Park Archives, Antietam, Md.

Mallory, Stephen R. Diary and Reminiscences. Manuscript Division. Library of Congress, Washington, D.C.

9th New Hampshire Infantry. File. Antietam National Military Park Archives, Antietam, Md.

Palmetto Sharpshooters. File. Antietam National Military Park Archives, Antietam, Md.

Rice, David R. Diary. Manuscript Collection. Library of Congress. Washinton, D.C.

Ross, Albert B. Diary. Manuscript Department. New York Historical Society, New York, N.Y.

Rouse, John. Diary. Antietam National Military Park Archives, Antietam, Md.

2nd Georgia Infantry. File. Antietam National Military Park Archives, Antietam, Md.

2nd Maryland Infantry. File. Antietam National Military Park Archives, Antietam, Md.

Semmes, Paul J. Papers. Manuscripts Division. William R. Perkins Library, Duke University, Durham, N.C.

6th New Hampshire Infantry. File. Antietam National Military Park Archives, Antietam, Md.

Squires, Charles W. Transcripts. Miscellaneous Manuscript Collection, no. 224. Manuscript Division. Library of Congress, Washington, D.C.

35th Massachusetts Infantry. File. Antietam National Military Park Archives, Antietam, Md.

36th Ohio Infantry. File. Antietam National Military Park Archives, Antietam, Md.

Toombs, Robert A. Papers. Manuscripts Collection. University of Georgia Library. University of Georgia, Athens, Ga.

———. Papers. Manuscripts Division. Emory University Libraries, Atlanta, Ga.

———. Papers. Special Collections. William R. Perkins Library, Duke University, Durham, N.C.

20th Georgia Infantry. File. Antietam National Military Park Archives, Antietam, Md.

28th Ohio Infantry. File. Antietam National Military Park Archives, Antietam, Md.

21st Massachusetts Infantry. File. Antietam National Military Park Archives, Antietam, Md.

Waddell, James D. Papers. Special Collections Department. Robert W. Woodruff Library, Emory University, Atlanta, Ga.

Ware, Thomas L. Diary. Southern Historical Collection. University of North Carolina, Chapel Hill, N.C.

Washington Artillery. Files. Antietam National Military Park Archives, Antietam, Md.

Wren, James. Diary. Antietam National Military Park Archives, Antietam, Md.


## NEWSPAPERS

*Macon Central Georgian*
*Charleston (S.C.) Daily Courier*
*Augusta (Ga.) Daily Constitutionalist*
*Daily Columbus (Ga.) Enquirer*
*Milledgeville (Ga.) Southern Federal Union*
*Harper's Weekly*
*Norristown (Pa.) National Defender*
*New York Tribune*
*Richmond Dispatch*
*Richmond Enquirer*
*Savannah Republican*
*Atlanta Southern Confederacy*
*New Haven Connecticut War Record*
*Columbus (Ga.) Weekly Sun*
*Augusta (Ga.) Weekly Chronicle and Sentinel*


## MAPS

Carmen, Ezra A. Collection of Antietam Battlefield Maps. Antietam National Battlefield Archives, Antietam, Md.

Hudson, John Williams. Map. Letter to Sophy, 15 Oct. 1862. Western Maryland Room. Washington County Free Library, Hagerstown, MD.


## BOOKS

Adams, Michael C. C. *Fighting for Defeat: Union Military Failure in the East, 1861–1865.* Lincoln: University of Nebraska Press, 1992.

Allen, William. *The Army of Northern Virginia in 1862.* New York: Houghton, Mifflin, 1892.

Andrews, J. Cutler. *The South Reports the Civil War*. Princeton: Princeton University Press, 1970.

Andrews, William H. *Footprints of a Regiment: A Recollection of the 1st Georgia Regulars, 1861–1865*. Marietta, Ga.: Longstreet Press, 1992.

*Antietam: Report of the Ohio Antietam Battlefield Commission*. Springfield, Ohio: Springfield Publishing, 1904.

Austin, Aurelia. *Georgia Boys with "Stonewall" Jackson*. Athens: University of Georgia Press, 1967.

Baldwin, James T., III. *The Eagle Struck: A Biography of Brigadier General Micah Jenkins: A History of the 5th South Carolina and the Palmetto Sharpshooters*. Shippensburg, Pa.: White Mane Publishing, 1996.

Barrett, John G., ed. *Yankee Rebel: The Civil War Journal of Edmund DeWitt Patterson*. Chapel Hill: University of North Carolina Press, 1966.

Barron, Lee, and Barbara Barron. *The History of Sharpsburg*. Sharpsburg, Md.: privately printed, 1972.

Bauer, Jack. *Zachary Taylor*. Baton Rouge: Louisiana State University Press, 1985.

Beringer, Richard E., Herman Hattaway, Archer Jones, and William N. Still. *The Elements of Confederate Defeat: Nationalism, War Aims, and Religion*. Athens: University of Georgia Press, 1988.

Blackford, Charles M., III, ed. *Letters From Lee's Army*. New York: Perpetua Books, 1962.

Boatner, Mark M., III. *The Civil War Dictionary*. New York: David McKay, 1959.

Bonner, James C. *Milledgeville: Georgia's Antebellum Capital*. Macon, Ga.: Mercer University Press, 1985.

Bridges, Hal. *Lee's Maverick General: Daniel Harvey Hill*. Lincoln: University of Nebraska Press, 1991.

Caldwell, J. F. J. *The History of a Brigade of South Carolinians*. Philadelphia: King and Baird Printers, 1866.

Calkins, Chris M. *The Battles of Appomattox Station and Appomattox Court House, April 8–9, 1865*. Lynchburg, Va.: Howard Publishing, 1987.

Candler, Allen D. *The Confederate Records of the State of Georgia*. Atlanta: Charles P. Byrd, State Printer, 1909.

Canfield, Cass. *The Iron Will of Jefferson Davis*. New York: Fairfax Press, 1978.

Cannan, John. *The Antietam Campaign: August–September 1862*. Conshohocken, Pa.: Combined Publishing, 1994.

Casdorph, Paul D. *Lee and Jackson: Confederate Chieftains*. New York: Dell Books, 1992.

Catton, Bruce. *The Army of the Potomac: Mr. Lincoln's Army.* Garden City, N.Y.: Doubleday, 1962.

Coleman, Kenneth, and Charles Stephen Gurr. *Dictionary of Georgia Biography.* Athens: University of Georgia Press, 1983.

Commager, Henry Steele. *The Blue and the Gray.* 2 vols. New York: Fairfax Press, 1982.

Committee of the Regimental Association. *History of the Thirty-Fifth Regiment Massachusetts Volunteers, 1862–1865.* Boston: Mills, Knight, 1884.

Connelly, Thomas L. *The Marble Man: Robert E. Lee and His Image in American Society.* Baton Rouge: Louisiana State University Press, 1977.

Conrad, James Lee. *The Young Lions: Confederate Cadets at War.* Mechanicsburg, Pa.: Stackpole Books, 1997.

Cottingham, David T. *Bridges: Our Legacy in Stone.* Washington County, Md.: Washington County Board of County Commissioners, 1977.

Coulter, E. Merton. *Georgia: A Short History.* Chapel Hill: University of North Carolina Press, 1947.

Craven, Avery. *The Coming of the Civil War.* Chicago: University of Chicago Press, 1974.

Cullen, Joseph P. *The Peninsula Campaign, 1862: McClellan and Lee Struggle for Richmond.* New York: Bonanza Books, n.d.

Cutrer, Thomas W., ed. *Longstreet's Aide: The Civil War Letters of Major Thomas J. Goree.* Charlottesville: University Press of Virginia, 1995.

Davis, Burke. *Gray Fox: Robert E. Lee and the Civil War.* New York: Fairfax Press, 1981.

———. *Our Incredible Civil War.* New York: Ballantine Books, 1974.

———. *The Civil War: Strange and Fascinating Facts.* New York: Fairfax Press, 1982.

Davis, Varina Howell. *Jefferson Davis, Ex-President of the Confederate States of America: A Memoir by His Wife.* 1890. Reprint, Freeport, N.Y.: Books for Libraries Press, 1971.

Davis, William C. "A Government of Our Own." In *The Making of the Confederacy.* Baton Rouge: Louisiana State University Press, 1994.

———. *Jefferson Davis: The Man and His Hour.* New York: HarperCollins Publishers, 1991.

Derry, Joseph T. "Georgia." In *Confederate Military History.* Ext. ed. Wilmington, N.C.: Broadfoot Publishing, 1987.

———. "South Carolina." In *Confederate Military History.* Ext. ed. Wilmington, N.C.: Broadfoot Publishing, 1987.

Douglas, Henry Kyd. *I Rode with Stonewall.* Greenwich, Conn.: Fawcett Publications, 1961.

Dowdey, Clifford. *The Seven Days: The Emergence of Lee*. Boston: Little, Brown, 1964.

Dowdey, Clifford, and Louis H. Manarin, eds. *The Wartime Papers of R. E. Lee*. New York: Bramhall House, n.d.

Durkin, Joseph T., ed. *John Dooley: Confederate Soldier*. Washington, D.C.: Georgetown University Press, 1945.

Eaton, Clement. *Jefferson Davis*. New York: Free Press, 1977.

Eisenhower, John S. D. *So Far from God: The U.S. War with Mexico*. New York: Doubleday Books, 1990.

Everson, Guy R., and Edward W. Simpson, Jr. *"Far, Far from Home": The Wartime Letters of Dick and Tally Simpson, Third South Carolina Volunteers*. Oxford: Oxford University Press, 1994.

Farwell, Byron. *Stonewall: A Biography of General Thomas J. Jackson*. New York: W. W. Norton, 1992.

Frassanito, William A. *Antietam: The Photographic Legacy of America's Bloodiest Day*. New York: Charles Scribner's Sons, 1978.

Freehling, William W., and Craig M. Simpson. *Secession Debated: Georgia's Showdown in 1860*. New York: Oxford University Press. 1992.

Freeman, Douglas Southall. *Lee's Lieutenants: A Study in Command*. 3 vols. New York: Charles Scribner's Sons, 1942–44.

———. *R. E. Lee: A Biography*. 4 vols. New York: Charles Scribner's Sons, 1934–35.

Gallagher, Gary W., ed. *Antietam: Essays on the 1862 Maryland Campaign*. Kent, Ohio: Kent State University Press, 1989.

———., ed. *Fighting for the Confederacy: The Personal Recollections of General Edward Porter Alexander*. Chapel Hill: University of North Carolina Press, 1989.

Gambone, A. M. *Major-General John Frederick Hartranft: Citizen Soldier and Pennsylvania Statesman*. Baltimore: Butternut and Blue, 1995.

Garrison, Webb. *Civil War Curiosities: Strange Stories, Oddities, Events, and Coincidences*. Nashville: Rutledge Hill Press, 1994.

———. *A Treasury of Civil War Tales*. New York: Ballantine Books, 1988.

Goldsborough, W. W. *The Maryland Line in the Confederate Army*. Baltimore: Press of Guggenheimer, Weil, 1900.

Gordon, John R. *Reminiscences of the Civil War*. New York: Charles Scribner's Sons, 1904.

Harwell, Richard B., ed. *The Confederate Reader*. New York: Dorset Press, 1992.

Hassler, William W. *A. P. Hill: Lee's Forgotten General*. Chapel Hill: University of North Carolina Press, 1962.

————., ed. *The General to His Lady, The Civil War Letters of William Dorsey Pender.* Chapel Hill: University of North Carolina Press, 1988.

————., ed. *The General to His Lady, The Civil War Letters of William Dorsey Pender to Fanny Pender.* Gaithersburg, Md.: Ron R. Van Sickle, 1988.

Hattaway, Herman. *General Stephen D. Lee.* Jackson: University Press of Mississippi, 1976.

Hays, Helen Ashe. *The Antietam and Its Bridges: The Annals of an Historic Stream.* New York: G. P. Putnam's Sons, 1910.

Hendrick, Burton J. *Statesman of the Lost Cause.* New York: Literary Guild, 1939.

Hennessy, John J. *Return to Bull Run: The Campaign and Battle of Second Manassas.* New York: Simon and Schuster, 1993.

Heysinger, Isaac W. *Antietam and the Maryland and Virginia Campaigns of 1862.* New York: Neale Publishing, 1912.

Hoogenboom, Ari. *Rutherford B. Hayes.* Lawrence: University of Kansas Press, 1995.

Houghton, William R., and Milton B. Houghton. *Two Boys in the Civil War and After.* Montgomery, Ala.: Paragon Press, 1912.

Hoyt, James A. *The Palmetto Riflemen: Historical Sketch.* Greenville, S.C.: Hoyt and Keys, 1886.

Huebner, Richard Alden. *Antietam from the Book: Meserve Civil War Record.* Oak Park, Mich.: RAH Publications, 1987.

Hunt, Alfred N. *Haiti's Influence on Antebellum America: Slumbering Volcano in the Caribbean.* Baton Rouge: Louisiana State University Press, 1988.

Huntsberry, Thomas V., and Joanne M. Huntsberry. The North. Vol. 2, *Maryland in the Civil War. Baltimore:* J. Mart Publishing, 1985.

Jackson, Lyman. *History of the Sixth New Hampshire Regiment in the War for the Union.* Concord, N.H.: Republican Press Association, 1891.

Jamieson, Perry D. *Death in September: The Antietam Campaign.* Fort Worth: Ryan Place Publishers, 1995.

Johnson, Allen, ed. *Dictionary of American Biography.* New York: Charles Scribner's Sons, 1985.

Johnson, Curt, and Richard C. Anderson, Jr. *Artillery Hell: The Employment of Artillery at Antietam.* College Station: Texas A&M University Press, 1995.

Johnson, Robert Underwood, and Clarance C. Buel, eds. *Battles and Leaders of the Civil War.* 4 vols. New York: Thomas Yoseloff, 1956.

Johnson, Rossiter. *Campfires and Battlefields: A Pictorial Narrative of the Civil War.* New York: Civil War Press, 1967.

Jones, John B. *A Rebel War Clerk's Diary.* Baton Rouge: Louisiana State University Press, 1993.

Katcher, Philip. *American Civil War Armies: Vol. 5, Volunteer Militia.* London: Osprey Publishing, Men-At-Arms Series, 1990.

———. *The Army of Robert E. Lee.* London: Arms and Armour Press, 1994.

Keegan, John, and Richard Holmes. *Soldiers: A History of Men in Battle.* New York: Viking Books, 1986.

Kegel, James A. *North with Lee and Jackson: The Lost Story of Gettysburg.* Mechanicsburg, Pa.: Stackpole, 1996.

King, Spencer B., Jr. *Georgia Voices: A Documentary History to 1872.* Athens: University of Georgia Press, 1966.

———. *Sound of Drums: Selected Writings of Spencer B. King from His Civil War Centennial Columns Appearing in the* Macon (Georgia) Telegraph-News, *1960–1965.* Macon, Ga.: Mercer University Press, 1984.

Klein, Maury. *Days of Defiance: Sumter, Secession, and the Coming of the Civil War.* New York: Alfred A. Knopf, 1997.

Krick, Robert K. *Lee's Colonels: A Biographical Register of the Field Officers of the Army of Northern Virginia.* Dayton, Ohio: Morningside Bookshop, 1992.

Lane, Mills, ed. *"Dear Mother: Don't Grieve about Me. If I Get Killed, I'll Only Be Dead": Letters from Georgia Soldiers in the Civil War.* Savannah: Beehive Press, 1977.

Leckie, Robert. *None Died in Vain.* New York: Harper Perennial, 1991.

Lee, Fitzhugh. *General Lee.* 1894. Reprint, Da Capo Press, 1994.

Lewis, Richard. *Camp Life of a Confederate Boy.* Charleston, S.C.: News and Courier Book Presses, 1883.

Longacre, Edward G. *Army of Amateurs: General Benjamin F. Butler and the Army of James, 1863–1865.* Mechanicsburg, Pa.: Stackpole Books, 1997.

Longstreet, James. *From Manassas to Appomattox: The Memoirs of the Civil War in America.* 1896. Reprint, Bloomington: Indianna University Press, 1960.

Luvass, Jay, and Harold W. Nelson. *The U.S. Army War College Guide to the Battle of Antietam: The Maryland Campaign of 1862.* New York: Harper and Row Publishers, 1987.

McCaffrey, James M. *Army of Manifest Destiny: The American Soldier in the Mexican War, 1846–1847.* New York: New York University Press, 1992.

McConnell, William F. *Remember Reno: A Biography of Major General Jesse Lee Reno.* Shippensburg, Pa.: White Mane Publishing, 1996.

McIntosh, John H. *The Official History of Elbert County, Georgia*. Elberton, Ga.: Daughters of the American Revolution, Stephen Hear Chapter, 1940.

McPherson, James M. *Battle Cry of Freedom: The Civil War Era*. New York: Oxford University Press, 1988.

McWhiney, Grady, and Perry D. Jamieson. *Attack and Die: Civil War Military Tactics and the Southern Heritage*. Tuscaloosa: University of Alabama Press, 1982.

Mahon, John K. *History of the Second Seminole War, 1835–1842*. Gainesville: University Presses of Florida, 1967.

Manakee, Harold R. *Maryland in the Civil War*. Baltimore: Maryland Historical Society, 1968.

Marvel, William. *Burnside*. Chapel Hill: University of North Carolina Press, 1991.

———. *Race of the Soil: The Ninth New Hampshire Regiment in the Civil War*. Wilmington, N.C.: Broadfoot Publishing, 1988.

Mellichamp, Josephine. *Senators from Georgia*. Huntsville, Ala.: Strode Publishers, 1976.

Miller, William J. *The Training of an Army: Camp Curtin and the North's Civil War*. Shippensburg, Pa.: White Mane Publishing, 1990.

Millett, Alan R. and Peter Maslowski. *For the Common Defense: A Military History of the United States of America*. New York: Free Press, 1984.

Moneyhon, Carl, and Bobby Roberts. *Portraits of Conflict: A Photographic History of Louisiana in the Civil War*. Fayetteville: University of Arkansas Press, 1990.

Moore, Frank, ed. *The Rebellion Record*. 11 vols. New York: n.p., 1862–68.

Murfin, James V. *The Gleam of Bayonets*. New York: Curtis Books, 1965.

Myers, Robert Manson, ed. *The Children of Pride: A True Story of Georgia and the Civil War*. 6 vols. New York: Popular Library, 1977.

Newman, Harry Wright. *Maryland and the Confederacy*. Annapolis: privately printed, 1976.

Nisbet, James Cooper, ed. *Four Years on the Firing Line*. Jackson, Tenn.: McCowat-Mercer Press, 1963.

Nolan, Alan T. *Lee Considered: General Robert E. Lee and Civil War History*. Chapel Hill: University of North Carolina Press, 1991.

Oates, Stephen B. *To Purge This Land with Blood: The Biography of John Brown*. New York: Harper and Row Publishers, 1970.

O'Connell, Robert L. *Of Arms and Men: A History of War, Weapons, and Aggression*. Oxford: Oxford University Press, 1980.

Owen, William M. *In Camp and Battle with the Washington Artillery of New Orleans*. Boston: Griffith-Stillings Press, 1903.

*Papers of the Military Historical Society of Massachusetts.* Boston: Griffith-Stillings Press, 1903.

Parker, Thomas H. *History of the 51st Regiment of Pennsylvania Volunteers.* Philadelphia: King and Baird Printers, 1869.

Parsons, William T., ed. *Pennsylvania Soldier Life, 1861–65.* Huntingdon, Pa.: Juniata College, 1986.

Pendleton, Constance, ed. *Confederate Memoirs: Early Life and Family History: William Frederic Pendleton.* Bryn Athyn, Pa.: privately printed, 1957.

Perrett, Bryan. *Last Stand! Famous Battles against the Odds.* London: Arms and Armour Press, 1994.

Perry, Mark. *Conceived in Liberty: Joshua Chamberlain, William Oates, and the American Civil War.* New York: Viking Books, 1997.

Phillips, Ulrich B. *The Correspondence of Robert Toombs, Alexander H. Stephens, and Howell Cobb.* New York: Da Capo Press, 1970.

———. *The Life of Robert Toombs.* New York: Burt Franklin, 1968.

Piston, William Garrett. *Lee's Tarnished Lieutenant: James Longstreet and His Place in Southern History.* Athens: University of Georgia Press, 1987.

Pleasants, Henry, Jr. *The Tragedy of the Crater.* Philadelphia: Eastern National Park and Monument Association, 1975.

Pollard, Edward A. *Southern History of the War: The Second Year of the War.* New York: Charles B. Richardson, 1863.

Priest, John M. *Antietam: The Soldier's Battle.* Shippensburg, Pa.: White Mane Publishing, 1989.

———. *Before Antietam: The Battle of South Mountain.* New York: Oxford University Press, 1996.

———., ed. *Captain Wren's Civil War Diary: From New Bern to Fredericksburg.* New York: Berkley Books, 1991.

Quaife, Milo M. Introduction to *Civil War Letters of General Apheus S. Williams: From the Cannon's Mouth.* Detroit: Wayne State University Press and Detroit Historical Society, 1959.

Regan, Geoffrey. *Great Military Disasters: A Historical Survey of Military Incompetence.* New York: M. Evans and Company, 1987.

Rhea, Gordon C. *The Battle of the Wilderness, May 5–6, 1864.* Baton Rouge: Louisiana State University Press, 1994.

Rivers, William James. *Rivers' Account of the Raising of Troops in South Carolina for State and Confederate Service, 1861–1865.* Columbia, S.C.: Bryan Printing, State Printers, 1899.

Robertson, James I., Jr. *General A. P. Hill: The Story of a Confederate Warrior.* New York: Vintage Books, 1992.

———. *Stonewall Jackson: The Man, the Soldier, the Legacy.* New York: Simon and Schuster, 1997.

Roland, Charles P. *The Confederacy.* Chicago: University of Chicago Press, 1960.

Rollins, Richard, ed. *Black Southerners in Gray: Essays on Afro-Americans in Confederate Armies.* Murfreesboro, Tenn.: Southern Heritage Press, 1994.

Royster, Charles. *Light-Horse: Harry Lee and the Legacy of the American Revolution.* Cambridge: Cambridge University Press, 1986.

Schildt, John W. *Drums along the Antietam.* Parsons, W.V.: McClain Printing, 1972.

———. *September Echoes: The Maryland Campaign of 1862: The Places, the Battles, the Results.* Middletown, Md..: Valley Register Publishers, 1960.

———. *The Ninth Corps at Antietam.* Chewsville, Md.: privately printed, 1988.

Schmitt, Martin F., ed. *General George Crook: His Autobiography.* Norman: University of Oklahoma Press, 1986.

Sears, Stephen W. *George B. McClellan: The Young Napoleon.* New York: Ticknor and Fields, 1988.

———. *Landscape Turned Red: The Battle of Antietam.* New York: Warner Books, 1983.

———., ed. *The Civil War Papers of George B. McClellan: Selected Correspondence, 1860–1865.* New York: Ticknor and Fields, 1989.

———. *To the Gates of Richmond: The Peninsula Campaign.* New York: Ticknor and Fields, 1992.

Sergent, Mary Elizabeth. *They Lie Forgotten: The United States Military Academy, 1856–1861.* Middletown, N.Y.: Prior King Press, 1986.

Shackleford, George Green. *George Wythe Randolph and the Confederate Elite.* Athens: University of Georgia Press, 1988.

Smith, Gerald J. *Smite Them Hip and Thigh!: Georgia Methodist Ministers in the Confederate Military.* N.p.: privately printed, 1993.

Sorrell, G. Moxley. *Recollections of a Confederate Staff Officer.* 1905. Reprint, Wilmington, N.C.: Broadfoot Publishing, 1995.

———. *Recollections of a Confederate Staff Officer.* Dayton, Ohio: Morningside Bookshop, 1978.

Spear, William E. *The North and South.* Boston: privately printed, 1908.

Stackpole, Edward J. *Drama on the Rappahannock: The Fredericksburg Campaign.* New York: Bonanza Books, n.d.

Standard, Diffee William. *Columbus, Georgia: Georgia in the Confederacy: The Social and Industrial Life of the Chattahoochee River Port.* New York: William-Frederick Press, 1954.

Stiles, Robert T. *Four Years under Marse Robert.* New York: Neale Publishing, 1910.

Stovell, Pleasant A. *Robert Toombs: Statesman, Speaker, Soldier, Sage.* New York: Cassell Publishing, 1892.

Swinton, William. *Army of the Potomac.* New York: Smithmark Publishers, 1995.

Swisher, James K. *Prince of Edisto: Brigadier General Micah Jenkins, C.S.A.* Berryville, Va.: Rockbridge Publishing, 1996.

Symonds, Craig L. Introduction to *Jubal Early's Memories: Autobiography Sketch and Narrative of the War between the States.* Baltimore: Nautical and Aviation Publishing, 1989.

Taylor, Richard. *Destruction and Reconstruction: Personal Experiences of the Late War.* New York: Longmans, Green, 1955.

Terrill, Helen Elize. *History of Stewart County, Georgia.* 2 vols. Columbus, Ga.: Columbus Supply, 1958.

Thomas, Emory M. *Bold Dragon: The Life of J. E. B. Stuart.* New York: Vintage Books, 1988.

———. *Robert E. Lee: A Biography.* New York: W. W. Norton, 1995.

———. *The Confederate Nation, 1861–1865.* New York: Harper and Row, 1979.

Thomas, John P. *Career and Character of General Micah Jenkins, C.S.A.* Columbia, S.C.: State, 1908.

Thompson, William Y. *Robert Toombs of Georgia.* Baton Rouge: Louisiana State University Press, 1966.

Toomey, Daniel Carroll. *The Civil War in Maryland.* Baltimore: Toomey Press, 1988.

Tower, R. Lockwood, ed. *Lee's Adjutant: The Wartime Letters of Colonel Walter Herron Taylor, 1862–1865.* Columbia: University of South Carolina Press, 1995.

Trass, Adrian G. *From the Golden Gate to Mexico City: The United States Topographical Engineers in the Mexican War.* Washington, D.C.: U.S. Government Printing Office, 1992.

Tuchman, Barbara W. *The March of Folly: From Troy to Vietnam.* New York: Alfred A. Knopf, 1984.

Tucker, Glenn. *High Tide at Gettysburg: The Campaign in Pennsylvania.* New York: Bobs-Merrill, 1958.

U.S. War Department. *The War of the Rebellion: A Compilation of the Official Records of the Union and Confederate Armies.* 130 vols. Washington, D.C.: U.S. Government Printing Office, 1895–1919.

Vandiver, Frank E. *Ploughshares into Swords: Josiah Gorgas and Confederate Ordnance.* College Station: Texas A & M University Press, 1994.

Vetter, Charles Edward. *Sherman: Merchant of Terror, Advocate of Peace.* Gretna, La.: Pelican Publishing, 1992.

Wakelyn, Jon L. *Biographical Dictionary of the Confederacy.* Westport, Conn.: Greenwood Press, 1977.

Walcott, Charles F. *History of the 21st Massachusetts Volunteers in the War for the Preservation of the Union.* Boston: Houghton, Mifflin, 1882.

Walker, William and Robert Houston. *The War in Nicaragua.* Tucson: The University of Arizona Press, 1985.

Warfield, Edgar. *The Civil War Memoirs of Private Edgar Warfield.* McLean, Va.: EPM Publications, 1996.

Wert, Jeffrey D. *General James Longstreet: The Confederacy's Most Controversial Soldier.* New York: Simon and Schuster, 1994.

Wheeler, Richard. *Lee's Terrible Swift Sword: From Antietam to Chancellorsville: An Eyewitness History.* New York: HarperCollins, 1992.

Wiley, Bell Irvin. *The Life of Johnny Reb: The Common Soldier of the Confederacy.* Baton Rouge: Louisiana State University Press, 1978.

Williams, Benjamin A., ed. *A Diary from Dixie by Mary Chesnut.* Boston: Houghton, Mifflin, 1949.

Wise, Jennings Cropper. *The Long Arm of Lee.* 2 vols. Lincoln: University of Nebraska Press, 1991.

Wood, William N. *Reminiscences of Big I.* Wilmington, N.C.: Broadfoot Publishing, 1987.

Woodard, C. Vann, and Elisabeth Muhlenfield, eds. *The Private Mary Chesnut: The Unpublished Civil War Diaries.* New York: Oxford University Press, 1984.

Worsley, Etta B. *Columbus on the Chattahoochee.* Columbus, Ga.: Office Supply, 1951.

Wyckoff, Mac. *A History of the 2nd South Carolina Infantry: 1861–65.* Fredericksburg, Va.: Sergent Kirkland's Museum Historical Society, 1994.

Yeary, Mamie, ed. *Reminiscences of the Boys in Gray, 1861–1865.* Dallas: Press of Wilkinson Printing, 1912.

ARTICLES

Andrews, William H. "Tige Anderson's Brigade at Sharpsburg." *Confederate Veteran* 16 (1908).

Benning, Henry L. "Notes by General H. L. Benning on the Battle of Sharpsburg." *Southern Historical Society Papers* 16 (1888).

Cleveland, Henry Whitney. "Robert Toombs." *The Southern Bivouac* 1 (1886).

Cochran, Jai S. "The Contentious Robert Toombs." *Civil War Magazine* 11 (1993).

Conrad, James L. "Training in Treason." *Civil War Times Illustrated* 30 (1991).

Dawson, Joseph G. "The Confederacy Revisited: Encyclopedia of the Confederacy." *Civil War History* 40 (1994).

Dimon, Theodore. "A Federal Surgeon at Sharpsburg." Edited by James I. Robertson, Jr. *Civil War History* 6 (1960).

Evans, Thomas H. "Eyewitness Accounts of Antietam." *Civil War Times Illustrated* 7 (1968).

Flanagan, W. A. "Account of How Some Flags Were Captured." *Confederate Veteran* 13 (1905).

Greene, A. Wilson. "The Bridge and Beyond: Ambrose Burnside and the Ninth Corps at Antietam." *Civil War: The Magazine of the Civil War Society* 9 (1987).

Hunter, Alexander. "The Battle of Antietam." *Southern Historical Society Papers* 31 (1905).

Jones, Charles C., Jr. "Brigadier-General Robert Toombs." *Southern Historical Society Papers* 14 (1886).

McIntosh, D. G. "McIntosh's Battery at Sharpsburg." *Confederate Veteran* 20 (1912).

Mockbee, R. T. "Why Sharpsburg Was 'a Drawn Battle.'" *Confederate Veteran* 16 (1908).

Napier, D. J. "McIntosh's Battery at Sharpsburg." *Confederate Veteran* 19 (1911).

Parker, George C. "I Feel . . . Just like Writing You a Letter . . ." *Civil War Times Illustrated* 16 (1977).

Richardson, C. A. "Incidents of Sharpsburg." *Confederate Veteran* 15 (1907).

Roach, Harry. "John F. Hartranft: Defender of the Union." *Military Images* 4 (1982).

Sears, Stephen W. "Antietam." *Civil War Times Illustrated* 27 (1987).

Seker, Richard. "Fighting under the Influence." *America's Civil War* 11
     (1998).
Shingleton, Royce Gordon. "South from Appomattox: The Diary of Abner
     R. Cox." *South Carolina Historical Magazine* 77 (1974).
Thompson, William Y. "Robert Toombs: Confederate Soldier." *Civil War
     History* 7 (1961).


## ANONYMOUS ARTICLES
"Last Colonel of Artillery, A. N. V." *Confederate Veteran* 20 (1912).
"New Commander of the Georgia Division." *Confederate Veteran* 12
     (1904).
"The Burke County Sharpshooters." *Confederate Veteran* 32 (1924).


## INTERVIEWS
Fry, Dennis. Interview by author. National Park Service, 19 Feb. 1991.


## CORRESPONDENCE
Plotts, Richard A. Letter to author, 11 Feb. 1995.
Toombs, DuBose Lewis, Jr. Letters to author, 10 June 1990, 27 Sept.
     1990, and 19 Oct. 1990.

# INDEX